# *When* PROPHECY FAILS

A Social and Psychological Study
of a Modern Group that Predicted
the Destruction of the World

BY *Leon Festinger*

*Henry W. Riecken* AND *Stanley Schachter*

Martino Publishing
Mansfield Centre, CT
2011

*Martino Publishing*
*P.O. Box 373,*
*Mansfield Centre, CT 06250 USA*

ISBN 1-891396-98-6

© *2011  Martino  Publishing*

Cover design by T. Matarazzo

*Printed in the United States of America On 100% Acid-Free Paper*

# When
# PROPHECY FAILS

A Social and Psychological Study
of a Modern Group that Predicted
the Destruction of the World

BY *Leon Festinger*

*Henry W. Riecken* AND *Stanley Schachter*

HARPER TORCHBOOKS ❧ The Academy Library
Harper & Row, Publishers
New York

WHEN PROPHECY FAILS

© Copyright 1956 by the University of Minnesota.

Printed in the United States of America.

This book was originally published in 1956 by the University
of Minnesota Press and is here reprinted by arrangement.

First HARPER TORCHBOOK edition published 1964 by
Harper & Row, Publishers, Inc.
10 East 53 rd Street
New York , N. Y. 10022.

Library of Congress Catalog Card Number: 56-11611

75 76 77 78 79 80   12

# Foreword

THE study reported in this volume grew out of some theoretical work, one phase of which bore specifically on the behavior of individuals in social movements that made specific (and unfulfilled) prophecies. We had been forced to depend chiefly on historical records to judge the adequacy of our theoretical ideas until we by chance discovered the social movement that we report in this book. At the time we learned of it, the movement was in mid-career but the prophecy about which it was centered had not yet been disconfirmed. We were understandably eager to undertake a study that could test our theoretical ideas under natural conditions.

That we were able to do this study was in great measure due to the support obtained through the Laboratory for Research in Social Relations of the University of Minnesota. This study is a project of the Laboratory and was carried out while we were all members of its staff. We should also like to acknowledge the help we received through a grant-in-aid from the Ford Foundation to one of the authors, a grant that made preliminary exploration of the field situation possible.

A number of individuals also contributed importantly to the success of the field study. Our chief debt of personal gratitude is to the participant observers who bore the brunt of the day-to-day work: Doris Bosted, Elizabeth Williams Nall, Frank Nall, Marsh Ray, and Donald Salzman. We regret that we cannot here give them credit for their individual deeds of ingenuity, endurance, and self-sacrifice, since our attempt to disguise the persons, places, and times in our narrative makes it desirable to conceal who did what and where.

Dr. John G. Darley, director of the Laboratory for Research in Social Relations, deserves our gratitude for his logistic support. While we were entangled in the innumerable problems of data collection, dashing off at frequent intervals to attend meetings of the movement or to supervise the work of the observers, he kept a cool head and brought order out of the administrative chaos we dumped on his desk.

Finally, we want to acknowledge the insightful criticisms of the manuscript we received from Gardner Lindzey, Seymour M. Lipset, and Pauline S. Sears. Their many helpful suggestions are reflected in the final draft.

All the persons and places we mention have been given fictitious names and any resemblance between these names and those of actual people anywhere is unintentional. We have not changed the essential nature of any of the events we report, but by the disguises employed we have tried to protect the actual people involved in the movement from the curiosity of an unsympathetic reader.

The publication of a collaborative work sometimes raises questions among readers about what share of the credit (or blame) should be given to each author. We all contributed equally to the study and have tried to avoid the problem of seniority of authorship by arraying our names on the title page alphabetically.

LEON FESTINGER
HENRY W. RIECKEN
STANLEY SCHACHTER

*December 21, 1955*

# Table of Contents

**CHAPTER I** ～～～～～～ *Unfulfilled Prophecies and Disappointed Messiahs*

A MAN with a conviction is a hard man to change. Tell him you disagree and he turns away. Show him facts or figures and he questions your sources. Appeal to logic and he fails to see your point.

We have all experienced the futility of trying to change a strong conviction, especially if the convinced person has some investment in his belief. We are familiar with the variety of ingenious defenses with which people protect their convictions, managing to keep them unscathed through the most devastating attacks.

But man's resourcefulness goes beyond simply protecting a belief. Suppose an individual believes something with his whole heart; suppose further that he has a commitment to this belief, that he has taken irrevocable actions because of it; finally, suppose that he is presented with evidence, unequivocal and undeniable evidence, that his belief is wrong: what will happen? The individual will frequently emerge, not only unshaken, but even more convinced of the truth of his beliefs than ever before. Indeed, he may even show a new fervor about convincing and converting other people to his view.

How and why does such a response to contradictory evidence come about? This is the question on which this book focuses. We hope that, by the end of the volume, we will have provided an adequate answer to the question, an answer documented by data.

Let us begin by stating the conditions under which we would expect to observe increased fervor following the disconfirmation of a belief. There are five such conditions.

3

1. A belief must be held with deep conviction and it must have some relevance to action, that is, to what the believer does or how he behaves.

2. The person holding the belief must have committed himself to it; that is, for the sake of his belief, he must have taken some important action that is difficult to undo. In general, the more important such actions are, and the more difficult they are to undo, the greater is the individual's commitment to the belief.

3. The belief must be sufficiently specific and sufficiently concerned with the real world so that events may unequivocally refute the belief.

4. Such undeniable disconfirmatory evidence must occur and must be recognized by the individual holding the belief.

The first two of these conditions specify the circumstances that will make the belief resistant to change. The third and fourth conditions together, on the other hand, point to factors that would exert powerful pressure on a believer to discard his belief. It is, of course, possible that an individual, even though deeply convinced of a belief, may discard it in the face of unequivocal disconfirmation. We must, therefore, state a fifth condition specifying the circumstances under which the belief will be discarded and those under which it will be maintained with new fervor.

5. The individual believer must have social support. It is unlikely that one isolated believer could withstand the kind of disconfirming evidence we have specified. If, however, the believer is a member of a group of convinced persons who can support one another, we would expect the belief to be maintained and the believers to attempt to proselyte or to persuade nonmembers that the belief is correct.

These five conditions specify the circumstances under which increased proselyting would be expected to follow disconfirmation. Given this set of hypotheses, our immediate concern is to locate data that will allow a test of the prediction of increased proselyting. Fortunately, there have been throughout history recurring instances of social movements which do satisfy the conditions adequately. These are the millennial or messianic move-

4

ments, a contemporary instance of which we shall be examining in detail in the main part of this volume. Let us see just how such movements do satisfy the five conditions we have specified.

Typically, millennial or messianic movements are organized around the prediction of some future events. Our conditions are satisfied, however, only by those movements that specify a date or an interval of time within which the predicted events will occur as well as detailing exactly what is to happen. Sometimes the predicted event is the second coming of Christ and the beginning of Christ's reign on earth; sometimes it is the destruction of the world through a cataclysm (usually with some select group slated for rescue from the disaster); or sometimes the prediction is concerned with particular occurrences that the Messiah or a miracle worker will bring about. Whatever the event predicted, the fact that its nature and the time of its happening are specified satisfies the third point on our list of conditions. *don't most religions satisfy these conditions?*

The second condition specifies strong behavioral commitment to the belief. This usually follows almost as a consequence of the situation. If one really believes a prediction (the first condition), for example, that on a given date the world will be destroyed by fire, with sinners being destroyed and the good being saved, one does things about it and makes certain preparations as a matter of course. These actions may range all the way from simple public declarations to the neglect of worldly things and the disposal of earthly possessions. Through such actions and through the mocking and scoffing of nonbelievers there is usually established a heavy commitment on the part of believers. What they do by way of preparation is difficult to undo, and the jeering of nonbelievers simply makes it far more difficult for the adherents to withdraw from the movement and admit that they were wrong.

Our fourth specification has invariably been provided. The predicted events have not occurred. There is usually no mistaking the fact that they did not occur and the believers know that. In other words, the unequivocal disconfirmation does materialize and makes its impact on the believers.

Finally, our fifth condition is ordinarily satisfied — such movements do attract adherents and disciples, sometimes only a handful, occasionally hundreds of thousands. The reasons why people join such movements are outside the scope of our present discussion, but the fact remains that there are usually one or more groups of believers who can support one another.

History has recorded many such movements. Some are scarcely more than mentioned, while others are extensively described, although sometimes the aspects of a movement that concern us most may be sketchily recounted. A number of historical accounts, however, are complete enough to provide an introductory and exploratory answer to our central question. From these we have chosen several relatively clear examples of the phenomena under scrutiny in an endeavor simply to show what has often happened in movements that made a prediction about the future and then saw it disconfirmed. We shall discuss these historical examples before presenting the data from our case study of a modern movement.

Ever since the crucifixion of Jesus, many Christians have hoped for the second coming of Christ, and movements predicting specific dates for this event have not been rare. But most of the very early ones were not recorded in such a fashion that we can be sure of the reactions of believers to the disconfirmations they may have experienced. Occasionally historians make passing reference to such reactions as does Hughes in his description of the Montanists:

Montanus, who appeared in the second half of the second century, does not appear as an innovator in matters of belief. His one personal contribution to the life of the time was the fixed conviction that the second coming of Our Lord was at hand. The event was to take place at Pepuza — near the modern Angora — and thither all true followers of Our Lord should make their way. His authority for the statement was an alleged private inspiration, and the new prophet's personality and eloquence won him a host of disciples, who flocked in such numbers to the appointed spot that a new town sprang up to house them. *Nor did the delay of the second advent put an end to the movement. On the contrary, it gave it new life and form* as a kind of Christianity of the elite,

6

whom no other authority guided in their new life but the Holy Spirit working directly upon them. . . . [Italics ours.] [1]

In this brief statement are all the essential elements of the typical messianic movement. There are convinced followers; they commit themselves by uprooting their lives and going to a new place where they build a new town; the Second Advent does not occur. And, we note, far from halting the movement, this disconfirmation gives it new life.

There is somewhat better documentation of millennial movements in more recent history. For example, the Anabaptists of the early sixteenth century believed that the millennium would occur in 1533. As Heath puts it:

But these high thoughts were obscured by Hoffmann's prediction that the end of all things was at hand. Strassburg, according to him, had been chosen as the New Jerusalem; there the magistrates would set up the kingdom of righteousness, while the hundred and forty and four thousand would maintain the power of the City, and the true Gospel and the true Baptism would spread over the earth. No man would be able to withstand the power, signs and wonders of the saints; and with them would appear, like two mighty torches, Enoch and Elias, who would consume the earth with the fire proceeding from their mouths. The year 1533 was the time in which, Hoffmann declared, the great fulfillment would begin. [2]

This adventist prediction was apparently proclaimed with vigor and was accepted by many persons who then acted accordingly, that is, they began to prepare for the Second Advent and the end of the temporal world. Heath says, for example:

. . . The followers of Rothmann [a disciple of Hoffmann], were at this time, as was their leader, distinguished for earnestness and self-sacrificing devotion. They sought to exemplify equality and brotherhood in their lives. Well-to-do Brothers and Sisters gave all their goods to the poor, destroyed their rent-rolls, forgave their debtors, renounced worldly pleasures, studying to live an unworldly life. [3]

Such was the situation in 1533, when the end of the world was due. Many people had accepted this belief and some were even

7

disposing of their worldly goods. What happened as the end of 1533 approached and, indeed, when 1534 arrived, without the Second Coming having materialized?

From all accounts it would seem that instead of dampening the ardor of the Anabaptists, the disconfirmation of the predicted Second Coming increased their enthusiasm and activity. They poured greater energy than ever before into obtaining new converts, and sent out missionaries, something they never had done before. The following excerpts from Heath's study illustrate this increase of enthusiasm and activity following the disconfirmation:

> ... The year 1533 was almost at an end, the half-year during which it had been prophesied Hoffmann should be imprisoned had nearly elapsed, the two years' cessation from baptism had nearly run out when a new prophet [Matthysz] arose.
>
> The Dutch Baptists felt that a leader had risen up amongst them, and they yielded themselves to his guidance. Matthysz began by sending out apostles . . . These apostles went forth announcing, among other things, that the promised time had come, that no more Christian blood would be poured out, but that in a short time God would overthrow the tyrants and blood-shedders with all the rest of the wicked. They travelled through many states and visited many cities, going to the gatherings of the faithful, and offering them the kiss of peace. They baptized, and ordained bishops and deacons, committing to the former the duty of ordaining others.
>
> The new tide of enthusiasm rose higher than ever. Jakob van Kampen, who, assisted by Houtzager, worked among the poorer homes in Amsterdam, baptized in February, 1534, in one day, a hundred persons. About two months later it was estimated that two-thirds of the population at Monniaendam were adherents of Jan Matthysz, and it is said to have been the same in the neighbourhood of most of the great cities of Holland.[4]

Another, and rather fascinating, illustration of the reaction to disconfirming evidence is provided by the messianic movement of which Sabbatai Zevi was the central figure.[5] Sabbatai Zevi was born and raised in the city of Smyrna. By 1646 he had acquired considerable prestige through living a highly ascetic life and devoting his whole energy to the study of the cabala. Indeed, though

8 *severe self discipline
*Jewish tradition of mystical Biblical interp.

he was only twenty years old, he had already gathered around him a small group of disciples. To these disciples he taught and interpreted the highly mystical writings of the cabala.

Prevalent among Jews at that time was the belief that the Messiah would come in the year 1648. His coming was to be accompanied by all manner of miracles and the era of redemption would dawn. Sometime in 1648 Sabbatai Zevi proclaimed himself as the promised Messiah to his small group of disciples. Needless to say, the year 1648 passed and the era of redemption did not dawn and the expected miracles were not forthcoming.

There is but scant information about immediately subsequent events but apparently this disconfirmation of his messiahship did not daunt Sabbatai or his disciples. Indeed, it seems that after 1648 he made his claim known to the community at large. Graetz writes: "When Zevi's pretensions became known some years later, the college of rabbis, at their head his teacher Joseph Eskapha, laid him and his followers under a ban . . . Finally, he and his disciples were banished from Smyrna [about 1651]." [6] The significant point for our interest is that it was *after* the year 1648 had passed and nothing had happened that Zevi proclaimed his messiahship to people outside his small circle of disciples.

His banishment, however, certainly does not end the story. About this time some segments of the Christian world were expecting the year 1666 to usher in the millennium, and Sabbatai Zevi appears to have accepted this date. From 1651 until the autumn of 1665 he moved about among the cities of the Near East which had large Jewish communities, making known his claims to be the Messiah and gradually acquiring more and more followers even though the rabbinate continued to oppose him. By 1665 his following was very large and a number of disciples had helped him spread his name and pretensions throughout the Jewish world. The atmosphere in Smyrna had so changed by the autumn of 1665 that when he returned to his native city in that year he was received with great joy. In September or October of 1665 he proclaimed himself the Messiah in a public ceremony in Smyrna:

9

The madness of the Jews of Smyrna knew no bounds. Every sign of honor and enthusiastic love was shown him. . . . All prepared for a speedy exodus, the return to the Holy Land. Workmen neglected their business, and thought only of the approaching Kingdom of the Messiah. . . .

These events in the Jew's quarter at Smyrna made a great sensation in ever-widening circles. The neighboring communities in Asia Minor, many members of which had betaken themselves to Smyrna, and witnessed the scenes enacted in the town, brought home exaggerated accounts of the Messiah's power of attraction and of working miracles, were swept into the same vortex. Sabbatai's private secretary, Samuel Primo, took care that reports of the fame and doings of the Messiah should reach Jews abroad.[7]

The movement gradually spread to almost the whole of Jewry, and Sabbatai was accepted and heralded everywhere as the Messiah. Furthermore, since this was no idle belief, people took steps to prepare for the promised events. They neglected their work and their businesses, and many prepared for the return to Jerusalem.

Since one of the predicted events was that the Sultan would be deposed (a necessary preliminary to the return of the Jews to the Holy Land), at the very beginning of the year 1666, Sabbatai together with a number of followers set out for Constantinople to accomplish this task. The party landed on the coast of the Dardanelles where Sabbatai was immediately arrested by Turkish officials and was brought in fetters to a small town in the neighborhood of Constantinople. Graetz writes:

Informed by a messenger of his arrival . . . his followers [from Constantinople] hastened from the capital to see him, but found him in a pitiable plight and in chains. The money which they brought with them procured him some alleviation, and on the following Sunday [February 1666] he was brought by sea to Constantinople — but in how different a manner to what he and his believers had anticipated! [8]

Clearly, we may regard his arrest as a serious disappointment to the followers of Sabbatai and a disconfirmation of his predictions. Indeed, there were evidences of shock and disappointment. But then there began to emerge the familiar pattern: recovery of conviction, followed by new heights of enthusiasm and proselyting. Graetz describes the ensuing events very well:

> For some days they kept quietly at home, because the street boys mocked them by shouting, "Is he coming? Is he coming?" But soon they began again to assert that he was the true Messiah, and that the sufferings which he had encountered were necessary, a condition to his glorification. The prophets continued to proclaim the speedy redemption of Sabbatai and of all Israel. . . . Thousands crowded daily to Sabbatai's place of confinement merely to catch a glimpse of him. . . . The expectations of the Jews were raised to a still higher pitch, and the most exaggerated hopes fostered to a greater degree.[9]

The very fact that Sabbatai was still alive was used by the Jews to argue that he was really the Messiah. When he was moved to another jail and his incarceration became milder (largely through bribery) the argument was complete. A constant procession of adoring followers visited the prison where Sabbatai held court, and a steady stream of propaganda and tales of miracles poured out all over the Near East and Europe. Graetz states:

> What more was needed to confirm the predictions of prophets of ancient and modern times? The Jews accordingly prepared seriously to return to their original home. In Hungary they began to unroof their houses. In large commercial cities, where Jews took the lead in wholesale business, such as Amsterdam, Leghorn and Hamburg, stagnation of trade ensued.[10]

The memoirs of a contemporary European Jewess vividly confirm Graetz' assertions:

> Our joy, when the letters arrived [from Smyrna] is not to be told. Most of them were addressed to the Sephardim who, as fast as they came, took them to their synagogue and read them aloud; young and old, the Germans too hastened to the Sephardic synagogue.
>
> Many sold their houses and lands and all their possessions, for any day they hoped to be redeemed. My good father-in-law left his home in Hameln, abandoned his house and lands and all his goodly furniture and moved to Hildesheim. He sent on to us in Hamburg two enormous casks packed with linens and with peas, beans, dried meats, shredded prunes and like stuff, every manner

of food that would keep. For the old man expected to sail any moment from Hamburg to the Holy Land.[11]

Finally, in an effort to cope with the problem, without making a martyr of Sabbatai, the Sultan attempted to convert him to Islam. Astonishingly enough, the plan succeeded and Sabbatai donned the turban. Many of the Jews of the Near East still kept faith in him. Explanations were invented for his conversion and many continued their proselyting, usually in places where the movement had not previously been strong. A considerable number of Jews even followed his lead and became Moslems. His conversion proved to be too much for most of his followers in Europe, however, and the movement there soon collapsed.

The Sabbataian movement strikingly illustrates the phenomenon we are concerned with: when people are committed to a belief and a course of action, clear disconfirming evidence may simply result in deepened conviction and increased proselyting. But there does seem to be a point at which the disconfirming evidence has mounted sufficiently to cause the belief to be rejected.

In the preceding examples many of the facts are not known, others are in dispute, and much is vague. There is, however, a more recent movement about which considerable detail is known — the Millerites, who flourished in mid-nineteenth-century America. Many of the original documents of the Millerite movement have been preserved and there are two fairly lengthy summary accounts available. One, by C. E. Sears,[12] tends to ridicule the Millerites while the other, by F. D. Nichol,[13] is a careful and vigorous defense of them.

William Miller was a New England farmer with a belief in the literal fulfillment of biblical prophecy. In 1818, after a two-year study of the Bible, Miller reached the conclusion that the end of the world would occur in 1843. Nichol's account reads:

Specifically, he put his first and greatest emphasis on the prophetic declaration, "Unto two thousand and three hundred days; then shall the sanctuary be cleansed." Daniel 8:14. Believing that the "cleansing" of the sanctuary involved the purging of this earth by fire, the "days" in symbolic prophecy stand for years, and that this time prophecy began about 457 B.C., he reached this final conclusion: "I was thus brought, in 1818, at the close of my two years' study of the Scriptures, to the solemn conclusion, that in about twenty-five years from that time all the affairs of our present state would be wound up." (William Miller, *Apology and Defense*, p. 5).[14]

For another five years he continued to study the Bible and to check his calculations before he acquired the confidence to talk much about it to others. Even then he talked only to his neighbors and to a few ministers, none of whom seemed to manifest much interest. He continued talking about his views, however. By 1831 he had evoked enough interest to receive invitations to address various groups. For eight years Miller continued to devote a great deal of his time to giving lectures in which he explained the basis for his prediction of the millennium in 1843. He gradually persuaded more and more people, including a number of ministers, of the correctness of his belief. In 1839 he met and convinced Joshua V. Himes, who helped change the movement from a one-man affair into an organized activity. A newspaper was started, and in 1840, only three years before the Second Coming was due, a general conference of interested ministers was called. Proselyting activity increased and Miller's views began to spread as the adventist prediction became the focus of a mass movement.

Many of the leading figures in the Millerite movement had still not fully accepted the specific date of 1843 as the time of the Second Coming. In the spring of 1842, a general conference was held in Boston. Nichol states:

In this conference the significance of the time element in the preaching of the advent came definitely to the front as indicated in this resolution that was passed:

"*Resolved*, that in the opinion of this conference, there are most serious and important reasons for believing that God has revealed the time of the end of the world, and that that time is 1843." (*Signs of the Times*, June 1, 1842, p. 69).

The very fact that an increasing emphasis was being placed on the time element meant that all who accepted this phase of the teaching felt an increasing sense of urgency in discharging their responsibility to warn the world. They believed that the time had come to proclaim with vigor what they described as "the midnight cry." [15]

In other words, as the year 1843 approached, belief in the correctness of the predicted date grew stronger. At the same time activity in spreading the word was on the increase. The general conference had decided to hold a series of camp meetings during the summer of 1842, and these were almost all highly successful. In four months, ending the middle of November, the Millerites held thirty camp meetings at which the attendance was in the thousands. The number of adherents was growing steadily.

In addition to the newspaper *Signs of the Times*, which had been started in Boston in 1840, the Millerite leaders now started another, *The Midnight Cry*, in New York. Many other newspapers were published in various cities for shorter periods of time, usually in connection with a special series of lectures being given locally:

For example, the *Philadelphia Alarm* was started in 1843, as an adjunct to a series of lectures. Thirteen numbers were issued. Thus a local color could be given to the literature in any city while an initial endeavor was being made there. Afterward the more permanently established publications could be used for promotion and educating the believers in the movement. [16]

While the movement was growing the opposition was also increasing. By the beginning of 1843 many ministers were preaching against the Millerites and newspapers were ridiculing them. Rumors were current and printed widely in the newspapers of the day that Miller's followers were fanatics and that his doctrines drove people insane. A single example should suffice to show the kind of attack directed against the movement:

The Millerites have very properly been shut out of the buildings in which they have for some time been holding their orgies in Philadelphia, and we are happy to learn that the grand jury of the Boston municipal court has represented the great temple itself as a dangerous structure. After some half-dozen more deaths occur and a few more men and women are sent to madhouses by

14

this miserable fanaticism perhaps some grand jury may think it worth-while to indict the vagabonds who are the cause of so much mischief.[17]

In spite of such opposition, the movement continued to attract believers — so many that it became difficult to find a hall large enough for general meetings. Early in 1843, therefore, the leaders decided to erect a tabernacle in Boston. It was dedicated before an audience of some 3500 people — a capacity crowd that included a number of clergymen of the city. The new building made it possible to speed the word to even larger audiences in the city, while the campaign of pamphlets and newspapers continued unabated.

As one might expect, the beginning of 1843 coincided with an upsurge of interest in the specific date of the Advent. Until the beginning of the year, Miller had usually referred to the Second Coming as taking place "about the year 1843." On January 1, 1843, Miller published a synopsis of his beliefs, and therein stated his expectations about the date:

I believe the time can be known by all who desire to understand and to be ready for His coming. And I am fully convinced that sometime between March 21st, 1843, and March 21st, 1844, according to the Jewish mode of computation of time, Christ will come, and bring all His Saints with Him; and that then He will reward every man as his work shall be.[18]

Nichol comments:

Miller set no date or day within this period. The leaders who were associated with him likewise refused to name a specific date. In the first issue of January, 1843, the *Signs of the Times* declared, in refutation of a widely circulated charge that the Millerites had set on a certain day in April:

"The fact is, that the believers of the second advent in 1843, *have fixed* NO TIME *in the year* for the event. And Brethren Miller, Himes, Litch, Hale, Fitch, Hawley, and other prominent lecturers, most decidedly protest against . . . fixing the day or hour of the event. This we have done over and over again, in our paper." (*Signs of the Times*, Jan. 4, 1843, p. 121. See also issue of Jan. 18, 1843, p. 141, in which George Storrs, another Millerite minister, protests against the fixing of any day; also issue of April 5, 1843, pp. 33–35, 37.)

It is true that individual preachers or limited groups here and there sought to find a Scriptural analogy or by a certain reading of the prophecy a warrant for predicting the advent on some particular day during the year.[19]

The fact that Miller had specified an interval of time, namely, March 21, 1843, to March 21, 1844, rather than a single day, tended to be temporarily overlooked by many followers. Two predictions of specific days had some currency although it is impossible to be sure how widely they were believed. Some Millerites expected the Advent to occur on April 23, 1843, although the leaders never endorsed this date. Those who had given credence to the April date reacted to its passing in the following way:

At first there was evidence of surprise and disappointment among the Millerites, but it quickly gave way to renewed confidence. "After all," they reminded one another, "there is a whole year in which to look for the Coming;—we looked for it too soon, that was all."—and the singing and exhorting took on a new fervor.[20]

Here once again we note the appearance of increased enthusiasm and conviction after a disconfirmation.

In spite of the official position of the leaders, that the end of the period in which the Second Coming was expected was March 21, 1844, many Millerites placed their hopes on the end of 1843. The leaders took note of this specific expectation and, early in 1844, issued statements concerning it. For example, the opening paragraph of a New Year's address by Miller goes as follows:

"Brethren, The Roman [year] 1843 is past [the Jewish sacred year would end in the spring of 1844] and our hopes are not realized. Shall we give up the ship? No, no . . . We do not yet believe our reckoning has run out. It takes all of 457 and 1843 to make 2300, and must of course run as far into '44 as it began in the year 457 before Christ." [21]

The situation generally at the beginning of 1844 is described by Sears:

16

. . . Then a fluttering of doubt and hesitation became apparent in certain communities, but soon those were dispelled when it was recalled that as far back as 1839 Prophet Miller had stated on some occasion, which had been forgotten in the general excitement, that he was not *positive* that the event would take place during the *Christian* year from 1843 to 1844, and that he would claim the whole *Jewish* year which would carry the prophecy over to the 21st of March, 1844. An announcement to this effect was sent broadcast, and by this time the delusion had taken such a firm hold upon the imaginations of his followers that any simple explanation, however crude, seemed sufficient to quiet all doubts and questionings.

Having accepted this lengthening of the allotted time, the brethren who had assumed the responsibility of sounding the alarm entered into their work with renewed energy and outdid themselves in their efforts to terrify the army of unbelievers into a realization of the horrors that awaited them and to strengthen the faith of those already in he ranks.[22]

Again fervor increased; Millerite conferences in New York and Philadelphia were thronged, and, in Washington, there had to be a last-minute change to a larger hall. Popular interest greatly exceeded even the leaders' expectations.

But March 21, 1844, also came and went with no sign of the Second Coming. The reaction of the non-Millerites was strong and unequivocal:

The world made merry over the old Prophet's predicament. The taunts and jeers of the "scoffers" were well-nigh unbearable. If any of Miller's followers walked abroad, they ran the gauntlet of merciless ridicule.

"What! — not gone up yet? — We thought you'd gone up! Aren't you going up soon? — Wife didn't go up and leave you behind to burn, did she?"

The rowdy element in the community would not leave them alone.[23]

There was strong and severe disappointment among the believers, but this was of brief duration and soon the energy and enthusiasm were back to where they had been before and even greater:

. . . The year of the end of the world had ended, but Millerism had not. . . . Though some who had been only lukewarm in the movement fell away from it, many maintained both their faith and their fervor. They were ready to attribute the disappointment to some minor error in calculating chronology.[24]

But in spite of the failure of the prophecy the fires of fanaticism increased. The flames of such emotions cannot be quenched at will; like all great conflagrations they must burn themselves out. And so it was in 1844. Instead of decreasing, the failure seemed to excite even greater exhibitions of loyalty to the expectation of the impending Judgment Day.[25]

By the middle of July things were at a new fever pitch and the energy expended to convert more and more people was greater than ever. Miller and Himes traveled as far as Ohio to make converts, something that had never before been done. Himes described the general attitude of followers toward the Advent: "I have never witnessed a stronger, or more active faith. Indeed, the faith and confidence of the brethren in the prophetic word was never stronger. I find few, if any, who ever believed on Bible *evidence*, that are at all shaken in the faith; while others are embracing our views." [26] Following a visit to Philadelphia Himes, still very much aware of the disconfirmation in March, showed his elation at the revival of belief: "The trying crisis is past, and the cause is on the rise in this city. The calls for lectures in the vicinity were never more pressing than now. The minister in charge of the Ebenezer station, Kensington, (Protestant Methodist) has just come out on the doctrine in full." [27]

As Nichol puts it:

From Cleveland, Himes wrote early in August of his plan to go to England in October, "if time be prolonged," for the purpose of quickening the interest already present there. Literature had been sent out. Various ministers in other lands had taken up the cry, "Behold, the Bridegroom cometh." But Himes thought that now he and others with him from America should go forth to strengthen the endeavors abroad. Said he:

"If time be continued for a few months, we shall send the *glad tidings* out in a number of different languages, among Protestant and Catholic nations. . . .

"A press shall be established at London, and lecturers will go out in every direction, and we trust the Word of the Lord shall have a free course and be glorified. What we shall accomplish we can not tell. But we wish to do our duty." (*The Advent Herald*, Aug. 21, 1844, p. 20)

Thus even as Himes and Miller moved westward expanding the work, they envisioned a still greater work overseas.[28]

About this time more and more Millerites were accepting a new prediction first promulgated by one of their number, the Reverend Samuel S. Snow, who believed that the date of the Second Coming would be October 22, 1844. Although it might not seem possible for the enthusiasm and fervor to exceed what had already been shown in the first few months of 1844, that is just what happened. The two partial disconfirmations (April 23, 1843, and the end of the calendar year 1843) and one complete and unequivocal disconfirmation (March 21, 1844) served simply to strengthen conviction that the Coming was near at hand and to increase the time and energy that Miller's adherents spent trying to convince others:

Perhaps not so much from the preaching and writing of Snow, as from a deep conviction that the end of all things could not be far away, some of the believers in Northern New Hampshire, even before summer began, failed to plow their fields because the Lord would surely come "before another winter." This conviction grew among others in that area so that even if they had planted their fields they felt it would be inconsistent with their faith to take in their crops. We read:

"Some, on going into their fields to cut their grass, found themselves entirely unable to proceed, and, conforming to their sense of duty, left their crops standing in the field, to show their faith by their works, and thus to condemn the world. This rapidly extended through the north of New England." (*The Advent Herald*, Oct. 20, 1844, p. 93)

Such conviction naturally prepared men to give a sympathetic ear to the proclamation that the day of the Lord would come on October 22. By midsummer a new stimulus had been given to Millerism in New England. Backsliders were reclaimed, and new ardor controlled those Adventists who accepted Snow's reckoning, as they went out to proclaim the cry, "Behold, the Bridegroom cometh, go ye out to meet Him." Indeed, Snow declared that only now was the true midnight cry being given.[29]

It is interesting that it was the insistence of the ordinary members of the Millerite movement that the October date be accepted. The leaders of the movement resisted it and counseled against it for a long time but to no avail. A Millerite editor, writing in retrospect, commented:

At first the definite time was generally opposed; but there seemed to be an irresistible power attending its proclamation, which prostrated all before it. It swept over the land with the velocity of a tornado, and it reached hearts in different and distant places almost simultaneously, and in a manner which can be accounted for only on the supposition that God was [in] it. . . .

The lecturers among the Adventists were the last to embrace the views of the time. . . . It was not until within about two weeks of the commencement of the seventh month [about the first of October], that we were particularly impressed with the progress of the movement, when we had such a view of it, that to oppose it, or even to remain silent longer, seemed to us to be opposing the work of the Holy Spirit; and in entering upon the work with all our souls, we could but exclaim, "What were we, that we should resist God?" It seemed to us to have been so independent of human agency, that we could but regard it as a fulfillment of the "midnight cry." [30]

In the period from mid-August to the predicted new day, October 22, 1844, things reached an incredible pitch of fervor, zeal, and conviction:

Elder Boutelle describes the period thus: "The 'Advent Herald', 'the Midnight Cry', and other Advent papers, periodicals, pamphlets, tracts, leaflets, voicing the coming glory, were scattered broadcast and everywhere like autumn leaves in the forest. Every house was visited by them. . . . A mighty effort through the Spirit and the word preached was made to bring sinners to repentance, and to have the wandering ones return."

The camp meetings were now so crowded that they were no longer orderly as they had been. If there had been a time when an undesirable element could be kept out, it was now impossible to do so; and as a matter of fact the world was so near its end, as they claimed, whatever precautions were taken before seemed hardly worth while any longer. [31]

The most active endeavors were made by the Millerites during these closing weeks to broadcast what they believed was the truth concerning the exact time of Christ's advent. Extra issues of *The Midnight Cry* and *The Advent Herald* were published. The editor of *The Midnight Cry* stated that in order to provide the literature needed they were keeping "four steam presses almost constantly in motion." [32]

Further evidence on the extent of the conviction and the drive to persuade and convert others is the fact that now even many of the leaders were advocating partial cessation of normal activities on the part of believers so they would have more time to convert others and spread the word. An editorial in the final issue of *The Midnight Cry* proclaimed:

Think for eternity! Thousands may be lulled to sleep by hearing your actions say: "This world is worth my whole energies. The world to come is a vain shadow." O, reverse this practical sermon, *instantly!* Break loose from the world as much as possible. If indispensable duty calls you into the world for a moment, go as a man would run to do a piece of work in the rain. Run and hasten through it, and let it be known that you leave it with alacrity for something better. Let your actions preach in the clearest tones: "The Lord is coming" — "The Time is short" — "This world passeth away" — "Prepare to meet thy God." [33]

A news story in *The Midnight Cry* stated:

Many are leaving all to go out and warn the brethren and the world. In Philadelphia, thirteen volunteered at one meeting (after hearing Brother Storrs) to go out and sound the alarm. . . . In both cities [New York and Philadelphia], stores are being closed, and they preach in tones the world understands, though they may not heed it. [34]

And Nichol points out:

There were several reasons why the believers in a number of instances sold their possessions in part or in whole. First, they wished to have more money with which to support the cause. It took money to support four presses running constantly, pouring out literature on Millerism. Second, they wished to have all their dealings with their fellow men honorably concluded before the advent, including full payment of all their debts. Third, with the fervent love for others, which true religion certainly ought to generate in the hearts of men, Millerites who owed no debts themselves sought to help others pay their debts. Some Millerites, stimulated by the realization that soon earthly gold would be worthless, and warmed in their hearts with a love for their fellow men, wished to make gifts to the poor, both within and without the faith.[35]

But October 22 came and went, and with it all the hopes of the Millerites. This was the culminating disconfirmation and, at last, conviction was shattered and proselyting was stilled. The plight of the heavily committed followers was pitiable indeed. They had to bear the taunts and jeers of a hostile world and many were left pauperized. Their cruel disappointment and the hardship are well attested to. Nichol quotes two extracts from the writings of convinced believers that tell the sad story:

"Our fondest hopes and expectations were blasted, and such a spirit of weeping came over us as I never experienced before. It seemed that the loss of all earthly friends could have been no comparison. We wept, and wept, till the day dawn. I mused in my own heart, saying, My advent experience has been the richest and brightest of all my Christian experience. If this had proved a failure, what was the rest of my Christian experience worth? Has the Bible proved a failure? Is there no God, no heaven, no golden home city, no paradise? Is all this but a cunningly devised fable? Is there no reality to our fondest hope and expectation of these things? And thus we had something to grieve and weep over, if all our fond hopes were lost. And as I said, we wept till the day dawn." [36]

"The 22nd of October passed, making unspeakably sad the faithful and longing ones; but causing the unbelieving and wicked to rejoice. All was still. No *Advent Herald*; no meetings as formerly. Everyone felt lonely, with hardly a desire to speak to anyone. Still in the cold world! No deliverance—the Lord [had] not come! No words can express the feelings of disappointment of a true Adventist then. Those only who experienced it can enter into the subject as it was. It was a humiliating thing and we all felt it alike . . ." [37]

The disconfirmation of October 22 brought about the collapse of Millerism. It had taken three or perhaps four disconfirmations within a period of eighteen months, but this last one was too much. In spite of their overwhelming commitments, Miller's followers gave up their beliefs and the movement quickly disintegrated in dissention, controversy, and discord. By the late spring of 1845 it had virtually disappeared.

The history of the Millerites shows again the phenomenon we have noted in our other examples. Although there is a limit beyond which belief will not withstand disconfirmation, it is clear that the introduction of contrary evidence can serve to increase the conviction and enthusiasm of a believer.

Historical records are replete with further instances of similar movements of a millennial or messianic character. Unfortunately for our purpose, however, in most instances the data which would be relevant to our hypotheses are totally absent. Even in cases where considerable data are available, there will frequently be some crucial point which is equivocal, thus destroying the cogent relevance to our hypotheses. The best instance of such a movement where there is one single controversial point on a crucial issue is the very beginnings of Christianity.[38]

There is quite general agreement among historians that the apostles were both convinced and committed. None would question that the apostles fully believed in the things Jesus stood for and had altered their lives considerably because of this belief. Burkitt, for example, states that Peter, at one point, "exclaimed that he and his companions really had left all to follow Jesus." [39] Thus, we may assert that the first two conditions which we stated early in the chapter are fulfilled.

There is no denying that the apostles provided support for one another and that they went out to proselyte following the crucifixion of Jesus. Thus, we may accept as fact that the fifth condition we mentioned is satisfied, and that there was a point at which proselyting increased.

But the third and fourth conditions remain in doubt. Was there, in essence, something in the belief system that was amenable to clear and unequivocal disconfirmation and, if so, did such disconfirmation occur? In spite of many things which are not disputed, the major issue is shrouded in disagreement among various historians. There is general agreement that Jesus, in various ways, implied that he was the Messiah or Christ. More important, it is also clear that his disciples recognized him as such. For example, Scott states: "When directly challenged by Jesus, Peter speaking for the group of disciples said, 'Thou art the Messiah.'" [40]

It is also clear that, at least so far as other Jewish sects of that day were concerned, the Messiah could not be made to suffer pain. Thus Simpson states: "With equal certainty it may be affirmed that no department of Judaism had ever conceived of a suffering Messiah." [41] If this were all there were to it one would assert that the crucifixion and the cry Jesus uttered on the cross were indeed an unequivocal disconfirmation.

But this is not all there is to it. Many authorities assert unequivocally that it is precisely on this question that Jesus introduced new doctrine. Jesus and the apostles, these authorities state, did believe that the Messiah had to suffer and Jesus even predicted that he would die in Jerusalem. Burkitt says: ". . . we end with Peter declaring, 'Thou art the Messiah' and with Jesus saying, practically, in reply, 'Yes, and I go now to Jerusalem; but whoever wants to follow Me there must renounce all ambitious hopes and accompany Me — to execution.'" [42] If this view is maintained then the crucifixion, far from being a disconfirmation, was indeed a confirmation of a prediction and the subsequent proselyting of the apostles would stand as a counter-example to our hypotheses. The authorities we have quoted from above accept this latter interpretation and, in fact, they are in the majority.

But not all authorities agree. At the other extreme of interpretation is Graetz, who states:

When the disciples of Jesus had somewhat recovered from the panic which came upon them at the time he was seized and executed, they re-assembled to mourn together over the death of their beloved Master. . . . Still, the effect that Jesus produced upon the unenlightened masses must have been very powerful; for their faith in him, far from fading away like a dream, became more and more intense, their adoration of Jesus rising to the highest pitch of enthusiasm. The only stumbling-block to their belief lay in the fact that the Messiah who came to deliver Israel and bring to light the glory of the kingdom of heaven, endured a shameful death. How could the Messiah be subject to pain? A suffering Messiah staggered them considerably, and this stumbling-block had to be overcome before a perfect and joyful belief could be reposed in him. It was at that moment probably that some writer relieved his own perplexities and quelled their doubts by referring to a prophecy in Isaiah, that "He will be taken from the land of the living, and will be wounded for the sins of his people." [43]

Was it or was it not a disconfirmation? We do not know and cannot say. But this one unclarity makes the whole episode inconclusive with respect to our hypotheses.

There are many more historical examples we could describe at the risk of becoming repetitive and at the risk of using highly unreliable data. Let the examples we have already given suffice.

We can now turn our attention to the question of why increased proselyting follows the disconfirmation of a prediction. How can we explain it and what are the factors that will determine whether or not it will occur?

Since our explanation will rest upon one derivation from a general theory, we will first state the bare essentials of the theory which are necessary for this derivation. The full theory has wide implications and a variety of experiments have already been conducted to test derivations concerning such things as the consequences of decisions, the effects of producing forced compliance, and some patterns of voluntary exposure to new information. At this point, we shall draw out in detail only those implications that are relevant to the phenomenon of increased proselyting following disconfirmation of a prediction. For this purpose we shall introduce the concepts of consonance and dissonance. [44]

Dissonance and consonance are relations among cognitions — that is, among opinions, beliefs, knowledge of the environment, and knowledge of one's own actions and feelings. Two opinions, or beliefs, or items of knowledge are *dissonant* with each other if they do not fit together — that is, if they are inconsistent, or if, considering only the particular two items, one does not follow from the other. For example, a cigarette smoker who believes that smoking is bad for his health has an opinion that is dissonant with the knowledge that he is continuing to smoke. He may have many other opinions, beliefs, or items of knowledge that are consonant with continuing to smoke but the dissonance nevertheless exists too.

Dissonance produces discomfort and, correspondingly, there will arise pressures to reduce or eliminate the dissonance. Attempts to reduce dissonance represent the observable manifestations that dissonance exists. Such attempts may take any or all of three forms. The person may try to change one or more of the beliefs, opinions, or behaviors involved in the dissonance; to acquire new information or beliefs that will increase the existing consonance and thus cause the total dissonance to be reduced; or to forget or reduce the importance of those cognitions that are in a dissonant relationship.

If any of the above attempts are to be successful, they must meet with support from either the physical or the social environment. In the absence of such support, the most determined efforts to reduce dissonance may be unsuccessful.

The foregoing statement of the major ideas about dissonance and its reduction is a very brief one and, for that reason, it may be difficult to follow. We can perhaps make these ideas clearer to the reader by showing how they apply to the kind of social movement we have been discussing, and by pointing out how these ideas help to explain the curious phenomenon we have observed.

Theoretically, what is the situation of the individual believer at the pre-disconfirmation stage of such a movement? He has a strongly held belief in a prediction — for example, that Christ will return — a belief that is supported by the other members of the movement. By way of preparation for the predicted event, he has engaged in many activities that are entirely consistent with his belief. In other words, most of the relations among relevant cognitions are, at this point, consonant.

Now what is the effect of the disconfirmation, of the unequivocal fact that the prediction was wrong, upon the believer? The disconfirmation introduces an important and painful dissonance. The fact that the predicted events did not occur is dissonant with continuing to believe both the prediction and the remainder of the ideology of which the prediction was the central item. The failure of the prediction is also dissonant with all the actions that the believer took in preparation for its fulfillment. The magnitude of the dissonance will, of course, depend on the importance of the belief to the individual and on the magnitude of his preparatory activity.

In the type of movement we have discussed, the central belief and its accompanying ideology are usually of crucial importance in the believers' lives and hence the dissonance is very strong — and very painful to tolerate. Accordingly we should expect to observe believers making determined efforts to eliminate the dissonance or, at least, to reduce its magnitude. How may they accomplish this end? The dissonance would be largely eliminated if they discarded the belief that had been disconfirmed, ceased the behavior which had been initiated in preparation for the fulfillment of the prediction, and returned to a more usual existence. Indeed, this pattern sometimes occurs and we have seen that it did happen to the Millerites after the last disconfirmation and to the Sabbataians after Zevi himself was converted to Islam. But frequently the behavioral commitment to the belief system is so strong that almost any other course of action is preferable. It may even be less painful to tolerate the dissonance than to discard the belief and admit one had been wrong. When that is the case, the dissonance cannot be eliminated by giving up the belief.

Alternatively, the dissonance would be reduced or eliminated if the members of a movement effectively blind themselves to the fact that the prediction has not been fulfilled. But most people, including members of such movements, are in touch with reality and cannot simply blot out of their cognition such an unequivocal and undeniable fact. They can try to ignore it, however, and they usually do try. They may convince themselves that the date was wrong but that the prediction will, after all, be shortly confirmed; or they may even set another date as the Millerites did. Some

Millerites, after the last disconfirmation, even ventured the opinion that the Second Coming had occurred, but that it had occurred in heaven and not on the earth itself. Or believers may try to find reasonable explanations and very often they find ingenious ones. The Sabbataians, for example, convinced themselves when Zevi was jailed that the very fact that he was still alive proved he was the Messiah. Even after his conversion some stanch adherents claimed this, too, was part of the plan. Rationalization can reduce dissonance somewhat. For rationalization to be fully effective, support from others is needed to make the explanation or the revision seem correct. Fortunately, the disappointed believer can usually turn to the others in the same movement, who have the same dissonance and the same pressures to reduce it. Support for the new explanation is, hence, forthcoming and the members of the movement can recover somewhat from the shock of the disconfirmation.

But whatever explanation is made it is still by itself not sufficient. The dissonance is too important and though they may try to hide it, even from themselves, the believers still know that the prediction was false and all their preparations were in vain. The dissonance cannot be eliminated completely by denying or rationalizing the disconfirmation. But there is a way in which the remaining dissonance can be reduced. *If more and more people can be persuaded that the system of belief is correct, then clearly it must, after all, be correct.* Consider the extreme case: if everyone in the whole world believed something there would be no question at all as to the validity of this belief. It is for this reason that we observe the increase in proselyting following disconfirmation. If the proselyting proves successful, then by gathering more adherents and effectively surrounding himself with supporters, the believer reduces dissonance to the point where he can live with it.

In the light of this explanation of the phenomenon that proselyting increases as a result of a disconfirmation, let us take another, and more critical, look at the historical examples we have offered in evidence. There are a number of grounds for feeling unsatisfied with them as proof.

In the first place there is a scarcity of data of the sort required by our analysis. It is an understandable lack, for the people collecting historical records were not concerned with our particular problem, but it is a lack nonetheless. Even our best documented example, the Millerites, contains little evidence on actual proselyting behavior, especially among the mass members. Statements about proselyting must be inferred largely from evidence about the number of adherents and the size and frequency of meetings. But such signs as these are dependent not only on the effort made to proselyte — the desire to convince others — but also on the effectiveness of the efforts and on the state of mind of prospective converts.

Even where there is direct evidence about proselyting attempts, such as the number of speeches made, the fact that Miller and Himes traveled widely, or that the Millerite presses worked twenty-four hours a day, these are activities of the leaders. There is very little concrete evidence of the proselyting activities of the ordinary members, whose behavior is most significant for our purposes. Leaders of a social movement may, after all, have motives other than simply their conviction that they have the truth. Should the movement disintegrate, they would lose prestige or other rewards.

And if the Millerite case is inadequately documented for our purposes, our other examples are even more poorly supported. On the Sabbataian movement we have virtually no data concerning the initial disconfirmation in 1648, for the very good reason that the movement attracted little attention (and, hence, there were few records of it) until it became very large and important.

A second reason for considering historical data alone as inadequate is the small likelihood that this kind of data could challenge our explanation. Suppose we could find record of a mass movement that had apparently collapsed immediately after disconfirmation. In the absence of adequate measurement, we might well conjecture that the members' commitment to the belief was small — so small that the dissonance introduced by disconfirmation was enough to force the discarding of the belief. Alternatively, if the commitment could be demonstrated to have been heavy, it is still possible that there were attempts to proselyte following disconfirmation, but that these attempts had been unsuccessful. This would be a tenable contention since it is the results of proselyting efforts that generally find their way into historical records rather than the efforts themselves.

There is a type of occurrence that would indeed disprove our explanation — namely, a movement whose members simply maintained the same conviction after disconfirmation as they had before and neither fell away from the movement nor increased their proselyting. But it is precisely such an occurrence that might very well go unnoticed by its contemporaries or by historians and never find its way into their annals.

Since the likelihood of disproof through historical data is small, we cannot place much confidence in the supporting evidence from the same sources. The reader can then imagine the enthusiasm with which we seized the opportunity to collect direct observational data about a group who appeared to believe in a prediction of catastrophe to occur in the near future. Direct observations made before, during, and after the disconfirmation would produce at least one case that was fully documented by trustworthy data directly relevant to our purpose.

One day in late September the Lake City *Herald* carried a two-column story, on a back page, headlined: PROPHECY FROM PLANET. CLARION CALL TO CITY: FLEE THAT FLOOD. IT'LL SWAMP US ON DEC. 21, OUTER SPACE TELLS SUBURBANITE. The body of the story expanded somewhat on these bare facts:

Lake City will be destroyed by a flood from Great Lake just before dawn, Dec. 21, according to a suburban housewife. Mrs. Marian Keech, of 847 West School street, says the prophecy is not her own. It is the purport of many messages she has received by automatic writing, she says. . . . The messages, according to Mrs. Keech, are sent to her by superior beings from a planet called 'Clarion.' These beings have been visiting the earth, she says, in what we call flying saucers. During their visits, she says, they have observed fault lines in the earth's crust that foretoken the deluge. Mrs. Keech reports she was told the flood will spread to form an inland sea stretching from the Arctic Circle to the Gulf of Mexico. At the same time, she says, a cataclysm will submerge the West Coast from Seattle, Wash., to Chile in South America.

The story went on to report briefly the origin of Mrs. Keech's experiences and to quote several messages that seemed to indicate she had been chosen as a person to learn and transmit teachings from the "superior beings." A photograph of Mrs. Keech accompanied the story. She appeared to be about fifty years of age, and she sat poised with pad and pencil in her lap, a slight, wiry woman with dark hair and intense, bright eyes. The story was not derogatory, nor did the reporter comment upon or interpret any of the information he had gathered.

Since Mrs. Keech's pronouncement made a specific prediction of a specific event, since she, at least, was publicly committed to belief in it, and since she apparently was interested to some extent in informing a wider public about it, this seemed to be an opportunity to conduct a "field" test of the theoretical ideas to which the reader has been introduced.

In early October two of the authors called on Mrs. Keech and tried to learn whether there were other convinced persons in her orbit of influence, whether they too believed in the specific prediction, and what commitments of time, energy, reputation, or material possessions they might be making in connection with the prediction. The results of this first visit encouraged us to go on. The three of us and some hired observers joined the group and, as participants, gathered data about the conviction, commitment, and proselyting activity of the individuals who were actively interested in Mrs. Keech's ideas. We tried to learn as much as possible about the events that had preceded the news story, and, of course, kept records of subsequent developments. The means by which the observers gained entree, maintained rapport, and collected data are fully described in the Appendix. The information collected about events before early October is retrospective. It comes primarily from documents and from conversations with the people concerned in the events. From October to early January almost all the data are first-hand observations, with an occasional report of an event we did not cover directly but heard about later through someone in the group of believers who had been there at the time.

The next three chapters are a narrative of events from the beginning of Mrs. Keech's automatic writing up to the crucial days in December just before the cataclysmic flood was expected.

These chapters provide background material. They will introduce the members of the group, describe their personal histories, their involvement in the movement, and the preparations they made for the flood. We shall also describe the ideology accompanying the prediction and some of the other influences to which the group was exposed. Such background is necessary to make understandable some of the behavior and the events that led up to the night of December 21. Much of this material is not directly relevant to the theoretical theme of the book, but we hope that these details will re-create for the reader some of the vividness of these months.

CHAPTER II 〰〰〰 *Teachings and Prophecies from Outer Space*

THE first contact between a prophet and the source of his revelation is likely to be marked by confusion and astonishment, not to say shock. So it was with Mrs. Marian Keech, who awoke near dawn one morning in the early winter about a year before the events with which we are concerned. "I felt a kind of tingling or numbness in my arm, and my whole arm felt warm right up to the shoulder," she once remarked later, in describing the incident. "I had the feeling that someone was trying to get my attention. Without knowing why, I picked up a pencil and a pad that were lying on the table near my bed. My hand began to write in another handwriting. I looked at the handwriting and it was strangely familiar, but I knew it was not my own. I realized that somebody else was using my hand, and I said: 'Will you identify yourself?' And they did. I was much surprised to find that it was my father, who had passed away."

Although it was her most impressive experience with psychic phenomena, the message from her father was by no means the first contact Mrs. Keech had had with the occult, either as an interested student or as a participant. At least fifteen years earlier, while living in New York, she had been invited by an Indian acquaintance to attend a lecture on theosophy. She was fascinated by what she heard, and deeply impressed with the profundity of the lecturer's message. She attended several lectures on theosophy and, after each, picked up a mimeographed copy of the talk to study it more carefully.

In the years following her exposure to theosophy, Mrs. Keech's deep strain of curiosity about the cosmos and about her own

33

nature led her to explore a variety of sources of enlightenment. She read the works of Godfré Ray King (Guy Ballard), the founder of the I AM movement, and the idea that one might "walk in the light" of superior knowledge was communicated to her. During a lengthy convalescence she became absorbed in *Oahspe*, subtitled "A Kosmon Bible." The Reverend John Ballou Newbrough, who held the first copyright on *Oahspe*, disclaimed authorship in the ordinary sense when he asserted that the contents of the book were given to him by direct revelation; he served merely as the scribe of higher forces. *Oahspe* challenges the orthodox Christian account of human downfall by setting forth a story of the division of mankind into two forces: the "Faithists," who forswore war, dissipation, and drunkenness and followed God's commandments; and the "Uzians," signifying destroyers.

Besides her quest for cosmic knowledge, Mrs. Keech sought insight into herself. She joined a dianetics group and was "cleared" by an auditor and friend who later took up residence in Mrs. Keech's home. Discussing this experience later, she remarked: "I prefer to call it scientology, which is the art and science of taking someone back as far in his life as he can go. My friends have helped me take myself back to the period of my birth — in fact, even before my birth. I can remember the day I was conceived." On another occasion, Mrs. Keech explained that everyone knew his true identity when he was born, but, in growing up, lost this clear knowledge and, thus, his true self. One of the chief advances in scientology, she felt, was that it not only made possible an understanding of the circumstances of an individual's conception and birth, but also gave access to knowledge of one's identity in earlier incarnations.

At about the same time that she began to receive messages from nonterrestrial sources, Mrs. Keech had become actively interested in one of the major popular mysteries of our time — flying saucers. Her interest led her to attend one or more lectures on the subject by an expert on saucers who expounded the belief that these objects did indeed transport visitors from outer space or other

34

planets. The connection between extraterrestrial messages and such visitors was probably immediately apparent to Mrs. Keech.

With this background of esoteric knowledge, Mrs. Keech took her first active step into the occult when she transcribed her father's message. Like many beginnings, it was not especially impressive. It was a letter from her father to her mother giving some instructions to the latter for planting flowers that spring. There was a certain amount of information about her father's state of spiritual health, and a brief, and rather unclear, description of his present surroundings and his "way of life" in "the astral." Unclarity and incoherence were characteristic of this first message as well as of several of the immediately subsequent ones. They were written haltingly and contained many indecipherable words and perplexing neologisms. Mrs. Keech concluded that the fault lay at least partially in her, and set herself the task of developing, through concentration, through prayers for help and guidance, and through constant, obedient practice, a higher level of skill in transcribing the messages from the spiritual realm.

She soon learned that the world was populated with scoffers and unbelievers. At her father's command she had transmitted his first message to her mother, who answered by reprimanding her and ordering her to stop such nonsense or, at least, to stop inflicting it upon her living parent. Disheartened, but undeterred by this rebuff, Mrs. Keech continued to believe in her newly developed ability. She accustomed herself to sit each day for a message, or a lesson, and spent many hours in bitter frustration, often plagued by doubt, as she tried to grasp the meaning of the words and phrases her pencil wrote. On some days there were no messages at all.

As she struggled, she gradually became aware that other beings or intelligences were trying to "get through to" her. "It occurred to me," she subsequently said, "that if my father could use my hand, Higher Forces could use my hand. I have always been interested in my fellow men and I have always wanted to be of service to mankind. I don't mind telling you I prayed very diligently that I would not fall into the wrong hands." During this early phase

35

of message writing, Mrs. Keech apparently came to fear that she would "fall into the hands" of beings located in "the astral." She explained that the astral is overflowing with spirits who are desperate for communication with those left behind, and whose insistent clamor can confuse or obliterate the intelligence available from higher beings, who dwell at higher (i.e., less dense) spiritual vibration frequencies.

Mrs. Keech's prayers were answered. Within a short time she began to receive messages from a being who identified himself as "the Elder Brother" and informed her that her father was in considerable need of spiritual instruction in order that he might advance to higher levels. Between them, Mrs. Keech and the Elder Brother attempted to provide such instruction, but her father proved a recalcitrant pupil, overly concerned with the earthly affairs of those he had left behind. He was inattentive and mischievous, as is, apparently, the wont of astral spirits, and finally the Elder Brother gave up, instructing Mrs. Keech to turn her attention to a more feasible and important task — her own spiritual development.

Gradually, as spring wore on, she developed greater and greater facility at receiving messages, while the number of her communicators increased. Besides the Elder Brother, she began to receive writings from other spiritual beings who dwelt on the planets Clarion and Cerus. Toward mid-April she began to receive communications from Sananda, who was destined to become her most important source of information and instruction, as well as her principal link with orthodox Christian revelation, for Sananda subsequently identified himself as the contemporary identity of the historical Jesus — his new name having been adopted with the beginning of the "new cycle" or age of light.

In spite of her growing facility, Mrs. Keech was still concerned about her ability and fearful lest the superior beings abandon her as a promising pupil. On Easter morning her mind was set at ease on that point, however, when, just after she awakened at 7 A.M., she received the following message from the Elder Brother:

"I am always with you. The cares of the day cannot touch you.

We will teach them that seek and are ready to follow in the light. I will take care of the details. Trust in us.

"Be patient and learn, for we are there preparing the work for you as a connoiter. That is an earthly liaison duty before I come. That will be soon.

"You were directed to tell your experiences of my coming to you, for it prepares the way in their hearts. I will come again to teach each of you. They that have told you that they do not believe shall see us when the time is right."

Mrs. Keech often commented upon the significance of this message and on the spiritual comfort she found in it. It was apparently the first unequivocal promise to her of instruction and guidance from those she came to call the Guardians; it assured her, in the Elder Brother's own words, that her writing was genuinely from him, not from some inferior source; and it assured her again that she was to tell other mortals of her experiences in "extrasensory perception." This last point is important for our study. This is the first indication we have of anything that might be construed as proselyting on her part. We may hazard the guess, from the message as well as from her own subsequent description of this phase, that she did not tell very many people and was not very successful in convincing them that she was indeed endowed with special powers of reception.

Such messages, referring to proselyting, were infrequent during the spring. However, since attempts to proselyte followers are one of the main objects of concern in our study, we will do well to follow the thread of promptings to this end which are contained in Mrs. Keech's early messages, as well as to examine what we know of her behavior during this period.

A few days after the Easter message Mrs. Keech received a communication from one of Sananda's assistants promising to teach Mrs. Keech "Many truths you do not understand." The message continued:

"What can you do for us? Well, you can go tell the world that we have at last contacted the Earth planet with the waves of ether that have become tactable by the bombs your scientists have been exploding. This works like an accordian. When the condensation leaves the carceious level of the ether or atmosphere levels that support a large light layer of marine life, it causes a barrier to be set up. Now that the bombs have broken that barrier we can break through. That is what your scientists call the sonic barrier. We have been trying to get through for many of your years, with alcetopes and the earling timer."

In order to help her learn and "tell the world," Mrs. Keech was advised in another message later the same day:

"This is a new study for you and we will be lenient with you for the experience will be very shocking to you. You will need real level-thinking people around you. Get a couple of learned friends that can stabilize you. Let them know what you are doing. Let them watch with you to see that you are not misunderstood. Share what you have with each other. Share all — and be enlightened — to those who are ready."

In another message two weeks later, Sananda reassured Mrs. Keech that her prayers for protection and guidance were being heard and answered, then instructed her: "The connoiter's work is to spread the news, tell the story, and be fearless in the doing. The world mind is still in lethargy. It does not want to awaken."

To the extent that these messages reflect Mrs. Keech's own wishes rather than the will of superior beings on other planets, they tell us clearly enough that she was beginning to feel some urge to communicate the special knowledge she felt she possessed. But what did she do about these promptings?

Unfortunately, knowledge of her first efforts at finding fellow believers is scanty and somewhat confused, for both Mrs. Keech and the people who later surrounded her have been hazy about dates and places, and have sometimes contradicted not only each other but themselves. From our limited evidence, we can infer a few things, however. We know that she discussed her experiences with her husband, who was quite unreceptive. A man of infinite patience, gentleness, and tolerance amounting almost to self-abasement, he never believed that his wife could communicate with other worlds, yet he never actively opposed her activities or sought to dissuade her from her writing. He simply went about his ordinary duties in the distributing company where he was a traffic manager, and did not allow the unusual events in his home to disturb in the slightest his daily routine.

We can be fairly sure that she acted on the counsel of the Guardians to get a couple of friends and tell them what she was doing, for by June a female acquaintance from nearby Highvale was freely devoting time and energy to typing multiple copies of some of the more important messages Mrs. Keech had received. We know that it was through conversation with this woman that at least two of the most faithful of Mrs. Keech's followers learned about her. This same woman introduced Mrs. Keech to a small, informal circle of housewives who met in various Highvale homes to discuss dianetics, scientology, metaphysics, and occult topics. At one or more such meetings, Mrs. Keech read extracts from her "lessons" and described how she received these messages. We have good reason to conclude that she was in intermittent contact with a second group of students of dianetics in downtown Lake City.

Perhaps most important was the occasion when she discussed her writings with the lecturer and expert on the subject of flying saucers mentioned earlier. At one of his talks in Lake City, Mrs. Keech described her experiences and showed him some of the messages. He appears to have been impressed by her, for, some time later, while he was on a lecture tour that brought him to the Steel City Flying Saucer Club, he seems to have given Mrs. Keech a favorable notice. In particular, he talked about her work to Dr. Thomas Armstrong, a frequent attender at meetings of this club. Dr. Armstrong was a physician who lived in Collegeville, a small community about one hundred miles from Steel City. Since he and his wife, Daisy, were to play highly prominent parts in the subsequent development of the group that gathered around Mrs. Keech, we shall say more about them and explain as best we can the route by which they became involved.

Thomas and Daisy Armstrong, Kansas born and raised, had served as medical missionaries in Egypt for one of the liberal

Protestant churches. For about five years they spread gospel and health, returning on furlough to the United States just at the outbreak of World War II. The war prevented their return to the mission field until 1946, when they again set out, with high hopes and ideals, and with three children. This time, however, they had an unpleasant sojourn — at least Daisy Armstrong did, for she suffered a "nervous collapse" as she once described it. Bedeviled by nightmares that featured violence and bloody death, she could not rid herself of the obsession that her loved ones were in imminent danger of injury from sharp objects, especially knives, axes, swords, and the like. She had persistent dreams and fantasies of cuttings, stabbings, and beheadings. Even the simple tools on her husband's workbench had to be put out of sight, since they terrified her.

Mrs. Armstrong's anxieties did not yield to any of the attempts she and her husband made to overcome them. Although she recognized her feelings as unreasonable, she could not will them away. Nor did her husband's reassurances, changes in the household regimen, and a short vacation do any good. Even prayer did not help. The Armstrongs were especially distressed by this last disappointment. As Mrs. Armstrong once put it, they could not understand why they had been singled out for persecution by such malignant emotion; after all, they had always led a good life, had tried to do the right thing, and were certainly engaged in good works. Why they then? "We finally decided there must be a reason," she added, "and we started searching." This may be why the Armstrongs turned to the study of mysticism and the occult, in which they read widely and eclectically. They studied some of the sacred writings of Hinduism, the Apocrypha, *Oahspe*, and books and pamphlets on theosophy, Rosicrucianism, New Thought, the I AM movement, and the mystical (though not, apparently, the political) writings of William Dudley Pelley. The ideas they encountered in this literature, and discussed at length, seem to have opened their minds to possibilities that many people regard with incredulity. They believed in the existence of a spirit world, whose masters could communicate with and instruct people of the earth; were convinced that extrasensory communication and spiritual migration (without bodily change or motion) had occurred; and subscribed to many of the more common occult beliefs, including reincarnation.

In 1949 they returned to the United States and Dr. Armstrong took a post as a member of the Student Health Service staff at Eastern Teachers College. His work there was evidently of a routine nature and left his mind and time free to continue exploration of esoteric literature. The Armstrongs continued to participate in orthodox Christian religious activities. They attended a nondenominational Protestant church, where Dr. Armstrong organized "The Seekers," a group for young people, principally college students, which met once a week to discuss ethical, religious, metaphysical, and personal problems, always seeking truth. A tall man in his early forties, Dr. Armstrong had an air of ease and self-assurance that seemed to inspire confidence in his listeners.

Any topic was grist for the Seekers' mill, so it may have been no surprise to most of the members when Dr. Armstrong began to show considerable interest in flying saucers. Just why his attention was drawn to this phenomenon is not clear. But one winter he found reason to visit southern California. While there he sought out George Adamski who, in collaboration with another, had recently published *The Flying Saucers Have Landed*. This book related Adamski's meeting with a being who is alleged to have landed in a flying saucer near Desert Center, California. Adamski says that he talked with the man and his book contains a drawing of the footprints that the visitor left behind when he climbed back into the saucer and blasted off for Venus, his home base. Dr. Armstrong enjoyed a lengthy interview with Adamski and came away convinced that flying saucers were real, not illusory, that they came from other planets, and that they carried men, or beings, who were visiting the earth on missions of exploration and observation. He also came away with an enlarged copy of the drawing of the Venusian footprints, whose curious interior markings seemed to him symbols of a mysterious sort.

Upon Dr. Armstrong's return to Collegeville, his wife also became interested and charged herself with the task of interpreting the message carried by these footprints—a task which she had completed to her satisfaction by May 22 of the year they met Marian Keech. Her interpretation of the footprints forecast a rising of the submerged continents of Mu and Atlantis, an event that would be consistent with the flooding of the North American continent. Much later on, in August, when Marian Keech received the prediction of a flood on December 21, Daisy Armstrong emphasized that this prediction was all the more likely to be correct since her own interpretation, arrived at independently, was corroborative evidence.

Sometime during late April or early May the Armstrongs learned of Mrs. Keech from the expert on flying saucers. The Armstrongs wrote to Mrs. Keech shortly thereafter, expressing an interest in her work and telling her something of their own explorations in the occult.

Meanwhile, according to Mrs. Keech, she had received a message from Sananda to "Go to Collegeville. There is a child there to whom I am trying to get through with light." Since she knew no one in that town, she was extremely puzzled, and uncertain about what to do. She seized upon the Armstrongs' letter with delight; it was too fitting to be a coincidence, she felt. This contact with people who had only yesterday been strangers in a town populated by strangers must have great significance. She subsequently decided that Daisy Armstrong was the "child" referred to in the instruction, a decision to which Mrs. Armstrong quickly assented since she felt that the Guardians had been trying to "get light through to her" for a long time and she felt that her own blindness and unreceptivity to these attempts had been the root of her "nervous collapse" in Egypt.

From the initial contact, developments proceeded rapidly, and not even the two hundred miles between Lake City and Collegeville inhibited the growth of a close friendship. Letters were exchanged during May and June and, in late June, the Armstrongs drove to Lake City to pay a visit to Mrs. Keech. It was evidently a meeting of like minds, for the Armstrongs not only prolonged their stay but invited Mrs. Keech to return their visit. She spent the Fourth of July weekend in Collegeville. The change in locale did not seem to interrupt the flow of communication from outer space. During July Mrs. Keech's productivity remained high. She sometimes received as many as ten messages or "lessons" in a single day, and scarcely a day passed without a communique of some kind from outer space.

The contents of these messages were diverse, and they covered a vast range of topics from brief descriptions of the physical environment and diet on other planets to warnings and forebodings of war and destruction soon to plague the earth, intermingled with promises of enlightenment, joy, and unparalleled new experiences in store for those who would "listen and believe." They varied considerably in length, from one or two sentences to as much as six or seven hundred words, although most were about two hundred fifty words long.

It is difficult to give a clear, simple picture of the entire belief system as it is revealed in these messages. The ideology was not only complex, but also pliant, changing this way and that in response to new influences (perhaps new people whom Mrs. Keech met, or new publications she saw). For the purpose of providing background, we shall set down the general propositions condensed from the messages, and illustrate them by extracts from the writings themselves. Wherever possible, we shall provide the "official" definitions of unfamiliar words or expressions, taken from the glossary provided by Mrs. Keech or from the usage current among believers at the time of our observations.

The first proposition is that there is a universe of planets beyond the solar system of the earth, which universe is at least partially inhabited by beings of superior intelligence, wisdom, and skill, possessing an enormously advanced technology. These beings bear some resemblance to humans but they exist at a higher "vibratory frequency" (i.e., lower density) than humans do, and are able to carry out, through thought or "knowing," what humans must depend upon action and manipulation of physical forces to accomplish.

43

Thus, for example, Sananda informed Mrs. Keech on July 8 that "The Guardians are beings of the UN [intelligence of the Creator; mind of the High Self] who have risen to the density seven or eight, who are UN as the Oneness with the Creator, who can and do create by the UN the casement or vehicle they chose to use in the seen." Another Guardian, on May 14, speaking from "the Seventh Sector Density of Creton" (presumably a planet in the "constellation of Cerus") explained: "We are in the avagada [space ship] of light force propulsion. We are like the human beings of Earth and have much in common; though there are millions of years difference in our culture, we are still brothers. What we enjoy as natural everyday enjoyments, you of the world cannot yet imagine." Sananda briefly commented on the planet Clarion, "It is a beautiful place to live. We have weather — snow and rain. We adjust our bodies to the temperature." He described the diet of the Guardians as "the bread of increase, which is like a snowflake."

On April 24 several messages provided this information: "We are coming through your atmosphere and being seen by your astronomers. They say it is large sun spots. The various methods of communication with the people of Earth can be explained by the various frequencies that we operate on. Our systems are very complicated to you; in reality they are very simple. . . . I am coming via inter-conscious-perception, which you call telepathy . . . It is our common means of communication and is used between our own planet and all the others we have communication with. How many you ask? We cannot number them for you have not enough paper to write the 000s on. This is staggering to you, for we have been learning for millions of years. . . . We know no death, as you do. It is as a cocoon turns into a moth — very consciously and voluntarily — *when we need or desire* the change. We never go back to the former lear [our Earth body]." Sananda further described the communication technique in these words: "The thermin ["that which records our thoughts, actions etc. in the Losolo"] you heard was really from Cerus. It is the engine-like affair that we use for timing the vibratory impulses

44

that come from your Earth. This communication is being recorded by your thermin. It looks much like a large looking glass and your thoughts are recorded on it as quickly as you think. And we beam back our impulses in the form of magnetic energy. It is done with a celecoblet, something your scientists have not yet imaged."

The second major proposition is that the Guardians are instructors or teachers in a school of the universe, called "the Losolo" (located on Cerus), who are communicating with Mrs. Keech in order to teach her — and, through her, other humans — those principles, ideas, and guides to right conduct that are necessary to advance the spiritual development of the human race and to prepare the people of the earth for certain changes that lie ahead. Thus, Mrs. Keech was told that "It is ignorance of the Universal Laws that makes all the misery of the Earth"; and that "We see and know that you struggle in darkness and want to bring real light, for yours is the only planet that has war and hatred. . . . We feel no sadness but are interested in the progress of the people of your Earth. Why? We are all brothers. Need I tell you more?"

Elder Brother encouraged Mrs. Keech with a report of progress: "Since we have been in contact with your planet, your people have been responding to our forces of light for the advancement of the human race on your Earth." "Surely," remarked Sananda on a later occasion, "there is light and it shall be revealed to you. You are coming to the end of the age of darkness. The light of the world shall be made manifest by the coming of the earlings. The earlings are the beings who are inhabiting the regions you call the atmosphere. The atmosphere is alive with beings of such a vibratory rate that the dense people of Earth cannot see them."

A number of messages promised visitation from outer space and gave some hint of the visitors' interest in earth. Early in April Sananda said: "The saucers are over West Virginia taking listings of the world's industrial people that make war material and profit from war assets. They are going to land and make contact with you people of Earth in May. . . . It may be June when they land in West Virginia." In mid-May Elder Brother mentioned that "we are coming into your Earth vision in numbers and will be seen by many over the city of New York, Washington, D.C., Seattle, and Chicago. We will land in various places, including West Virginia, the Carolinas, and Vermont. We have contacts there." Elder Brother also promised an even more interesting project — visits to other planets: "We are planning to take some people for a trip to our *plane* — that is, planet. We are trying to make arrangements for a party of six from Westinghouse to visit our territory. Is that a surprise to you? We have had people from your world with us. There is one in Syracuse, New York, one in Schenectady, New York, one in Rockford, Illinois, one in California — there are more than one in California and Arizona and Oregon. Two of them are now on our planet *Union*. They were there on Earth for a special mission."

By early summer portents of the flood prediction had already made their appearance. It gradually becomes apparent, as one leafs through the messages of that period, that the teaching of Mrs. Keech and the schemes for interplanetary exchange of persons have behind them the rationale of averting or mitigating an expected universal disaster.

The earliest messages hint darkly of trouble ahead for the earth but they are vague in intent. On May 23, however, Sananda came right out and said: "We are planning to come in great numbers in the weeks ahead, as the war preparations are being formulated . . . [certain earth dwellers] will be gathered up and relieved of the experiences of the holocaust of the coming events." The theme of war is adumbrated in a number of other messages during the late spring and early summer, and there are many references to the blessedness of harmony and peace, to the misery, futility, and madness of conflict. In several places, the Guardians promise Mrs. Keech that those who "instruct the people of Earth in slaughter" will meet a dark and awful justice soon, and warn: "the people of Earth are rushing, rushing toward the suicide of themselves. . . . To this we are answering with signs and wonders in the sky." There are, however, no explicit references to the nature of the "holocaust" or to any specific catastrophe on the earth during May, June, or July. It is not until late August that the messages begin to warn her more directly of what is ahead for humanity.

There are many other interesting lessons in the collection — far more than we have space to cite. In part the contents reflect the events of Mrs. Keech's daily life — the presence of guests and visitors in her home, the appearance of a new inquirer (for whom there is almost always praise and promise of great things to come), or the disappearance of a former disciple (usually with rueful comments from the Guardians on the difficulty of enlightening the people of the earth). There are messages of reassurance, of protection against "the dark forces" around her. There are fulminations against warmongers, scientists, nonbelievers, and materialists. And there are many, many messages of exhortation: to love thy neighbor; to "seek the light"; to cease thinking ("To think is of the second density" and "There is no advantage to thinking when we are studying the teaching of the Creator") and "to be still of the five senses" so that there may be "direct knowing" or "inner knowing," achieved by believing in the words of "the Father," or "the Creator." Above all she was urged to be patient, obedient, and faithful. These qualities were often put to severe tests.

From time to time the Guardians had given Mrs. Keech predictions of specific future events, such as the landing of flying saucers and visits by space people. She had also been issued a number of "orders" to carry out simple tasks or to go to certain places. Thus, in April, Sananda told her: "When you go to the lecture you will be contacted by a man from Langley Field. He has been on our planet for a brief stay. He will say to you: 'You are early.' That will be his sign to you that he knows you. He came through the atmosphere on a beam of light." On another occasion she was "ordered" to go to a certain street corner in downtown Lake City, and she waited there for nearly an hour, wearying, although nothing unusual occurred. Several times she was promised saucer "sightings" at or near her home, but was disappointed. The strongest test of her convictions and her loyalty to her teachers, however, came as a result of a prediction she received late in July.

On the morning of July 23, Mrs. Keech's pencil wrote this momentous message: "The cast of light you see in the southern sky is of our direction and is pulsating with a turning, spinning motion of the craft of the 'tola' [space ship] which is to land upon the planet in the cast of the day of August first — at the Lyons field. It will be as if the world was coming to an end at the field when the landing occurs. The operators will not believe their senses when they see the craft of outer space in the midst of the field." This message concluded: "It is a very accurate cast that we give."

In further communications, Mrs. Keech got word to be at Lyons field — a military air base — by noon in order to witness the landing. A number of her acquaintances learned of her plan, apparently through the offices of the friend who was currently typing copies of the lessons. Mrs. Keech subsequently made it plain that she had no intention of gathering a crowd for the occasion, yet she evidently did not regard her mission as a secret one. "I didn't want to start a traffic jam by telling anybody that there was going to be a landing at Lyons field on August the first, because I knew that if all the saucer enthusiasts got on the highway to see the saucers there would be a jam. So I wasn't going to say anything about it." But the news leaked out and several people asked if they might join the expedition or meet her at the field. Dr. Armstrong and his wife were in Lake City at the time, as weekend guests of Mrs. Keech, and asked if they might accompany her. The three of them reached the field just before noon.

Near the main gate of the field, the Armstrongs and Mrs. Keech were joined by another car or two of acquaintances, and the whole group sought out a lightly traveled road that bordered the field. Selecting a place that offered a good view of the runways and the sky, they parked and prepared to wait. "We didn't know what we were looking for; we were looking for saucers," Mrs. Keech once said, in describing the incident. "As we stood there

48

eating our lunch from the back of the car, just standing in the fields alongside the road and looking up at the sky through our polaroid pieces that we had brought with us, we must have looked very silly to the ones who didn't sit around the table [outsiders, or those who did not share the feast of knowledge provided by the Guardians]."

Suddenly Mrs. Keech became aware that an unknown man had approached the party. Although the road was long and straight and the fields bordering it offered neither cover nor concealment, she had not seen him walking toward them; it was as if he had materialized out of thin air. He crossed the highway toward the group and, as he drew nearer, she sensed something strange, almost eerie in his appearance and manner. She recalls a somewhat strange "look in his eye" and a curiously rigid bearing.

One of the ladies in the party was alarmed, and urged Mrs. Keech to "be careful; that man is crazy." But, instead of fear, Mrs. Keech felt only curiosity and sympathy for the stranger on this hot, dry road far from comfort or refreshment. From the back of her car she got a sandwich and a glass of fruit juice, and offered them to him, but he declined, slowly and politely.

"I couldn't imagine anybody that time of day on a lonely highway not wanting a cold drink. I asked him again, but he just said: 'No thank you.' I looked at his eyes — eyes that looked through my soul — and the words sent electric currents to my feet. Yet I wasn't on the beam. As we stood there looking in the sky for saucers, he would look up and then he would look at us, at me especially. After I had offered him food, he turned and walked away. I felt very sad. I didn't know why at the time. I thought 'what can I give him to eat? What else have we got that I can give him?' I turned to my car [to get a slice of watermelon] which was about twenty feet away. As I reached it, I looked back and he was gone — just gone. He was no place to be seen. And I felt, I became — oh I can't tell you; there's no word for it. I knew something was going on that I didn't understand. I knew I was close to something."

The remainder of the vigil was uneventful. No saucers landed at Lyons field in the next two hours and an air of disappointment pervaded the assembly. Mrs. Keech was grave. "I thought to myself: That message did come through my hand. I am more or less responsible if I have misled anyone today." And she prayed for guidance. The group dispersed, and, when she was again alone with the Armstrongs and another friend, she began to probe their collective feelings: "I said: 'Well, what do you people feel?' Everyone agreed that something had happened on the roadside, but we didn't know what it was or how to explain it. We were all sensitized to that degree — that something had happened though we had no mental concept of it."

She was not to remain in ignorance long. Early on the morning of August 2 her pencil traced these words: "It was I, Sananda, who appeared on the roadside in the guise of the sice." Although this word may be unfamiliar to the reader, Mrs. Keech recognized it at once. She had first encountered it in a curious story, transmitted to her on July 28, whose significance was not immediately apparent to her.* But when the message of August 2, from Sananda,

* As it will probably not be to the average reader, either, for whose edification the account is reproduced here, verbatim, from the mimeographed lessons: "Sara and Justine were cast as the boy and the girl; to each a love of the Creator. As they came to the great city of the center of the Earth, which is called the CITY of the self — the child, Sara, asks Justine: 'Which way to the Father's house?' To Sara, Justine said: 'To be a Carter, or one who finds his way, is the great cast for which he was created.' As they journeyed to the city of the Self, in the center of the Earth, they were overtaken by the coy little scice [variant spelling for sice], which was a mink. He was in disguise of the rabbit, which was a cousin to the grouse.

" 'What a coy little sice is the rabbit,' was the girl Sara's cry which, as the sice had said, 'a cousin of the grouse — the GROUSE — the RABBIT — the SCICE.' 'WHAT WAS WHAT?' cried Sara. The boy Justine cried, 'We have arrived in the land of thinking! The sice thinks he will cast a spell of thinking upon us in the darkness of night while we are lost.'

"To them the gates of the treasure of the kingdom swung open, where the greatest of all treasures were found — the scice in the garden of increase, where he was only the scice — NO COUSINS — NO ANCESTRY. He was just Mr. Scice, WHO was himself, as the girl and boy, to the great Creator of the City of Self. Each to his own, as a silent witness of the CITY in the Middle of the Earth . . . Scice and Child alike in the Creator's City. Each found his way to the GARDEN OF SELF, each in his Creator's Garden."

50

reached her, she drew the conclusion that "the sice" was the Guardians' term for "one who comes in disguise," or "one whose true identity is unknown," and she immediately attached significance to the fact that the "story of the sice" had been transmitted to her before she went to Lyons field.

This explanation of the "something" that had happened by the roadside appears not only to have satisfied Mrs. Keech intellectually, but to have brought to her a special joy, an exultation that far outweighed the disappointment over the disconfirmed prediction. For, although no saucers had landed at Lyons, a greater gift had been bestowed upon her. She had looked upon Jesus (in another body, of course, and in disguise), had talked with him, and had performed the simple Christian act of offering hospitality to the casual, undistinguished stranger. Her enlightenment was ecstatic, and tinged with awe. Why should she have been chosen to receive the reincarnated Son of God? More deeply than ever the conviction overcame her that she was especially selected, that the voices she heard and the presences she felt were real, were valid, were the very stuff of transcendent life — and she their humble earthly vehicle.

On August 3, Sananda prepared her for possible future visits when he said: "While the guest of Earth is in the seen, he has many guises — as the sice he comes — as the giver of love he comes — as the one who calls by telephone — the glad in heart for the proferred bread and drink."

Twelve people stood by the roadside at Lyons field that hot August noon, but only five remained disciples in December. To all of them, in various degrees, the failure of the predicted saucer landings must have been a disappointment; some never recovered, apparently, and dropped Mrs. Keech forthwith, as a false prophet. Two disappeared from her influence for a time, but returned later; only the Armstrongs remained steadfast throughout. They were with Mrs. Keech in the immediate aftermath, when they "all agreed that something had happened" at the field, and remained with her, as her house guests, the next day when the revelation from Sananda was dictated. If they had had doubts of

Mrs. Keech's extraordinary powers on Sunday afternoon, these must have been dispelled by Monday when they read Sananda's message and noted Mrs. Keech's radiant confidence, her renewed faith, and her touching humility. Indeed they seem to have felt the same sentiments themselves.

Theoretically, we would expect an increase in proselyting following the disconfirmation of the Lyons field prediction. Unhappily, our report of this incident suffers from the same lack of data as do most of the historical examples we discussed in Chapter I. There were no observers present to report Mrs. Keech's activities during August and we have no direct evidence of what she did. Although the messages she received during that month contain some urgings to proselyte, our collection of messages from this period is so fragmentary that we can hardly draw any conclusions.

A couple of weeks after the incident of the sice Mrs. Keech went for an extended visit to Collegeville. There she continued to receive extraterrestrial messages and wrote sometimes for as many as fourteen hours a day. Lengthy discussions with the Armstrongs about esoteric matters seem to have affected Mrs. Keech's beliefs. One notices an increasing emphasis in her lessons on religious matters, such as the nature of heaven, the crucifixion of Jesus, the power and glory of God, the relationship between "the God of Earth" and "the Creator." There is a lesson devoted to comments on the identity between angels and "higher density" beings from outer space, and, in this connection, a discussion of "the miracle of Fatima in the land of California." More and more frequent references to "the Father" and "the Father's children" (believers) occur in the lessons. Simultaneously, there begin to appear in the lessons references to geophysical prehistory, especially accounts of the submersion of Atlantis, and of its sister "continent" Mu, in the Pacific Ocean (which occurred during a deadly war of "atomic" weapons between Atlantis and Mu).

An account of the origin of the earth's population also begins to emerge. It seems that eons ago, on the planet Car, the population divided into two factions: "the scientists," led by Lucifer, and "the people who followed the Light," under the banner of

God and in the command of Christ. The "scientists," having invented something analogous to atom bombs — in those days, the name was "alcetopes" — threatened to destroy the hosts of Light and, through their fumbling cleverness, succeeded in blowing to pieces the planet Car. The disappearance of Car, as an integrated mass, produced enormous disturbances in the balance of the omniverse ("all universes") and nearly caused complete chaos. Meanwhile, the forces of Light had retreated to other planets, such as Clarion, Uranus, and Cerus, where they regrouped and considered their next strategy. Lucifer led his troops, their minds now obliterated of cosmic knowledge, to earth.

Since that prehistoric day, "the cycle" has begun anew, and threatens to repeat itself. Lucifer is abroad today, in disguise, and has been leading our contemporary scientists in their construction of ever greater weapons of destruction. If the headlong plunge into fission is allowed to continue, the tragedy of the destruction of Car may be repeated: Earth will be fragmented and the whole solar system disrupted. The forces of Light have not been idle; Christ's visit to earth, as Jesus, was the initial attempt to reclaim mankind, to persuade them to desert the Prince of Darkness, and it was partially successful. There is a portion of the population of the earth who are open and receptive to "the Light," who can hear the still voice of the Creator, or God, and act rightly in His service. But the forces of evil (and science) are extremely powerful, and the followers of Light may not be able to conquer in time to escape another explosion.

This sketchy account cannot do justice to the complexity of the rationale that the Armstrongs and Mrs. Keech appear to have assembled during July, August, and September, but it may orient the reader to the view they had of the future. It may also explain, to some extent, their deep concern with both the dimmest events of the distant past and the most awful possibilities of the immediate future. We have had to confine ourselves, in this account, to only the most salient features of the ideology and have omitted many of the elaborations it contains. Thus we have perhaps given an impression of greater orderliness than actually exists in the lessons themselves, for they contain an extraordinary range of material complexly interwoven from a whole host of sources. If nothing else, the Armstrongs and Marian Keech were eclectics.

We use this term advisedly, for we must make it perfectly clear to the reader that the ideology was not *invented*, not created *de novo*, purely in Mrs. Keech's mind. Almost all her conceptions of the universe, the spiritual world, interplanetary communication and travel, and the dread possibilities of total atomic warfare can be found, in analogue or identity, in popular magazines, sensational books, and even columns of daily papers.

The notions of reincarnation and spiritual rarification (through changes in "vibratory density") are likewise echoed in many "modern cults and minority religious movements." * There have been numerous accounts of the "continents" of Atlantis and Mu, and attempts to explain their "disappearance" into the oceans. The idea that heavenly representatives will visit earth to instruct mankind through chosen instruments and to rescue those whose conduct and beliefs have marked them for salvation is older than Christianity.

Furthermore, there is evidence that all these ideas, singly or in combinations, are sincerely and fully believed by a great many people. Certainly, the books and periodicals in which they appear are widely read. Equally certain is that many of the readers engage in various actions that testify to their faith, such as joining particular groups, adopting certain ritual practices, giving money, and trying to convince others that the ideas are true.

So, if the reader has come to the hasty conclusion that the ideology constructed by Mrs. Keech's pencil is merely the unique raving of an isolated madwoman and that only "crazy people" would be able to accept and believe it, let him take further thought. True, Mrs. Keech put together a rather unusual combination of ideas — a combination peculiarly well adapted to our

* To borrow a phrase from the subtitle of Charles S. Braden's book *These Also Believe* (New York: Macmillan, 1949), which see for an objective, scholarly, readable account of several marginal groups of believers in America. See especially his descriptions of theosophy, the I AM movement, Psychiana, spiritualism, and Jehovah's Witnesses.

contemporary, anxious age — but scarcely a single one of her ideas can be said to be unique, novel, or lacking in popular (though not, for the most part, majority) support.

The Armstrongs and Mrs. Keech had more than an abstract connection with other groups having interests similar to their own. The Armstrongs belonged to at least one flying saucer club and Mrs. Keech had often attended lectures on the subject. Both homes were on the subscriber lists for such publications as the *Proceedings* of the College of Universal Wisdom, the *Round Robin* of the Borderland Sciences Research Associates, and the *Newsletter* of the group called Civilian Research on Interplanetary Flying Objects. Such periodicals were often proffered to visitors at the Keech and Armstrong homes, and references to them were frequently made to substantiate Mrs. Keech's point of view. Mrs. Keech declared that there were a number of other groups in the United States that were also receiving enlightenment from outer space, although from a different set of teachers.

It was against the background of this ideology that the prediction of cataclysmic disaster began to emerge. With Mrs. Keech in Collegeville, she and the Armstrongs had formed a team. While Mrs. Keech wrote, Daisy Armstrong busied herself typing out carbon copies of the lessons, and the doctor scanned them, adding here and there a commentary or citing some evidence from another source that threw light on the more obscure passages in the Guardians' discourses.

The first explicit reference to the impending disaster had appeared among Sananda's messages on August 2, the day after the visit of the sice. That message read: "the Earthling will awaken to the great casting [conditions to be fulfilled] of the lake seething and the great destruction of the tall buildings of the local city — the cast that the lake bed is sinking to the degree that it will be as a great scoop of wind from the bottom of the lake throughout the countryside. You shall tell the world that this is to be, for such it is given. To you the date only is secret, for the panic of men knows no bounds."

This startling information was considerably expanded in a long communique from Sananda on August 15, which read in part:

"And the scenes of the day will be as mad. The grosser ones will be as mad. And the ones of the light will be as the sibets [students] of teachers who have drilled them for this day. . . . In the carting [plan] it is cast [conditions to be fulfilled] that the event will begin at dawn and end swiftly as a passing cloud — in the seen.

"When the resurrected have been resurrected or taken up — it will be as a great burst of light . . . the ground in the earth to a depth of thirty feet will be bright . . . for the earth will be purified.

"In the midst of this it is to be recorded that a great wave rushes into the rocky mountains — the ones of the covered area will be as the com [group] of the newly dead. The slopes of the side to the east will be the beginning of a new civilization upon which will be the new order, in the light. As it is recorded the three mountain ranges to stand at the cast of the guards, are the Alleghenies, the Catskills, the Rocky Mts.

"Yet the land will be as yet not submerged, but as a washing of the top to the sea, for the purpose of purifying it of the earthling, and the creating the new order. Yet will it be of the LIGHT, for all things must first be likened unto the housecleaning, in which the chaos reigns first, second the ORDER.

"THIS IS DATED NOT IN SYMBOLOGY . . . THE REAL! OF REAL — REALITY YET."

Ten days later came the third great message which made explicit the further ramifications of the great events:

"This is not limited to the local area, for the cast of the country of the U.S.A. is that it is to break in twain. In the area of the Mississippi, in the region of the Canada, Great Lakes and the Mississippi, to the Gulf of Mexico, into the Central America will be as changed. The great tilting of the land of the U.S. to the East will throw up mountains along the Central States, along the Great New Sea, along North and South — to the South. The new mountain range shall be called The Argone Range, which will signify the ones who have been there are gone — the old has gone past — the new is. This will be as a monument to the old races; to the new will be the Altar of the Rockies and the Alleghenies."

On August 27, Sananda filled out the picture of world-wide upheaval and change in a long, elaborate message that specifically forecast that Egypt would be remade and the desert would become a fertile valley; Mu would rise from the Pacific; the "uprising of the Atlantic bottom" would "submerge the land of the Atlantic seaboard"; France would sink to the bottom of the Atlantic, as would England; and Russia would become one great sea.

We can only imagine the awe, the reverence, with which the Armstrongs and Mrs. Keech received these momentous pronouncements. Here, in the hands of three fairly ordinary people (by the world's standards) had been placed the most important news of our time, if not of all recorded history. A grave responsibility, an incomparable privilege had been thrust upon them.

It was Dr. Armstrong who saw his duty clearly and promptly did it. On August 30, he dispatched more than fifty copies of a seven-page mimeographed "Open Letter to American Editors and Publishers." In it he proclaimed the coming catastrophe, cited precedents from the submersion of Mu, and Christian parallels from chapters of Luke, and gave an account, with examples, of Mrs. Keech's "ESP lessons." The body of the letter did not mention the specific date predicted but stated in several places that the cataclysm was "very, very near." Copies of the release that we saw in October carried a handwritten addendum: "latest release — Date of evacuation Dec. 20." Some of the releases actually sent to the press may have also borne this legend.

The mailing of this press release marks the end of the first phase of Mrs. Keech's and the Armstrongs' activities. Up till now, the "lessons" had been virtually a private matter among Mrs. Keech and her friends. Dr. Armstrong's action changed things. In one gesture, he made the news of the flood public property, he committed himself and his reputation to a specific prediction of world-wide cataclysm, and he took the first step toward the organization of a movement.

57

CHAPTER III ⸺⸺⸺⸺⸺⸺ *Spreading the Word on Earth*

THE publicity release that Thomas Armstrong mailed to "American Editors and Publishers" on August 30 was an important move for the believers personally, since it represented their first attempt to "tell the world"; but its practical, social effect was disappointing. Apparently not even one of the more than fifty recipients published the announcement or requested further information. We have no record of how the triad of leaders felt about this failure, but it is clear what they did. On September 17, Dr. Armstrong sent out a second, much briefer, release.

The second dispatch was addressed to the same audience and signed by Dr. Armstrong. The letter consisted of a single-page synopsis of a "cosmic play" in which "we are all actors on the world stage" and "We are also the audience and know not the plot." "Two thousand years ago we played the scenes of the time of Jesus. Now, as Sananda, the Great Director is to put on the final show of the season." The two final paragraphs of the release contained the crucial material:

"The scene is Lake City and the country around. The date is December 21. As the scene opens it is dawn but still dark. The actors are awakened to the sound of a terrible rumbling. The earth shakes; the tall buildings topple. The waters of Great Lake rise in a terrific wave which covers the city and spreads east and west. A new river forms and flows from the lake to the Gulf of Mexico.

"Glad are the actors who have awaited the coming of the Guardians. Amid the cries of anguish the question is heard: 'Why didn't someone tell us that we might have moved to safety?' But in the days of the warnings they were told of the safe places — the eastern slopes of the Rockies, the Catskills, and the Allegheny Mountains — but they said, 'It can't happen here!'"

It was apparently this second dispatch which led to the story in the Lake City *Herald* on September 23. A reporter telephoned Mrs. Keech for an interview and was invited to call at her house. She received him graciously and willingly devoted between two and three hours to answering his questions and showing him the verbatim messages in her several notebooks. But there was a curious lack of a sense of urgency on Mrs. Keech's part. She felt, apparently, no need to preach, to threaten, to cajole or convert either the reporter or her fellow citizens. Her function, as she saw it, was to pass along the information given her by the Guardians. Those who were "ready" would see and heed the warning; those who were not would be swept away in the swirling waters of Great Lake. But even their drowning was of little importance because the victims would lose only their "physical bodies" and would be subsequently transported to planets appropriate to their spiritual development.

The two press releases were not the only proselyting activity of the three believers. Sometime during early September, Mrs. Keech gave two or three readings from her written messages at the Metaphysical Bookstore in Lake City. We know little about these readings but their outcome was evidently disappointing and the series was abruptly ended. Mrs. Keech almost never referred to this episode afterward.

The burst of proselyting between the end of August and the middle of September stands in marked contrast to the absence of such activity during the spring and early summer. Until the press release of August 30, proselyting had been on an extremely limited scale, virtually confined to word-of-mouth dissemination among Mrs. Keech's circle of acquaintances and among their friends. During the spring and summer, Mrs. Keech apparently received a number of individual callers by this route, but she seems to have made no effort to attract widespread attention. Indeed, as the incident at Lyons field illustrates, she kept her plans a secret until the last minute and then merely gave permission to others to accompany her rather than actively inviting their participation. Her attitude toward the seekers who called at her home seems to have been the same: she received them graciously and answered their questions, but did not try to draw them in or to persuade them to believe. She had taken an extraordinarily passive role in the proselyting process.

What, then, accounts for this burst of proselyting in early September? The most plausible explanation is that it was a response to the importance and urgency of the flood prediction itself — an initial surge of enthusiasm. Dr. Armstrong actually signed and sent the press releases, but Mrs. Keech must have agreed to their composition. She may even have had a hand in it, for she allowed her name to be mentioned in the first one, but she probably did not initiate it. Dr. Armstrong was, as we shall see later, consistently more active in publicizing his beliefs and had a greater sense of the urgency of his mission than Mrs. Keech had. He was also, perhaps, better trained for it and more experienced through his missionary activity.

Whatever the cause of the eruption of proselyting, the effects of it were remarkably small. Two or three other newspapers picked up the story from the Lake City *Herald* but none of them displayed it prominently or attempted to follow it up. A few letters trickled in to the Lake City paper inquiring for further details, and a few more were addressed directly to Mrs. Keech. But the impact of Mrs. Keech's news on the public at large was trifling. The citizens of the United States, even of Lake City, apparently greeted the warning of their coming destruction with apathy.

Only one consequence of the newspaper publicity is worth more than casual mention, and that is the visit of the "spacemen." One morning shortly after the appearance of the newspaper story in Lake City, Mrs. Keech answered a knock at her front door to find two men who asked to talk to her. The spokesman for the pair seemed quite conversant with Mrs. Keech's extrasensory communications, with the forecast of the flood, and with her recent publicity. He appeared to be a perfectly ordinary human being, according to Mrs. Keech's subsequent account of the interview, while his companion had a strange appearance and, furthermore, uttered not a word during the entire visit. When she inquired their identity, the spokesman replied, "I am of this planet, but he is not," and Mrs. Keech could not obtain any more information than that. Although the discussion lasted at least half an hour, the burden of the visitors' message was simple: Mrs. Keech was not to publish or publicize her messages any further. Instead, she was to seal the books in her possession and wait for further orders which, presumably, would come from outer space. No further authority or reason for this command was given than that "the time is not right now." Having conveyed their message, the two men left.

This visit puzzled Mrs. Keech, for she could not decide whether the two men were representatives from outer space bearing a genuine message from Sananda, or agents of Lucifer, bent on silencing the earth's only liaison with Clarion. Whatever the explanation of this unusual visit, there is no doubt that it diminished Mrs. Keech's impulse to publicize her beliefs, for it caused her to abandon some tentative plans she had made to publish her lessons as a book.

When two of the authors paid their first call on Mrs. Keech in early October, they found her receptive, friendly, and voluble about most of her beliefs. About the predicted cataclysm, however, she was taciturn and almost secretive. It required repeated inquiry to find out whether there were any people besides the Armstrongs who believed in the genuineness of her messages and in the prediction; and to learn what, if anything, the believers planned to do to prepare for or cope with the flood. Not only was she reluctant to divulge specific facts and plans, but she seemed to want to avoid all discussion of the cataclysm.

She made absolutely no explicit attempt to persuade or convert the two observers, but simply stated what she believed in a "take it or leave it" manner. At several points in the interview she reiterated the warning she had received to "avoid panic" and to try to calm those around her. There was no excitement, no fervor in her manner, but almost a *belle indifférence* to the awful possibility of world destruction that she was discussing. She did not attempt to enroll the observers as followers, to persuade them to return for further information or enlightenment, or to get them to commit themselves or express their agreement with her views. Her nearest approach to overt proselyting was to respond graciously, when she was asked if they could call again or write, "My latchstring is always out. I have been told that my door is to be always open to those who are ready." She was sure that those who were "ready" would be "sent" by higher spiritual forces, and would somehow find her house — in effect, there was no need for her to recruit or proselyte.

So evasive was Mrs. Keech in the matter of talking about the flood and about followers, and so lackadaisical was she about proselyting that the observers would have learned much less and would have underestimated the vitality of the group if it had not been for the chance presence of Daisy Armstrong in Mrs. Keech's home when they called. Although Mrs. Keech dominated the interview and the observers directed most of their questions to her, it was Mrs. Armstrong who revealed the plans the group had to go to the Allegheny Mountains just before the flood was due. There they planned to establish an "altar" or spiritual community of believers who would presumably survive the flood and remain on the earth until Christmas of the following year when they would be taken, bodily as well as spiritually, to Clarion, Venus, or some other planet. There they would be spiritually indoctrinated, preparatory to being sent back to the earth, a cleansed and innocent earth, to repopulate it with good people who "walked in the Light." It was Daisy Armstrong, too, who made known the existence of the knot of believers in Collegeville, the Seekers, led by herself and her husband. We shall have more to say of this group in a moment, after we have summarized briefly the state of proselyting, conviction, and commitment in the Lake City area around the beginning of October.

It is clear that Mrs. Keech fully believed in the legitimacy of her messages and had publicly committed herself to the prediction of the flood both through Dr. Armstrong's press release and the interview she gave the Lake City *Herald*, and in discussing her beliefs with between one and two dozen friends and acquaintances in the Lake City area. Thus, her conviction and commitment were high, and they remained so throughout the course of the group's existence. Of proselyting, we cannot make definite statements. Such evidence as we have leads us to believe that Mrs. Keech gave only one group talk during the spring, and that she addressed small audiences on perhaps two occasions during the flurry of proselyting in early September. We also have reason to believe that she talked freely with callers who came to her home, two or three of whom she had encountered at earlier group meetings. As far as we can learn, however, the majority of the occasions on which Mrs. Keech informed others of her belief were initiated by someone other than herself. She welcomed overtures from others and did not discourage them from proselyting for her but rarely did she herself deliberately seek out opportunities to proselyte.

Our information about believers is scanty up till the end of October, but, as far as we can tell, Mrs. Keech had only a few followers at this point. Perhaps as many as a dozen people had become temporarily interested at various times during the spring and summer. Some of these maintained their interest; others either quickly lost interest or had quarreled with Mrs. Keech and withdrawn. Even Mrs. Keech's husband felt that she was "on the wrong track" as far as the prophecy was concerned. When we interviewed her in early October her reply to a question about whether there were others who believed as she did was plain: "I have very few friends." As of mid-October, Mrs. Keech had few, if any, local followers.

The Armstrongs, however, were more successful in obtaining followers. They were not reluctant to mention their beliefs to others. Dr. Armstrong, upon occasion, talked to members of the faculty and to patients at the college Health Service about mystical beliefs. Most of the Armstrongs' acquaintances in Collegeville were familiar with their attachment to occult interests. But most important was Dr. Armstrong's role in the organization and leadership of the Seekers at the Community Church.

The Seekers began in the previous spring when Dr. Armstrong was asked to act as a "resource person" at a student retreat sponsored by the church. His participation aroused considerable interest, and a number of students wanted to see his influence extended. They asked him to attempt some regular meetings during the college year and thus the Seekers group was born. It appears to have flourished during that fall when the discussions seem to have been confined chiefly to Christian mysticism with perhaps a kind of "comparative religions" orientation. The group met once a week at the Community Church under Dr. Armstrong's leadership; attendance varied, but at least a dozen or fifteen students affiliated with the church were in the habit of attending the meetings.

When the Armstrongs began to develop a serious interest in flying saucers, this topic then became one of the central concerns of the Seekers. The doctor also began to discuss saucers and interplanetary travel in space ships with his colleagues and patients. At first, the latter may have regarded him only as an exceptionally open-minded student of science-fiction. But when he began to talk in more concrete terms about his expectations of personal contact with outer space, tolerance seems to have given way in some quarters to alarm. That was evidently the case among the staff of the Community Church, for later in the spring, they requested Dr. Armstrong to eliminate discussion of flying saucers from the meetings of the Seekers or else to stop holding meetings in the church. He chose the latter alternative and the Seekers began to meet at his home on Sunday afternoons. Formerly the group had been open to all comers, but in its new site it was restricted to those who were invited by Dr. Armstrong or by old members. Beyond these simple facts, we know little of the activities of the Seekers during this spring. The group had disbanded for the summer vacation before the prophecy of the flood was given to Mrs. Keech.

When the students reassembled in the fall, Dr. Armstrong had news for them. During late September and early October, at the weekly Sunday afternoon meetings, he spelled out the prophecy and some of the belief system that accompanied it. Much of what he said fell upon already fertile ground, for most of his hearers were already convinced (or at least ready to believe) that messages from the spirit world and visitors from other planets were not only possible but actual phenomena. They listened readily and he talked just as readily. At only one point, and that a crucial one, did some balk; they were uncertain, or unconvinced, that a flood would occur on December 21. Since the extent of conviction is a question of the utmost importance to our study, we shall deal later with the evidence about belief and commitment. For the moment, let us merely say that Dr. Armstrong attempted to proselyte for belief in Mrs. Keech's messages and her prediction among some fifteen or twenty young men and women who attended the Seekers' meetings fairly regularly.

In mid-October, the Armstrongs began the systematic mimeographing of excerpts from Mrs. Keech's writings. This activity continued until the last week in November when they stopped, for reasons that we shall discuss below. These mimeographed copies of the lessons were distributed to members of the Seekers and also to a mailing list, whose exact size was never revealed to us by the Armstrongs, but was alleged by them to contain between 150 and 250 names of individuals and organizations such as flying saucer clubs and metaphysical societies. The lessons which were so mimeographed and distributed were entirely the *early ones*, the ones that Mrs. Keech had received *before* she was "given" the prediction of the flood and the date thereof. This failure to include the prediction may have come about through the Armstrongs' desire to avoid panic; or it may have stemmed from the concern of the principals that all potential converts begin at the very beginning of the series of lessons in order that their study might raise their vibratory frequency.

On the basis of the evidence we have, it seems fair to characterize the proselyting of the Armstrongs during the early fall as fairly active but rather selective. The list of recipients for the mimeographed lessons was composed of people who were known or believed to be sympathetic to the ideology. In Collegeville itself, the Armstrongs limited their discussion of Mrs. Keech's lessons and the flood prediction chiefly to a small circle — the Seekers who met at their home. Dr. Armstrong occasionally mentioned flying saucers, Venusian footprints, and the like to patients and colleagues at the college, but even there he seems to have followed the doctrine that had developed from his intensive collaboration with Mrs. Keech — namely, that those who were "ready" would be "sent" to him.

Of course, the relative inactivity of the Armstrongs outside the Seekers does not mean that the prophecy was a secret in Collegeville, for some of the Seekers themselves discussed the prediction with their acquaintances and their relatives. We do not know what instructions, if any, they were given by the Armstrongs regarding proselyting, but it seems extremely doubtful that the Seekers were encouraged to proselyte. Our evidence indicates that they too were cautious in discussing the prediction, that most were careful to choose their audiences from among those whom they considered most receptive and least likely to scorn them. When we discuss the behavior of individual members of the Seekers in more detail, we shall see that some of them proselyted by inviting acquaintances to attend the Sunday afternoon meetings at the Armstrong home, and some took part in bull-sessions with "outsiders." Certainly, however, they never preached the prophecy publicly or declared it at meetings or gatherings.

Our general impression of selective proselyting is further borne out by the experience of one of our observers in his attempt to join the Seekers. A brief background is necessary here. At some point during the early fall (probably in October), Dr. Armstrong arranged to have the Seekers reinstated at the Community Church, apparently by promising the staff there to omit any mention of flying saucers, interplanetary travel, and the like. This move back into the church did not mean the shift of all meetings, however, but rather a kind of stratification of audiences. The old-timers continued to meet, as the advanced Seekers, on Sunday afternoons at the Armstrongs' and to discuss doctrines and "lessons" without restriction. The discussions of the "elementary" Seekers in their public meetings at the church were confined exclusively to such innocuous topics as Christian mysticism and occasional excursions into comparative religion. At the two public meetings of this group which our observer attended in November, Dr. Armstrong never so much as mentioned Mrs. Keech, her lessons, or the flood and never alluded more than vaguely to the possibility of communication with outer space. Thus, once again we have evidence that Dr. Armstrong refrained from proselyting for the belief system to the world at large.

Dr. Armstrong's retreat from indiscriminate publicity seeking in September to selective proselyting in October finds its rationale in a number of passages from Mrs. Keech's lessons of this period. In several places, the Guardians counsel an over-all attitude of passivity toward recruiting members and convincing nonbelievers. Again and again the lessons as well as the discourse of the three principals state that "those who are ready will be sent," that there is no need to take action because the die has been cast: all the inhabitants of the earth will be treated according to the level of their present spiritual development. Those who are most ethereal will be taken to planets of the highest density and there trained to be the future rulers of a cleansed earth; those who are of a lower density will be left behind to suffer discomfort and bodily death, but their spirits will eventually be taken to planets of a (spiritual) density appropriate to their own development. In short, while there will be differential treatment, everyone will get his just deserts. The possibility for elevating one's spiritual development in the short time remaining before the flood is slight, and those who could profit from intensive study of the lessons and discussion of their meaning will be alerted, will be sent, by some higher agency or through the stirrings and urgings of their own souls. Finally, the lessons contained the admonition to avoid panic; and what could cause more panic than indiscriminately raising the cry of imminent disaster?

Such a passive philosophy of recruiting at this time makes one wonder why the Armstrongs and Mrs. Keech ever decided to send out press releases or mimeograph lessons at all. Their own explanation revolves around the need for the cry of warning to be uttered at least so that those who were on the brink of eligibility for salvation could be roused to action, triggered off, so to speak, by the warning, but moved, in the last analysis, by their own inner resources and readiness. Thus, from the point of view of the leaders, their duty was done: they had shouted the alarm, and this was enough. Those who responded were to be taught, but those who remained aloof were lost and it would be wrong to force them into the movement to save themselves. To be sure, the rolls were not closed by mid-October; both the Armstrongs and Mrs. Keech were explicit on this point. "There will be those who are sent even up to the eleventh hour" was one of their favorite sayings, and they welcomed inquirers without seeking them.

So far we have discussed proselyting, conviction, and commitment up through the month of October. This date is a convenient one for dividing our narrative, for it is approximately at this point that we begin to get firsthand reports from our observers. Up to early November, we have had to depend upon documents, upon the recall of events by the participants, and upon material supplied, at a later date, by persons who had some acquaintance with what had happened in the movement but who were not intentionally observing it. Beginning in early November we arranged to have observers join the movement and gather data while participating. We shall reserve a detailed discussion of the role of our observers and their effect on the group for the Appendix. Since their reception well illustrates the policy of selective proselyting, we shall describe how our observers gained entree into the group.

During the second week in November one of our male observers, a student in sociology, attended an open meeting of the "elementary" Seekers at the Community Church. He found about ten students there, listening to Dr. Armstrong discuss a miscellany of spiritual, ethical, and religious topics. Representing himself simply as an interested member of the audience, our observer talked privately to Dr. Armstrong following the meeting, indicating interest in questions of mysticism. While Dr. Armstrong responded with interest, he still made no attempt to recruit our observer, mentioning neither the flood nor the lessons, nor even the Sunday afternoon group meetings. In further conversation about unusual experiences Dr. Armstrong casually remarked that he had a friend who was in contact with people on another planet; but he failed to amplify this remark, and did not mention Mrs. Keech's name.

During the ensuing week, our observer made a couple of attempts to attract Dr. Armstrong's attention to himself, but failed to arouse any more interest than the loan of a book on flying saucers. The next meeting of the elementary Seekers was attended by our observer and only one other person. Under these circumstances Dr. Armstrong chose not to hold a formal meeting and our observer seized this opportunity to tell the doctor of an alleged encounter he had had with the spirit world in Mexico. The anecdote revolved around a supposed meeting with a crone who appeared mysteriously, predicted dire events in the future, then disappeared.

Shortly thereafter Dr. Armstrong adjourned the meeting and told our observer about the "advanced" Seekers, inviting him to come the next Sunday. The observer had finally won his invitation after a week of persistent effort, climaxed by the story of his mystical experience. Perhaps the embarrassingly small size of the audience that evening also played a part in eliciting Dr. Armstrong's invitation. Whatever the reasons, it is clear that Dr. Armstrong was anything but eager to make a convert of the observer.

Forewarned by the difficulties our male observer had had in being accepted, our female observer in Collegeville was forearmed. She, too, was a student in sociology, but for the purposes of this research represented herself as an ex-student, currently doing part-time secretarial work. She by-passed the elementary

Seekers and went directly to call upon the Armstrongs. Mrs. Armstrong was at home alone when the observer called. She asked for Dr. Armstrong and said that she had, over a year before, consulted with him at the Health Service and had been impressed by one of his admonitions to her: "Get in tune with the universe." Now, she said, she was somewhat disturbed over a recent experience she had had, and was coming to seek guidance from the doctor.

Mrs. Armstrong's response to this plea was immediate and almost frightening in its initial ambiguity: "You've been sent," she declared. "They sent you." Fortunately for our observer's poise, Mrs. Armstrong went on to explain that "they" referred to the Guardians or people of outer space who were watching over the chosen on earth and guiding their actions. She asked what was troubling our observer who, according to plan, then related a "dream" she said she had had the previous night. She had dreamed she was standing near the foot of a hill on which stood a man, surrounded by an aura of light; there were torrents of water raging all about, and the man reached down and pulled her up to safety.

This "dream," completely fictitious, proved the open sesame for our female observer. Mrs. Armstrong welcomed her into the house and there began showering her with information about flying saucers, the universal cycles of Light and Darkness, and similar matters. Within ten minutes of their meeting, Mrs. Armstrong had mentioned the prophecy of the flood that would destroy the earth, although she did not immediately reveal the exact date, because, she said, she did not want to frighten her visitor. Mrs. Armstrong continued to discuss the belief system and to press reading matter upon our observer until Dr. Armstrong's return to the house. He too was fascinated by the observer's "dream" and concurred with his wife's enthusiastic conclusion that the visitor had been "sent" by higher powers. He questioned her closely about previous psychic experiences (none, she said) and about her interpretation of the dream (a mystery

70

to her, she stated), and concluded at last that she had come, like Nebuchadnezzar, to have her dream interpreted.

During the remainder of our observer's visit, the Armstrongs elaborated their beliefs and told her in great detail of the coming catastrophe, automatic writing, communication from other planets, reincarnation, and flying saucers. The visitor was immediately welcomed into the fold, so to speak, and no information was withheld from her. The Armstrongs nodded meaningfully as they informed her that she "had much to learn," predicted that she would return often, and invited her to come back as soon and as often as she pleased, but especially to return for the meeting of the Sunday afternoon group.

This pair of incidents well documents the attitude the Armstrongs seemed to take toward proselyting, and also illustrates the degree of their conviction about the validity of their beliefs. They did believe that "those who are ready will be sent" and welcomed them with open arms. They believed that one ought not to force, push, or harry people into belief. And they believed that "strange things are happening all around us"; and that these strange things were simply confirmation of their fundamental orientation toward the occult world.

The meeting of the Seekers at the Armstrong home the following Sunday shed some light on the extent and nature of the movement, but was, on the whole, an unexciting affair. Some fifteen people, almost all students, assembled in the living room of a perfectly ordinary home. The atmosphere was calm and serious, as it might be among any group of young people of religious bent, forgathering on a Sunday afternoon.

The meeting opened with a brief meditation period during which all present sat quietly with their eyes closed. Dr. Armstrong spoke briefly about adjusting "our vibrations" and "getting in tune with each other," the better to listen to an inner voice. Following the silence, the doctor prayed aloud to our Father for guidance — an ordinary, nonsectarian sort of Christian prayer. In an equally unexcited way he then proceeded to read aloud the latest lesson from Mrs. Keech — a lesson consisting primarily of messages of reassurance and comfort from Sananda.

He interrupted his reading from time to time to explain the meaning of an unfamiliar term or neologism, and sometimes strayed farther into an exposition of some phase of mysticism, geophysics, interplanetary travel, transmigration of spirits, biblical allusions, or cosmosgenesis that he thought might enlighten his audience. An occasional question, usually a request for clarification, spurred his explorations of these byways. In the main, his discourse consisted in the affirmation of the belief system we have already outlined, and its elaboration and refinement. His audience for the most part sat in placid silence, apparently absorbing what he said. Toward the end of his talk, a letter was passed around for everyone to sign; it was addressed to President Eisenhower, asking him to make public the "secret information" the air force had accumulated on flying saucers.

About two hours after the formal meeting had started, it broke up, for refreshments, into small groups of two or three. Some discussed spiritual transmigration, others college football. Some of the girls served the tea and cake — a handsome monument covered with pink and blue frosting in the design of a "mother ship" and three small flying saucers, bearing the words "Up in the Air." One or two of the members seemed to be of an experimental turn of mind, for they had brought a ouija board which they attempted to use. Dr. Armstrong warned them that it wouldn't work because the "charges" around the house were "positive" whereas the ouija board was "negatively charged," in addition to being of "low vibration," again unlike the atmosphere of the house. Later, a few of the young people attempted levitation of one another, though this venture also failed.

After perhaps an hour of this easy informality, some of the guests departed. Apparently the ones who remained behind were the more seriously interested, for the group again became focused on Dr. Armstrong, and some serious topics were brought up. One student raised the important problem of proselyting; how much and under what circumstances should one attempt to proselyte for the beliefs of the group? He mentioned that he had talked about the coming catastrophe to certain of his college acquaintances and had apparently encountered some scorn and disbelief. Dr. Armstrong's reply was characteristic: You can't explain the prophecy or the coming catastrophe to anyone who isn't ready, and those who are ready will be sent to this house. The Guardians will see to that. This house is guarded and no one can come into it who isn't supposed to be here. Those who are destined to survive the flood will come to the house. But you mustn't turn your back on those who don't come. If they make some overture to you, if they show some interest, you mustn't reject them. You should tell them, calmly and without creating panic, what lies ahead. Then it will be up to them, individually, to decide what to do.

It is interesting to note, parenthetically, that earlier in the afternoon Dr. Armstrong had been telephoned by a young woman who declined to give her name, but said she was a student and had heard that he knew all about a prediction that there would be a disaster on December 21. She had also heard of the meetings and asked if she might attend. Dr. Armstrong confirmed the date of the prediction but refused her permission to come to the meetings; she might, however, come see him during office hours if she wanted to. Later that afternoon he remarked that the unknown lady who telephoned was probably a "stooge" of the college administration being planted to "spy on" the group. We shall observe further indications of this attitude later on, but it is important to note here that, by mid-November, Dr. Armstrong was suspicious and concerned over the attitude the college authorities might be taking toward his teaching of the occult and unearthly.

Some of the other topics that came up for discussion during the latter part of the Sunday afternoon meeting, when only the more convinced and involved members remained, shed light on the range and diversity of elements in the beliefs the group shared. For example, not only was the doctrine of reincarnation taken for granted, but there was considerable discussion of the identities

73

that those present had had in previous incarnations. Some of the fortunate, notably the two adult Armstrongs, their college-age daughter, Cleo, and Bob Eastman, a convinced student-member, had been told through Mrs. Keech's automatic writing what identities they had had when Jesus of Nazareth was on earth. Dr. Armstrong did not take a large part in the discussion of reincarnation, but he let it be known that "someone in the room" had been positively identified as Joseph, and later let slip the "fact" that Marian Keech had been Mary, the mother of Jesus.

There was also some discussion of the deleterious effects on one's spiritual state of eating meat and smoking. Smoking, it appeared, not only fouled the atmosphere but indicated a yielding to the cravings of one's animal nature. Although smoking did not mean damnation, it lessened one's chances for spiritual achievement. Eating the flesh of animals also dampened spiritual development, since it meant incorporating more of the very elements that one was trying to rise above. Furthermore, the Guardians took a dim view of meat eaters; since the spirits of animals slaughtered for meat were consigned to the astral, the carnivores of the world had been responsible for the huge black cloud of dense animal vibrations that disfigured space, especially over such cities as Chicago.

Finally, there was considerable discussion of Mrs. Keech's lessons themselves, of how "sacred writings" could be distinguished from mere automatic writing stemming from the subconscious, and of the evidence that tended to give weight to belief in the prophecy. Perhaps most important of all was Dr. Armstrong's exposition of the nature and progress of the flood. The 21st of December, he declared, would see great physical changes in the earth's surface; a flood would engulf Lake City that day and gradually spread across the country. He did not believe, however, that the inundation of the globe would be immediate; it might take up to a year for the task to be completed. But, by Christmas of the following year, he was sure, all the earth's surface would be water and the souls of the dead would have been raised. Those who were now ready, and qualified, would have been taken off to

Clarion or other high-density spiritual planets and would be in training for their new task of ruling the cleansed earth. But, he allowed, he could be wrong about the details. The only thing he knew positively was that the flood would occur on the 21st. Personally, he was ready to go any time; he was on twenty-four-hour alert. He didn't know what would happen, or when, but it was best to be ready.

We have described the Seekers' meeting of November 21 in some detail for several reasons. First, it should give the reader some sense of the atmosphere that prevailed: a blend of the ordinary and the esoteric, and a curious absence of a sense of excitement and urgency. Furthermore, it gives us a convenient opportunity to introduce some of the principal figures in Collegeville and describe their attachment to the group. In so doing, we shall not confine ourselves to the time period we have already discussed, but shall borrow against future data where it is necessary to clarify the degree of conviction, commitment, and proselyting.

The evidence we shall use was all gathered by our observers between the middle of November and December 20, the day before the flood was predicted to occur. Between these dates, our observers encountered a total of thirty-three persons who either attended meetings of the Seekers or visited the Armstrong home on some errand relevant to the movement. Of these, eight were heavily committed individuals — that is, they had taken some action consistent with the belief that the predicted flood would actually occur on December 21. These actions ranged from simply making public declaration of their belief to quitting their jobs or otherwise freeing themselves from obligations to the post-21st future, and were "committing" actions in the sense that they were difficult or impossible to undo. The extent of conviction varied somewhat among these eight people, and we shall discuss each one's strength of belief in turn. Finally, they had engaged in proselyting, again, in varying degrees.

There were seven other individuals who, though equally active in the group, were less heavily committed to belief in the flood, and were correspondingly more doubtful about the prediction as well as less active in proselyting for it. We shall discuss them too.

Lastly, there were eighteen persons who can hardly be called members. Many of them attended only one meeting and others were clearly sightseers or curiosity seekers. The extent of belief, among this group, varied from almost complete skepticism about every aspect of the ideology to belief in some parts of it — such as flying saucer phenomena, the existence of a spirit world, or the actuality of reincarnation — but with a strong doubt about the flood prediction. We shall not discuss any of these uncommitted individuals.

Of the two adult Armstrongs, we have undoubtedly said enough to persuade the reader that they were heavily committed, highly convinced individuals who engaged in proselyting to a considerable extent. Their daughter Cleo presents a more complex picture. She skipped occasional meetings of the Seekers and once passed up an opportunity to attend a rather crucial discussion in mid-December in order to go Christmas caroling with her friends. Yet, on another occasion, she traveled a considerable distance, under difficulty, to be present at a meeting that her parents had urged her to attend. She sometimes expressed dislike for other members of the group because they "got on her nerves" by always talking of the coming disaster, and said she liked one unconvinced person because he "had some plans for the future." Yet, in early December, she told one of our observers that she had bought a great many new clothes because she wanted to enjoy wearing pretty things while she could, before the flood came. A little later, while our observer was visiting the Armstrongs, Cleo told her to "use anything in the house you want; use it up. It won't be much good to us anyway in a little while."

Cleo's situation is perhaps best described in a remark she once made that, while most of the members of the Seekers had little to lose if the flood did not come as predicted, she would "lose everything." "I'll have to quit college and go to work," she said, referring to the fact that her father would probably be disgraced professionally and unable to support her education further. One

76

may regard her attachment to the movement as based primarily on loyalty to her parents, or as resulting from involuntary commitment. The ground moved under her feet, so to speak, and willy-nilly she was precipitated into a position where she *had to* believe. Her fate was intimately tied to that of her father, and thus we classify her as a heavily committed member.

Cleo's conviction wavered considerably, however. More intensely exposed to the ideology as it developed than any of the other students in the group, she frequently demonstrated her familiarity with it in discussion, yet she took a very casual attitude toward studying the mimeographed copies of Mrs. Keech's lessons. She had been told that her biblical identity was that of Martha, the sister of Lazarus, yet she almost never mentioned this. She frequently disputed with her father over the meaningfulness of some of Mrs. Keech's messages and, at one point, almost seemed convinced that the December 21 prediction was false. Yet she rallied from this low point and, in mid-December, doggedly asserted that the flood would come, though more gradually than Mrs. Keech had first predicted, and flatly refused to accept the statement of a medium in Steel City that the date was wrong. We have been unable to learn of any proselyting on Cleo's part among her college acquaintances. Often placed under their scrutinizing inquiry, she seems to have refused either to deny her belief in the prediction or to argue for its validity. During November and early December she was among the least convinced of the heavily committed group.

Quite different was the position of Bob Eastman, an undergraduate majoring in educational administration. Older than most students, he had seen three years of army duty which had, by his own estimate, made a pretty rough fellow of him. He smoked, drank, swore, and was cynical about religion and Christian ethics. After his discharge, he joined the Steel City Flying Saucer Club, and, at their recommendation, made himself known to Dr. Armstrong when he began to attend the Eastern Teachers College. They quickly developed a strong relationship, something like master and disciple.

Eastman attended every meeting of the Seekers and spent a great deal of time at the Armstrong home. He gave up smoking, drinking, swearing, and "other rough habits" and soon developed into one of the most apt and serious students of the movement. Not only did he read the lessons avidly and ask many questions about them, but he pursued the study of esoteric and mystical literature on his own, though with the doctor's guidance. When the Armstrongs began mimeographing the lessons, Eastman helped with typing, running off, and assembling them and even assisted Mrs. Armstrong with some of her "editorial work" on Mrs. Keech's manuscript.

He had learned "who he was in the Bible" and had given considerable thought to the problem of finding his soulmate. He was thoroughly conversant with the prediction of the flood, could cite it from memory, and believed it completely. Furthermore, he had reordered his life in expectation of it. Not only had he forsworn earthly pleasures in order to raise the density of his vibrations, but he was, as he said on several occasions, "giving up all earthly ties," and asserted often in December that he was "ready to go any time." He continued to attend his classes, but did so merely, he said, in order to preserve an outward appearance of normality and thus not arouse the panic in his college mates that might ensue if he were to quit completely. He had given up studying for courses and was devoting all his spare time to "the lessons," although he fully expected to fail in one or more courses.

He sold some property he valued a great deal in order to get money to pay off debts. He spent his Thanksgiving vacation in Steel City "winding up his affairs" and "saying goodbye" to his parents and friends. He did not sell his car, since he thought it might be useful transportation for him and other believers during the last days, but he drove it hard, demanding utmost performance from it, and once remarked, "I don't baby it any more. I've got to use it up; there isn't much time left." He talked freely with other students about his beliefs, answered their questions, and resisted their scorn. Bob Eastman tried at length to convince his parents of the coming flood and felt that he had succeeded in persuading his stepmother, an elementary school teacher, but that his father, a state civil service employee, was still unconvinced. Perhaps his most important act of proselyting, however, was to draw into the group Kitty O'Donnell, a girl he was friendly with.

Kitty O'Donnell attended her first Seekers meeting in mid-October, at Bob Eastman's urging. She came along for the ride, and, initially, considered the people she met at the Armstrongs as "a bunch of crackpots." A fairly worldly, though not sophisticated, young woman, she had been married twice, had a small child and an absent husband when Bob met her in a bar. One of the few nonstudent members of the Seekers, she had a job on the production line of a nearby factory. Though her first visit to the group was motivated by interest in Bob and a desire to please him, it was not long before Kitty became one of the most convinced and committed members of the Seekers.

In late October she had a dream that she reported as follows: She spied a flying saucer at rest on a hilltop, and saw someone in it beckoning to her; with some trepidation she climbed up and into the saucer, where she found a friendly group of people seated around a circular table, and she felt an immediate sense of tranquillity and comfort. When she reported this dream to Bob and Dr. Armstrong, they assured her it meant that she had been chosen, she was "ready" to be "taken up" to Clarion with the others. She was enormously pleased and, forgetting her earlier conception of the group, plunged herself into their activities.

Fully convinced that the flood would come on the 21st, she quit her job at the plant and decided to devote all her time to the movement, while living on her savings — some six hundred dollars. To that end she left her parents' home, where she had been living, and with her three-year-old son moved into a comparatively costly apartment in Collegeville, nearer to the seat of the movement and, at the same time, nearer to Bob whom she believed to be her soulmate. She developed a philosophy of "living from day to day," and gradually came to believe that she too might be picked up any time by a flying saucer and spared the flood.

Kitty's chief concern was her small son, since she had no way of knowing whether he too was among the "ready," but she hoped he was. Fortified by this hope she came almost to expect to find him missing one day, feeling sure that this would mean he had been picked up by a saucer and was already on his way to a Better Place. In order not to deprive him of pleasures, she gave him his Christmas presents three weeks early.

Kitty attended every meeting of the Seekers, often baking the elaborately decorated cakes that were served at them. She gave up drinking, tried hard not to smoke (and succeeded in refraining during meetings, and while she was in the Armstrong house), and adopted a vegetarian diet. She often did the telephoning to announce special meetings of the Seekers. She professed her new beliefs openly, even though her parents considered her demented and her former pals at the plant scoffed at her beliefs and her newly acquired "virtues." Once or twice during November she discussed the belief system with a few of her acquaintances.

Kitty was well accepted in the group and she had great confidence in Dr. Armstrong. On one occasion, for example, she was quite concerned over an impending visit from her former husband, the father of her child, for he had always been harsh and rough on the child. She telephoned Dr. Armstrong, who promised to "beam her in" over the phone — i.e., to place her in tune with the Guardians who would protect her from violence. She later reported that her former husband had never been more gentle and loving toward the boy, and she concluded that he had been "sent," unknowingly, to say goodbye to his son. Like Cleo, Kitty recognized the degree to which she had committed herself to belief in the prediction. On December 4 she remarked to one of our observers who had questioned her about the strength of her conviction: "I have to believe the flood is coming on the 21st because I've spent nearly all my money. I quit my job, I quit comptometer school, and my apartment costs me $100 a month. I have to believe."

Kitty's depth of commitment was rarely equaled, never surpassed by the student members, largely because they had less opportunity for commitment. Most of them were still under the parental wing, and had no particular financial responsibilities. Their chief commitments to the belief system are to be found in the amount of time they devoted to it rather than to studying, and in the degree to which they defended their beliefs against parental opposition.

Fred Purden and Laura Brooks typify high commitment among the students. Since they were virtually engaged to be married and were together so much they can be treated as a pair. Both of them were juniors, he majoring in music and she in education, and they both came from small cities about fifty miles from the college. Both very active in the students' groups at the Community Church, they had become acquainted with, and been impressed by, Dr. Armstrong in the spring of the previous year. They had attended the Seekers' meetings in the church and moved with the advanced group to the Armstrong house. They attended nearly every meeting during the fall of the current year and took an active part in all the discussions. Apparently fully convinced the flood would overtake the world on the 21st, they both quit studying, and Fred found himself likely to fail one of his most important courses. Furthermore, he had argued violently with his parents and they had threatened to throw him out. Near the middle of December Laura threw away many of her personal possessions expecting to need them no longer.

Fred had been told his biblical identity (he was Paul), and he and Laura were fairly sure they were soulmates. We are not aware of any particular proselyting activities on their part, but they both had attempted to convince their parents the flood was coming and were resisting considerable pressure to persuade them to change their minds.

Susan Heath, a student majoring in physical education, had been a member of the Seekers the previous spring. During the fall she attended almost all of the Seekers' meetings, and she frequently discussed her beliefs with a number of her acquaintances. The degree of her conviction and commitment is documented by several facts. Because of the opposition to Dr. Armstrong's teachings at the Community Church, Susan gave up her student religious activities there — activities that she had valued. She remained steadfast in her conviction even though one of the members of the Community Church staff tried to dissuade her by pointing out reasons for doubting the flood prediction. Susan also found herself in acute disagreement with her roommate, a girl with whom she had felt compatible until Susan began to talk about the flood, but whose friendship she sacrificed rather than change her beliefs.

Susan was among the most active propagandists for the belief system. She began, in November, to give systematic instruction to three or four students in her dormitory and she had talked freely and persuasively to several more. In mid-December after there had been a formal ban on proselyting, she gave a full and enthusiastic account of the belief system to a fellow student who came to her asking for enlightenment. Her parents, informed of her convictions, seemed to take a passive attitude toward them, neither accepting nor rejecting what she had to say.

These eight people — Thomas, Daisy, and Cleo Armstrong, Bob Eastman, Kitty O'Donnell, Fred Purden, Laura Brooks, and Susan Heath — had all engaged in activities that committed them to the movement and were, to various degrees, irreversible. All of them had demonstrated their conviction that the predicted flood would actually occur on December 21, and most of them had proselyted for that prediction. To be sure, the extent of their commitment varied, with the three Armstrongs having taken the most irrevocable steps, while Susan Heath had perhaps given up least.

Less committed than any of those we have so far described was George Scherr, a student majoring in social science. Besides attending almost all the meetings of the Seekers, he paid many additional visits to the Armstrong house, especially to study material about the flood prediction. He appears to have told his fellows in the cooperative house where he lived that there would be a flood on December 21, and to have resisted their scorn and their attempts to persuade him to retract his belief. He himself expressed his feeling of commitment to the prediction when he remarked that, if the flood did not occur, he wouldn't be able to return to the house and face his friends next term.

By mid-December he had begun to feel the pressure of parental disapproval of his association with the movement. George was one of the few students whose parents lived in Collegeville, and they were especially sensitive to public opinion about the movement. They pointed out that, if his name appeared in the newspapers as a believing member of the group, this fact might go against him when it came to getting a good job after college. This consideration seems to have increased his anxiety, but did not make him retract what he had told his housemates. During the Christmas vacation, when he moved in with his parents, he felt it necessary to conceal his true errand from them whenever he visited the Armstrong house to listen to forecasts about the flood, and learn about orders and activities.

From time to time, George indicated a considerable degree of doubt about the flood prediction, usually when talking to our observers and other members of the Seekers. He was sure, he once said, that disaster lay ahead at some time and in some form, but he wasn't positive about the flood on the 21st; maybe it would occur, maybe it wouldn't. On another occasion, when he was asked what he was going to do about the flood, he replied that, well, there wasn't much anyone could do but sit and wait; he wouldn't be heartbroken if nothing happened on the 21st, but he definitely expected something to happen. Waiting was an extremely trying exercise for him. During the last few days before the 21st, George was almost constantly in attendance at the Armstrongs' and our observers noticed that he seemed to be under great strain.

Rather difficult to classify is Hal Fischer, a senior student of social science. He had had considerable experience with occult matters. Earlier, while a student at another college, Hal had acted as amanuensis to a fellow student who claimed to be receiving messages from the spirit world and who had predicted a cataclysmic disaster to occur in the late summer of the previous year. His intimate connection with this incorrect prediction had made

Hal cautious. However, he was one of the most faithful in attending meetings of the Seekers and was a frequent caller at the Armstrongs' at other times. One of the most vocal discussants of the ideology, he was also one of the most challenging and doubting. He claimed to be devoting more time to studying Mrs. Keech's lessons than to his college work, and said he was letting his studies slide, not caring what grades he received.

Within the group of Seekers, Hal was not regarded as a firm believer, even though he was one of the more prominent members in the eyes of outsiders to whom he was the most active exponent of the ideology. To a much greater extent than the other Seekers, Hal adopted the stance of an expert during discussions, raising questions of logicality and consistency of evidence, and introducing comparative materials from "independent sources." In public discussion he did not make his doubts explicit, but only raised challenging questions. Privately, he sometimes took a skeptical position, sometimes a neutral one. "I don't believe and I don't disbelieve," he once told an observer, "but I am ready to serve if necessary." Among his fellow students, Hal had a reputation for "trying to be different," and they felt that he pretended disbelief while actually believing.

For a few days after he had heard what he called "independent confirmation" of the flood prediction through a medium from Steel City, Hal appeared to be more convinced that the flood would come; but, later, he began to express doubts again, doubts that revolved around the relative inexperience of Mrs. Keech who had, he pointed out, been receiving messages for less than a year. There is no doubt that Hal was publicly committed to a thorough belief in mysticism and communication with other worlds and that he had often argued publicly for the predicted cataclysm. He also seemed to be risking his scholastic standing by devoting so much time and energy to the affairs of the Seekers. But in conviction, Hal was a classic fence-sitter. The master, rather than the victim of the ideology, Hal played to the hilt his role of the cautious, objective, and neutral expert, reserving judgment until the data were in.

There were five other people who played as prominent a role in the activities of the group as those we have already described. We shall not detail the evidence for their involvement, however, because, for reasons that will become clear to the reader, they drop out of our sight after December 21. We shall simply mention them briefly here to round out the picture of the active Seekers. Two of them, one a close friend and housemate of George Scherr, the other a girl friend of Susan Heath, were both about as convinced and committed as their respective friends whom we have described above. Two more were atypical: one was a middle-aged woman for whom the Seekers was just one more in a long series of involvements in mystical activities; the other was a student prominent in campus religious affairs who, although an out-and-out skeptic, continued to attend meetings. Finally, we must mention the Armstrongs' teen-age son who, like his older sister, had been involuntarily committed to the movement by his parents' actions. He was more skeptical than his sister, less interested, and yet no less committed, for he was often a target for the ridicule of his high school classmates.

The remaining eighteen people whom our observers saw at one time or another at meetings in the Armstrongs' home can be dismissed without ado. Most of them put in only one appearance, usually at the invitation of one of the core members or one of the fence-sitters. They stayed to hear the show, but did not return. Perhaps they came for the refreshments, perhaps for the "fellowship" that was to be found there.

We were unquestionably fortunate to have observed the Seekers' meeting of November 21 for, as it turned out, this was the last one conducted under relatively normal circumstances. Beginning on Monday, the 22nd, a complex series of events began to alter the situation both in Collegeville and in Lake City, with consequent effects upon the movement.

The first important event was that Dr. Armstrong was asked to resign from his position on the college Health Service staff. The reason given him was candid: there had been complaints from parents and students that he was using his position to teach unorthodox religious beliefs and was "upsetting" some students. The action was taken quietly and discreetly, being known immediately only to a few members of the college administrative staff and to Dr. and Mrs. Armstrong. They did not reveal the dismissal to any members of the Seekers until nearly a week later, as far as we can learn. Dr. Armstrong's immediate response to his dismissal is unknown, but from his later actions and words we can be fairly confident in inferring that he considered it a "part of the plan" of the Guardians — an indication that he was being shaken loose from the ties of this world in order to make him more ready to leave it for a better one.

A second inference, less sure, is that he telephoned Marian Keech in Lake City on the day he was dismissed soon after he had met with the college staff. If so, she too must have seen the same significance in his dismissal, for we know that later that same day she received a message from Sananda ordering her to call a meeting at her home on Tuesday night, the 23rd. Toward midnight on the 22nd she telephoned Dr. Armstrong and instructed him to come to the meeting. Fortunately, our observers in Collegeville learned of his projected departure, and his destination, and promptly informed us. We, in turn, telephoned Mrs. Keech and arranged to be invited to that meeting — the first of its kind in Lake City and, for several reasons, an important event. Let us shift our attention, then, to the Lake City scene and summarize the events back in late October and November.

86

In late October, Marian Keech had invited some eight or ten people in the Lake City area to meet at her home on Halloween for a reading from the lessons. Two people appeared — Edna Post and her son, Mark. Mrs. Post was a tall, gaunt woman in her late forties whose features usually wore either an expression of apprehension and sadness or a sweet, eager smile. Divorced, she and her nineteen-year-old son maintained a home in Highvale, a suburb of Lake City, where she was the director of a private day nursery school. Mark had attended an institute of technology until the previous spring when he was asked to withdraw because of academic deficiency. Since September he had been employed as a clerk in a hardware store near his home, but was still dependent in part on his mother's earnings and her alimony. A tall, gangling youth, Mark was ordinarily quiet, friendly, and a trifle shy; good-humored and obliging, he seemed to lack definite aims and was content to drift along, following where his mother led. She led him, this time, directly into the center of the movement, where he ultimately came to take a useful though not prominent role.

Edna Post had a history of participation in quasi-mystical groups with an intellectual orientation. Like Marian Keech, Edna had been "cleared" by a dianetics auditor, and had gone on to a more advanced group that discussed scientology. It was at a meeting of this group that Edna met Marian Keech. Apparently impressed by Mrs. Keech's powers, Edna remained in touch with her during the spring and summer, long enough at least to accompany Marian on the Lyons field expedition. Mark and his current girl friend also went along, but neither of the Posts had seen

Marian again until they received her Halloween invitation. What led them back into her arms we do not know, nor are we sure what happened on that evening to cause Edna to visit Bertha Blatsky, another member of the scientology group, who had heard some of Mrs. Keech's lessons the previous spring, and persuade her to go with the Posts to Mrs. Keech's house several weeks later — on November 22, to be precise.

Our knowledge of Mrs. Keech's activities is extremely scanty for the period between our first call on her in October and the meeting of November 23. Her chief callers for a short time were the children who attended the grade school opposite her home. Somehow they had become acquainted with her beliefs and used to call on her and ask her to tell them about flying saucers. Apparently she had responded well to these requests and had developed a sizable following in the school when parents, school authorities, and the police teamed up to intervene. A special PTA meeting was held to discuss means of restraining her influence on the children and she was finally warned, she claimed, to stop her talks to the children or she would be taken before "a psychiatric examining board." This threat, apparently from the police, proved effective for it terrified her. Her chief regret was that the children had genuinely needed and wanted the truth and the light, and had recognized the value of her teaching. But their parents and teachers insisted that the children stay away from her.

We know that during October and November Marian was constantly receiving messages from Sananda and other Guardians in the higher spiritual densities. Sometimes the messages gave interpretations of recent events such as the visit of the spacemen; sometimes they offered reassurance and comfort in the face of a disbelieving world.

During this period too, Mrs. Keech began increasingly to "sit for" individual lessons — i.e., at the request of a particular person she would make a special request to the Guardians for personal advice, instruction, or answers to questions. The result often left the inquirer puzzled and sometimes Mrs. Keech too. Often she would frankly ask the inquirer, "What does it mean to you?"

before she made any suggestions at all; and occasionally she would admit that she was completely baffled by what her hand had written.

This drift toward personal instruction coincided with the movement toward highly selective proselyting we have already noted in Collegeville. For Mrs. Keech, whose urge to spread the word had never been as strong as Dr. Armstrong's, the word "proselyting" is an exaggeration, for her treatment of those who came was remarkably passive. This is illustrated by her reception of our two Lake City observers. When the male observer called, he told her he had learned of the flood prediction through the newspapers. She received him warmly and spent considerable time explaining the background of the messages to him, but made absolutely no attempt to recruit him or to urge him to return. As he was leaving, he was forced to ask if he might return, to which she replied politely, "My door is always open."

Our female observer was also welcomed and given an hour or two of general talk about flying saucers, Sananda, the Guardians, and other items of the belief system. This observer's introductory story did not include any mention of the predicted flood and Mrs. Keech did not herself refer to it. She did, however, ask if the observer would like her to "sit for" a personal message from "upstairs."

Later when the observer asked whether there were ever any group meetings of interested persons, Mrs. Keech replied in the negative; the rule, she said, was against meeting in groups. Lessons were to be given on an individual basis, and people came singly to see her and to have their lessons. She had received orders from the Guardians in September or October that she was to stay at home from now on in order to teach those who came to see her — that those who were ready would seek her out. She mentioned that one or two people had been coming to see her but was reluctant to discuss how frequently they came, how many there were, or who they were. Nor did she seem interested in obtaining new recruits, for this observer too was forced to ask for permission to return.

Against this background, it was all the more surprising to learn that a meeting had been scheduled for November 23, only a few days after our observers' first call. The reason for Mrs. Keech's calling the meeting was probably that news of Dr. Armstrong's dismissal had suggested to her that the time was near when the Guardians were going to take some action. That was the keynote of the evening and the first speech Mrs. Keech made to the assembled group was "We have been told by Sananda that there will be a message for us and we expect to get our orders." As we shall see, the remainder of the meeting was devoted principally to waiting for these orders.

By 7:30 that evening ten people, several of them new faces to us, were seated in a rough circle around the living room and adjoining sun porch of the Keech home. Edna and Mark Post had driven in from their suburban home. Bertha Blatsky, a tall, robust, powerful-looking woman in her early forties, had brought two of her neighbors from the northwest side of Lake City, May and Frank Novick. Mrs. Blatsky and the Posts were evidently well acquainted through their earlier membership in the scientology group, and Edna Post had at least met May Novick. The relationship between Bertha and May was even closer, for Bertha had "audited" May, a pale, slim girl, with a timid and anxious manner. Frank Novick seemed curiously out of place and uneasy. He was an electronics engineer who came only because of his wife's urging. Less insensitive to social pressure than defiant of it, he was the only person who continued to smoke during the evening, and he rarely said a word. The rest of the gathering included Marian Keech's patient but skeptical husband; Dr. Armstrong; the girl who acted as a local observer in Lake City; one of the authors; and, finally, Clyde Wilton, who had flown the five hundred miles from his home especially for the meeting.

Clyde Wilton was a tall, well-built man in his late thirties with a Ph.D. in one of the rigorous natural sciences. He was quiet, good-humored, intellectually very curious. He held a research position in an important laboratory, had published in scientific journals and was a well-placed and respected member of his profession. He had made the long trip at his own expense and evidently in response to a telephone invitation from Mrs. Keech. He had been introduced to Mrs. Keech in September while he was visiting Lake City. He had evidently been deeply impressed by Mrs. Keech's messages, and had kept up correspondence with her during October and November, after his return home.

It is clear that her writings were not his first adventure in the occult, for he referred occasionally to "other masters," and drew parallels between them and Marian's Guardians. He had had a long-standing interest in flying saucers, and had made a careful study of the available literature on the subject without having his curiosity satisfied. During the meeting of the 23rd and on subsequent occasions, Clyde Wilton did rather little talking, but appeared to listen very attentively to what went on. He demonstrated his familiarity with the lessons by quoting from them and referring to specific passages, and frequently engaged in discussions with Marian or Dr. Armstrong regarding the meaning of terms or the interpretation of passages.

His whole approach was intellectual, studious, even scholarly. Yet he appeared to believe completely in the legitimacy of the messages and in the prediction of the flood. He had talked at length of these matters with his wife, who, he confided, was still somewhat unconvinced. He had discussed Mrs. Keech's lessons with one of his neighbors who may have believed in the flood prediction too. In all, then, Clyde Wilton seems to have been a convinced member of the group who at least had discussed the beliefs with his neighbors. By his very presence at the meeting, and the investment of time (away from home and job) and money to attend, he seems also to have been committed.

Although both Mrs. Keech and Dr. Armstrong believed that they would receive their orders sometime during the meeting of the 23rd, neither apparently had any idea what the orders might be or in what form, or through what messenger they might be transmitted. Accordingly, they were prepared to consider almost anyone in the group a potential messenger from outer space and almost any declaration an order. They began by focusing their attention on the author present, the last person to arrive. He was met at the door by Mrs. Keech, who, after introducing him around the assembled circle, took him into an adjoining room and told him of the expected receipt of orders. She concluded by saying: "And we want you to lead us tonight."

The author-observer, attempting to maintain his neutrality, protested that he could not officiate, that he was not "ready." Mrs. Keech countered firmly that he *was* "ready," and she would not be put off by further protests: "We all have to face our great responsibilities and take them," she maintained.

Finally, the observer agreed to her demand. He was led into the living room and Mrs. Keech told the group that he would lead them tonight. With nine expectant gazes transfixing him, the observer fought for time: "Let us meditate," he ad-libbed, and bowed his head in silence. After a few minutes of silence, he asked Mrs. Keech to say a few words. She stated simply that the group had been called together for a special purpose, namely, the receipt of orders. She asked the observer if he had anything to add to that, but he had nothing, so the meeting returned to silent meditation as the tension mounted.

After perhaps twenty minutes more of complete, tense silence, Bertha Blatsky, who was seated on the couch with her head thrown back and her eyes closed, began to breathe very deeply in short, sighing breaths. She continued, almost panting, and interspersing an occasional low moan for perhaps two minutes, and then began to gasp "I got the words, I got the words" over and over again. Her heavy breathing continued at a more rapid rate, and she began to sob. Within a few moments Dr. Armstrong and Mrs. Keech had crossed the room to assist her. They helped her stretch out on the couch, where Dr. Armstrong felt her pulse and, satisfied, motioned that she should be left alone. Mrs. Keech sat next to the couch, but said not a word; and the rest of the gathering sat rooted to their chairs in uneasy silence.

Bertha's panting and sighing became louder, turning into great, racking sobs, followed by swift, lip-quivering inhalation, all interspersed with breathless phrases: "I got the words . . ." Then,

"I am the Lord thy God . . . thou shalt . . . have no other . . . thou shalt have no other gods . . . before me." Her eyes closed, her whole body quivering with emotion she struggled, pantingly through the First Commandment again, and then fell briefly silent.

After a brief interval Bertha began to speak again, haltingly, painfully, with many pauses: "This is Sananda," she gasped, "Sananda speaks, Sananda speaks. I am Sananda, I am Sananda. These are my sibets, my precious sibets . . ." She broke off suddenly with a shriek, a cry of pain, and began to protest: "Oh no, not me, not me, He can't mean me . . . [a pause] . . . I give you my sibets . . . oh, no, he can't mean me, Oh no." Her voice trailed off into moans as Mrs. Keech sped to her side, loudly and clearly repeating: "Oh yes, he does, Bertha. Yes, Bertha, he does mean you." Turning halfway toward the rest of the group she added: "I had a message today that you were to take over the sibets. Yes, that's just what he means." Apparently Mrs. Keech was pinning her hopes for orders on Bertha since her first choice had failed her. Her assurances to Bertha seemed to calm the medium and Bertha emerged from her trance a few minutes later.

Bertha Blatsky, married to a Lake City fireman, had once been a beautician but was currently employed as a clerk. She had been born in Poland, but raised in Iowa. She had attended Catholic schools, married when she was about nineteen, and remained faithful to her religious tenets until she was perhaps twenty-eight or twenty-nine when she began to feel disappointed in the church and broke off from it. She was deeply disturbed over the sterility of her marriage. In more than twenty years of marriage she had never been pregnant. Her energy and her lack of parental responsibilities had driven her restlessly from job to job until she learned the trade of beautician, which seemed to bring her gratification, especially for the period when she operated her own shop. There she met May Novick, who was a client and became a close friend. There too she met the woman who introduced her to dianetics and to "metaphysics."

Through her membership in the dianetics and scientology group to which Edna Post also belonged, Bertha was invited to hear Mrs. Keech talk and was impressed. When Mrs. Keech needed secretarial assistance to type copies of the lessons, it was Bertha who thought immediately of May Novick and persuaded her to help. Both Bertha and May were in contact with Mrs. Keech during the spring and summer, but stopped seeing her after she went to Collegeville in August, and did not hear from her again until early November. Up till this night, Bertha, while interested and attentive, had never played a prominent role.

Bertha was the center of attraction during the break which followed her emergence from her trance and virtually all talk centered around her performance. She declared herself baffled by what had just happened. "I've never had an experience like that," she said. She kept repeating that it had been a "terrific experience," and she couldn't put into words how it felt. She had been afraid and uncertain how to behave although she "sort of knew," she said, that someone else's voice had "taken possession of" her.

Marian Keech impressed on Bertha that her new job was a big one, a job requiring her to live up to great responsibilities. Mrs. Keech also added her envious congratulations when she mentioned that she had wanted, even prayed, for the "power of speech" but had been "given writing." Dr. Armstrong offered Bertha some advice about relaxation and letting one's mind go blank while the control's thoughts entered. Refreshed by these words as well as by a drink of bottled spring water, Bertha Blatsky readily returned to the couch, announcing that she would "try it again and see what happened."

No one knew it then but the high point of the evening had passed, and the remainder was a tedious, painful monotony as Bertha struggled to live up to the thunderbolt she had hurled. During the next hour she called each member of the group to her side, and gave them one by one some spiritual message, some word of comfort, or blessing, from Sananda. She took another break. About 10:30 P.M. she resumed her position on the couch, but only empty phrases, tediously repeated, came from her mouth. "And the blessings of Sananda, on these precious, precious, precious [repeated eleven times] . . . precious sibets . . . and so it

94

is, so be it, be it so, forever and ever, and ever [fourteen times] . . . and ever."

During the break at midnight she was visibly discouraged, and tentatively suggested to Mrs. Keech that perhaps she should try no more that night for messages. But Mrs. Keech would not hear of it: "This is just the beginning. You haven't seen anything yet. If you think the evening is over, you're mistaken. We don't know what this is all about, but I have the feeling they want us to go ahead. They're doing this for a purpose." Turning to the rest of the group, she warned in tones of grim elation: "If anybody thinks he's going to get any sleep tonight, he's got another think coming. There isn't time for sleep. They've got work for us to do."

About an hour later, after another round of "precious sibets," Bertha, speaking in her "own" voice, suggested again that it might be advisable to stop for the night. But Mrs. Keech was firm: "No, no, Bertha," she cried, "you haven't gone the last mile yet."

Toward 2 A.M. Dr. Armstrong quietly told Mrs. Keech that he felt Bertha was "off the beam," and that all this talk didn't amount to anything. In a distinctly audible tone, Mrs. Keech disagreed: "Oh no, no. I am not going to break the porter's form [i.e., the Guardians' plan]. This is the discipline. It's a hard discipline but you have to learn it. I'm not going to take the responsibility for stepping in to stop her."

A moment or two later the medium's voice declared that someone in the room was trying to break the porter's form, and warned everyone not to break the porter's form. Mrs. Keech nodded and smiled wisely at this admonition, while Dr. Armstrong appeared to accept the rebuke ruefully. Clearly Mrs. Keech was still hoping that specific orders would come through Bertha.

Although the session continued until eight o'clock in the morning, there was no appreciable change in the general pattern of Bertha's speech. The only interruption occurred when, about 2:30 A.M., Frank Novick, resisting the entreaties and tears of his wife, stalked out of the house to go home and get some sleep.

95

The other members of the group either remained in the living room, occasionally dozing, or retired to the Keech's attic, where they stretched out on one of the numerous beds or cots that gave the place the look of a dormitory.

The expected orders did not come through that night. Apart from her message about leading the sibets, Bertha said almost nothing that was relevant to the ideology of the movement. At one point, Edna Post asked Mrs. Keech whether Bertha's commission from Sananda would mean that the date of the flood "was moved up." Mrs. Keech vigorously denied this; no change in the date had been given, she asserted. She added, however, that if December 21 were a "wrong date," if the flood did not occur, it would be because the prediction had been a disciplinary preparation for us, a "test" of faith. For the group as a whole, Bertha's new role made no change in expectations about what would happen. Her performance was perplexing to the group and Mrs. Keech did nothing to resolve the confusion.

One of Bertha's last acts in her early morning trance had been to call a second meeting for that very night, November 24, at 11 P.M. She asserted this time would be "favorable" for the receipt of messages. It later turned out that her husband, who disapproved of her explorations in the occult, worked the swing shift and would be on duty after 11 P.M.

The intervening daylight hours passed quietly, with only four people remaining in the Keech house: Mrs. Keech, Dr. Armstrong, Clyde Wilton, and the author-observer. These four represented, to Mrs. Keech at least, a symbolic group — one from the East, one from the South, one from the North, and herself from the West. On the previous evening these four, and these alone, had shared unleavened bread and bottled spring water from special glasses in a ceremony Mrs. Keech described as "re-creating the Upper Room experience." On the following morning, ritual purity was preserved and "breakfast" consisted of some more matzoth and, this time, hot spring water served in coffee cups.

Some desultory discussion of Bertha's mediumship sparked Mrs. Keech to remark that she expected big things from the meeting on the coming night, perhaps even orders to unseal her secret books of writings. Once again, however, she asked the author who was present if he had brought a message for the group.

Dr. Armstrong discussed his dismissal from the college, and showed his eagerness to be receiving orders as to what he should do next. During the last portion of the all-night séance, Edna Post had asked whether she should resign from her job or not, and Armstrong had announced his dismissal, pointing out to the group that it had obviously been "part of the Plan" to prepare him for "some important job" (i.e., in the service of the Guardians). Finally, May Novick had told the group that she had recently been dismissed from her secretarial position.

Reviewing these developments at breakfast, Dr. Armstrong pointed out that they could not be coincidental—clearly, something was afoot, and "the boys upstairs" (within the group of believers he frequently used this term instead of the more formal "Guardians") were planning something. He expected to get his orders momentarily and hoped they would come this night. He was ready, he said, to go anywhere, do anything. When the observer asked him about the earlier plan to go to the safe places in the hills, he was vague. That plan was still on, he said; neither he nor Mrs. Keech had heard anything to the contrary from the Guardians. But he just didn't know because there hadn't been any more orders. Dr. Armstrong went on to elaborate his own opinions as to what might happen. Some of the group, he felt, might be picked up individually by flying saucers, especially those who had immediate or important tasks to do.

The Wednesday night meeting began at 11 P.M. with the same audience, except for the absence of Frank Novick and the addition of a male observer who had called in the morning to arrange his invitation for that night. Although the audience was the same, the performer was not. The group saw a new and forceful Bertha. Gone were the incoherence, the repetition, the appeals to Mrs. Keech for help. With an air of confidence, even of command, she took her place on the couch, flung one arm over her eyes and began to speak. No sobbing or panting preceded her perform-

97

ance. She slid into her role with professional ease and began to lecture, confidently, authoritatively, to the meeting.

Her assumption of authority was corroborated when it became clear that the voice speaking through her this night was not that of Sananda but the Creator Himself. Having thus trumped Mrs. Keech's ace, Bertha proceeded to discuss such matters as "the good," "the will," the "I," and the "Am." As she progressed in these instructions she became more forceful and more domineering.

Although most of the Creator's teachings were irrelevant to the ideology of the movement, and to the flood prediction, He laid considerable emphasis on questions of will, self-discipline, and obedience. In brief, the Creator's view was that everyone had the responsibility to organize and develop his own will, that action was a matter of individual decision and choice. This philosophy of self-determination, or, as it was later called, one's "inner knowing," became thoroughly accepted by the group.

At about 4:30 A.M., the Creator's spokesman suggested that there be a third meeting to be held on the following night. Clyde Wilton protested that he had already stayed away from his family one day longer than he had planned, that he had missed two days' work, and that if any more time had to be taken off, he would have to ask for a leave of absence, which would require his explaining his purpose at length to his supervisor. Furthermore, he added, the trip was expensive. He therefore outlined a plan: that those who dwelt out of town be allowed to meditate at home while the group was meeting, and that the instructional proceedings be recorded and sent to out-of-town members who could then read them.

The Creator promptly and flatly vetoed the plan. There would be no recording of anything that was said at a group meeting — that was a rule. Furthermore, it would not be sufficient to meditate at home; there were things to be learned and everyone must receive instruction. Finally, the Creator stipulated that there must be at least three more instructional sessions during the next three weeks, since time was short and much had to be accomplished. Thereupon, Clyde Wilton proposed a second plan, namely, three meetings in succession on the following weekend. After asking if there were any objections to this plan, the Creator announced His willingness to cooperate.

The events of this night had been irrelevant to the central interest of the group. No orders had been forthcoming, and, indeed, the cataclysm had not even been mentioned until shortly after 5 A.M., when the Creator spontaneously remarked: "I am wondering if I should bring up the question of the date. Let me see, I can't decide if I should or not. Are you desirous of knowing about the date?" Mrs. Keech seemed quite tense and anxious to hear what the Creator would say. The voice from the couch sighed: "Well, then I will bring it up. What do you wish to know?" The room was electric with tension during the pause that followed Mrs. Keech's inevitable question: "Has the date we have been given been invalidated?" The reply of the Creator was lengthy:

"It is not for me to invalidate that which has been given you. She who has given it to you has been faithful and has worked very hard and has been responsible for the work which led to this wonderful, precious meeting tonight. Her work has been well done and she has been faithful to those who instructed her and to whom I gave the task of fixing the date and telling her of it. Nor do I belittle her work when I say that she has been a good prophet, but tonight you are in the presence of the Creator who has chosen the greatest prophet, the Bertha, who ever was or ever will be."

The group meeting came to a bone-weary halt at 5:45, but activity did not cease, for each member was commanded to have a personal counseling session with the Creator, while the rest of the group stayed out of earshot, munching fruits, nuts, and matzoths, drinking Nescafé or spring water, and conversing.

Dr. Armstrong was more emphatic about the validity of the date than the Creator had been. In a conversation with one of the observers earlier in the evening he had made his views clear:

"We've had that date mentioned several times. I mean, it's come through in lots of messages: to our kids, to Marian, to us; and after all, we know it is a significant date too. It's not just an accident, like the equinox or something. You see, it's the day on which the Essenes moved out of their old house and went looking for a new master and teacher. They had prayed for a universal teacher, and on the 20th of December they moved out of their old house to go looking for him, so it's a very significant date. And, anyway, you know it's the 21st, not the 25th that Jesus was really born. So we're pretty sure of the date."

The topic of proselyting had come up during the meeting, when the Creator had remarked that the lessons were "closed," that they were restricted to the group presently assembled, but that they were to be used "for the enlightenment of the world." The Creator then clarified this by stating that members of the group were encouraged to instruct others and to disseminate information, "for the good of the world," but to do so "with discretion," not promiscuously, not by telling others precisely what had happened on this night in this room, nor by talking to unsympathetic people, who might ridicule the beliefs, but by enlightening people "who are sympathetic." There was also a strong implication that one ought not to mention the existence of the group. During his personal counseling period an observer pursued the matter further and was told by the Creator:

"Remember that you alone cannot save the world or anyone in it. Unless they will it, they cannot be taught or saved. You are not to grab anyone or seize him and try to teach him. You can very gently lead someone who is already willing and who will join his will with yours and mine to reach the light, but you cannot take anyone who is unwilling and save him. You are not to tire yourself with trying too hard to rescue others. Gently and a little at a time you can push people, but you must avoid rushing. You must avoid hurrying things. If you find yourself having to rush with a person, stop and give up. It would not be right."

In short, the new "source" of spiritual information preached a pattern of proselyting similar to that we have heard from Mrs. Keech and Dr. Armstrong: be cautious, be discreet in telling anyone about our beliefs; avoid ridicule; do not force anyone; and tell the secrets only to those who you are sure will listen with a sympathetic ear.

The net result of the two group meetings on November 23 and 24 was to heighten the ambiguity of an already unclear situation. Bertha's elevation to a position of influence, if not leadership, meant that there were now two "sources" of information from the beyond: the Creator, and Sananda. It was not immediately apparent that the two sources, or their earthly spokesmen, were in complete accord. Rather little of what the Creator had to say had any direct bearing on the ideology developed through Sananda.

Furthermore, it was not clear whether the Guardians had transmitted the "important message" that Mrs. Keech had anticipated. No one had received his orders — or had he? Were orders buried somewhere in the Creator's words? What had happened to the plan for evacuation to the "safe places"? Mrs. Keech was vaguer than ever on the subject, saying she was simply "waiting for orders." Dr. Armstrong was beginning to believe that he, personally at least, would be picked up by a flying saucer before the cataclysm.

By eight or nine o'clock on Thursday morning, which was Thanksgiving Day, the company had departed, leaving only Dr. Armstrong at the Keech home. In this vegetarian group, there was scarcely any interest in the holiday feast and even some jokes about it, so the doctor was in no hurry, apparently, to return to Collegeville and his family. When he did return to Collegeville that night or the following morning, he set about winding up the affairs of the Seekers in anticipation of his imminent departure from the earth.

Because many of the students were still absent from Collegeville on their Thanksgiving vacations, only twelve people (besides the observers) attended the Sunday Seekers' meeting of November 28. In addition to the two adult Armstrongs, their older daughter, Cleo, and their son, there were present Bob Eastman, Kitty O'Donnell, and five other more peripheral members. The meeting was fairly short, by Seekers' standards, but some important things were communicated.

Up to this point, news of Dr. Armstrong's dismissal had been confined to a limited circle — even Bob Eastman and Kitty O'Donnell did not know of it — but now he announced it to the group. He drew from this action two inferences: that "the boys upstairs" had arranged his discharge in order to free him for more important work with them; and that "the heat was on" not only him but anyone associated with him. Comparing himself somewhat elliptically to the early Christian martyrs (and, perhaps, to the earliest of them all) he pointed out that the administration of the college must have been very much impressed by what he was saying to take such a drastic step. It must be, therefore, that his beliefs and his teachings were upsetting to the administration and they would spare no pains to abuse him and his followers. Accordingly, it was very important to conceal any evidence of the belief system. Thus, from a position of ambivalence and hesitancy regarding proselyting, the Collegeville contingent began to move toward concealment of their beliefs and activities.

Mrs. Armstrong announced that she had stopped editing and duplicating lessons. She urged those who had copies of the lessons to "keep them under cover," and Dr. Armstrong said that he had received orders to destroy all extra copies of lessons, as well as the group's mailing list. Even the names of members of the Seekers and correspondence with interested individuals from out of town were to be taken out of the Armstrong house or burned in the fireplace. Dr. Armstrong had received these orders in Lake City before he left. By Sunday night, the Armstrongs had destroyed all the documents they felt were incriminating.

Dr. Armstrong also announced that this would be the last meeting of the Seekers, as a group in formal session. Visitors to the house would be welcome, of course, but there would be no more meetings. Furthermore, there would be no more new members accepted into the group. The "eleventh hour" had passed, and no one else might join.

Dr. Armstrong next told his audience that Sananda had changed his plans. It was now unclear whether he (Dr. Armstrong) would be going to one of the "safe places," but he rather doubted it.

He expected, instead, to be picked up directly by saucer. In any event, there would not be a movement of the Collegeville group, qua group, to one of the refuges in the hills. Rather, each person would receive his own orders, probably directly — he would hear a voice telling him where to go and what to do. Some would be told merely to remain in their houses; some would be told to go to specific places to be picked up. But, if one were among the chosen, he could be sure of this much: he would receive some orders.

Time was short, the doctor emphasized, but everyone must keep calm and get a grip on himself. He must not panic and he must be prepared for any eventuality. Some people had already been picked up by saucers for transportation to other planets, and more would follow them soon; others would be directed to "safe places," which might actually be rougher, since they would be without the comforts of civilization, there to stay for perhaps a year before being taken to other planets; and some of the chosen might even be ordered to go under in the coming flood, for reasons best known to the inscrutable Guardians.

Furthermore, Dr. Armstrong stated, it was not necessary to be enlightened — i.e., informed of the belief system — in order to be saved. In fact, some of the most important work of the chosen among this enlightened group would be to calm and comfort those who were picked up by saucer or directed to the "safe places" without knowing why or what was happening to them. For the present, he said in conclusion, orders were for all to go about the daily routine of living, and to attract as little attention as possible. He specifically instructed the group to "make no special effort to proselyte," since such actions would only bring investigations and pressure from the college authorities. This order did not forbid instructing someone who came to one of the enlightened in a sincere fashion wanting help — but the members should not broadcast what they knew.

Finally, near the end of the meeting, Dr. Armstrong played a tape recording to the group. It was a séance conducted by a medium from Steel City, Mrs. Ella Lowell, who spoke with the voice of "Dr. Browning, from the seventeenth chair of the seventh density" in the spirit world. The séance at which the recording was made had taken place during the fall (probably mid-October) at Dr. Armstrong's house, but, as far as we can tell, the recording had not been played publicly in a meeting until this time.

It contained a number of vague references to the coming flood —e.g., "within the next three years . . . everything you are accustomed to will be washed away"; "Some of you will be on a plateau and will see the world crumble about you"; "Most of the earth will be uninhabitable, being turned upside down and exposed to the cleansing power of water, coming up shining and clean. It's almost like an agitator in your washing machine. Very simple." Dr. Browning did not mention any date for the disaster, but he was quite positive in reassuring the people at the séance that they had all "been selected" to be saved and assured them that "Not anyone in this room will lose his life through any form of natural disaster."

Furthermore, Dr. Browning's talk included a great many general ideas and specific notions we have already noted in Dr. Armstrong's and Mrs. Keech's discourses. For example, Dr. Browning, on proselyting, said: "You are going to be willing to share your special knowledge but you are not going to care whether anyone accepts you or not. And you are not to be concerned whether anyone accepts this special knowledge or not . . . You are not here as a salvationist . . ." Much of the lore of flying saucers was also dispensed through Dr. Browning. "Certain ships cannot be lowered nearer the earth than the three-mile limit. You will be lifted bodily in peapod ships, which will take 8–10 people to a mother-ship."

Dr. Armstrong received special instructions, rather flattering ones, that indicated his importance in the coming time of trouble: "He will give power and be a beam of power. He will create an aura. He will be charged with an electro-magnetic force that will fill all the cells of his body and make him immune to any death or disease. And that will be done on a space craft."

Just how, when, or why Dr. Armstrong came in contact with

Mrs. Lowell is not clear. It is our guess that he met her through the Steel City Flying Saucer Club and it is highly probable that he discussed Mrs. Keech's messages with Mrs. Lowell during the late summer and fall, although the two ladies did not meet at that time. Mrs. Lowell had been a medium, in touch with Dr. Browning, for a number of years and was a highly experienced person in the art of communicating with the spirit world. Her performances were fluent, imaginative, and ingenious. It is clear that she took pains to flatter Dr. Armstrong and delivered messages that must have inflated his feeling of importance. He must have been correspondingly impressed by her skill and by the apparent knowledge of her mentor, and, in the weeks just before December 21, Mrs. Lowell played an important, if confusing, role in the activities of the group in Collegeville as well as that in Lake City.

Although the Sunday afternoon meeting of the Seekers had been announced to be the last formal meeting, it was not, as we have said, well attended by the college students. Dr. Armstrong therefore called another "last" meeting of the group for the following night, Monday, November 29. The turnout was excellent — some nineteen students, including all those whom we have described in detail. Two strangers who appeared at the door seeking admission were turned away, in accordance with the new "closed group" policy announced on Sunday. The members present heard essentially a repetition of the discussion on the previous day.

Without having discussed the recently concluded meetings in Lake City, Dr. Armstrong announced that he would be going to Lake City the following weekend and that he might well not return. He was on "twenty-four-hour call," he explained, and his orders might come through anytime. Mrs. Armstrong felt she would return, however; that "they" wouldn't be "taking her" just yet. The doctor advised the students to go about their daily routines and to await their orders. In effect, he abdicated his position of leadership and left his followers completely on their own. Since there was nothing to be done in preparation for the disaster, they did just that.

During the following week, the Armstrongs went about practicing what they had preached at the Sunday and Monday meetings. One afternoon a deputation of three high school students, classmates of his son, waited upon Dr. Armstrong, seeking an explanation of the rumor that the world was coming to an end. Calmly and patiently, the doctor explained that the rumor was exaggerated. He belittled the idea of a cataclysm and said that there were going to be extensive magnetic changes in the earth's surface but that this was not the same as the end of the world, and they were not to become panicky or excited. He shifted the topic to flying saucers then, and discoursed on communication with other planets. When the young people had left, Dr. Armstrong felt pleased at the way he had handled the situation. He pointed out again that it was currently necessary to play down the account of the cataclysm and to lower rather than raise fear of it. He felt he had been right in urging them to believe only what "appealed to their reason."

Relieved of her editing and circulation chores, Mrs. Armstrong busied herself in housework and seemed to be almost compulsively absorbed in that task. Yet her expectations had not changed. One night when Bob Eastman was watching her move clothes from the washer to the dryer, he said he would bet she'd be glad when "all this is over with," and she answered that it wouldn't be long now, and she certainly would be glad. Again, one night when our female observer was helping wash the dishes, she expressed surprise that the electric dishwasher was not in use. Mrs. Armstrong explained that the motor was worn out, and it would cost thirty-five or forty dollars to repair it. "It just isn't worth it," she continued, "because the time is so short now."

On Friday, December 3, Dr. Armstrong left for Lake City taking with him not only his wife, but his daughter Cleo and Bob Eastman. The Armstrongs left their ten-year-old daughter in Collegeville in the care of Kitty O'Donnell; their fifteen-year-old son stayed home, too, because he wanted to attend a formal dance at his high school.

Although few of the Collegeville student group had changed their daily routine, things were quite different in Lake City. On

Saturday or Sunday, Edna and Mark Post had received "orders" through Mrs. Keech's writings to move in with Marian Keech and help take care of her. She required some care evidently, because she went on a three-day fast, again dictated by orders, during which she appreciably lost weight, though she could ill afford to become any thinner, and suffered great pain, weakness, and loss of motor control. Edna and Mark had also fasted, though only for one day, again on orders from the Guardians.

Furthermore, there had been almost blanket orders about quitting jobs. Mark Post had given up his job in the hardware store; Edna Post had resigned, somewhat embarrassedly, from the directorship of the nursery school; and Bertha had quit her job as a clerk in an industrial concern—all on orders received from the Guardians. All of them were living "from day to day," but for Edna and Mark especially, the daily routine had changed radically. Not only were they living with Mrs. Keech, but all three were under orders not to leave the house—even to procure food. They were arranging for food by telephone orders or through the good offices of Mrs. Keech's husband who had accepted, though not welcomed, this change in his household, and who was greatly concerned over his wife's health. Yet he could not influence her to give up her fast, or to disobey any of her other orders.

It is hard to overestimate the power that such orders were able to exert over so convinced and sincere a believer as Edna Post. During the time that she was "under orders" to remain at Mrs. Keech's and not even to leave the house, Edna received a phone call from her sister, telling her that their mother was very ill and in much pain. Still Edna decided to obey the orders she had received and to remain in the house. In discussing this incident later on, Edna showed the strength of her conflict in her trembling hands and tearful expression. "It's a hard choice to make," was her main comment. Mrs. Keech, who was standing nearby, agreed that these were times of difficult choices, and pointed out that it was a question of deciding between one person and the universe of brotherhood—which was important? Edna stayed.

There had been a small number of callers at the Keech house

during the week, but no organized activity. Bertha Blatsky had dropped in one afternoon, and phoned a couple of times, usually with a problem of interpretation of something she had "received" from the Creator. Another caller was a complete stranger, a salesman of cemetery lots who probably received the most unusual reception of his career when he announced his trade. "That," retorted Mrs. Keech, "is the least of my worries." But she invited him into the house and she and Edna Post spent over an hour explaining the ideology and the prediction to him. He promised to return for further instruction, and they expected him, but, as far as we know, he never showed up again. One expected visitor, a man who came every Thursday evening for his lesson, Marian said, failed to turn up.

It was during this week that we first became aware of Mrs. Keech's growing conviction that her home was under surveillance by unfriendly people. Heretofore, she had frequently repeated that the house was protected by the Guardians who would see to it that no one would be admitted who should not be there. She had often mentioned that she left her doors and windows unlocked. But now she was concerned about attracting the attention of the police, who, she said, often drove by and flashed their spotlight in her front window. "They're very anxious to know what we're doing," she once remarked. "We've got to keep everything looking normal." She urged our observer not to park his car in front of her house every time he called, lest it attract the attention of the police. Her concern was intermittent, but clear and growing, paralleling Dr. Armstrong's interest in maintaining secrecy.

The meeting that Bertha Blatsky had scheduled for Friday, December 3, began in an unusual way. As each guest arrived for the evening meeting his attention was directed to a note on the coffee table in the living room: "I shall receive one sibet at a time as they arrive in the room over us for instructions where I shall remain until the evening meeting. Parich. Beleis." * Each sibet in

* "Parich" was the title Mrs. Keech assumed during this phase of the movement and signed to her communiques from the Beyond. "Beleis" was

turn climbed the stairs to the cramped attic where Mrs. Keech, thin and shivering, even though she huddled near the gas fire, delivered a personal message from Sananda.

Downstairs, in the brightly lighted dining room and living room, the members greeted each other, were brought up to date on recent events by Mark, Edna, or Bertha, speculated about the meaning of Marian's unusual consultations, and anticipated the events to be unfolded during the evening. It was a goodly throng. No longer strangers, the members talked easily and fluently, in an atmosphere that was relaxed and almost gay. All the people who had attended the meeting of Wednesday, November 23, had returned, including Frank Novick, who had evidently yielded to the persuasion of his wife, May. Clyde Wilton had returned by air again from his home, and Mr. Keech, patient, kindly, and a little lost, hung on the fringes of the crowd. Dr. Armstrong, accompanied by his wife and daughter and by Bob Eastman, had driven in from Collegeville during the afternoon. Edna and Mark Post were present, of course, as was Bertha Blatsky. With the addition of three observers, the total audience in the room came to fifteen.

In one room downstairs there was an air of excitement. Dr. Armstrong was busy ripping the zipper out of the fly of his trousers, while Mark Post energetically removed the eyelets from a pair of his shoes. Frank Novick was wearing a piece of rope in place of the belt that usually encircled his waist, as was Clyde Wilton. It turned out that all the members in their private consultations with Mrs. Keech had received orders to remove all metal from their persons and had zealously complied, not only by emptying their pockets of change and taking off wristwatches and eyeglasses, but by literally cutting apart and tearing out metallic portions of their clothes. The rationale for this odd action was simple, Dr. Armstrong explained: if you're going for a ride in a flying saucer, you must not wear or carry any metal on your body, because contact with metal would produce severe burns.

a recurring salutation and complimentary close to messages exchanged by the believers, as well as a greeting and farewell.

He added that the technical details were not, of course, clear since we humans were so woefully underdeveloped technologically; but he did not need to know everything at once; the order had come through and that was enough.

Meanwhile, the individual consultations with Mrs. Keech were continuing, even though the hour for which Bertha had called the meeting, 7:30, had passed, and she was growing restless. Toward 8:30, a newcomer, unknown to any of the people downstairs, appeared at the door and asked for Mrs. Keech. She explained that she hadn't seen Mrs. Keech since the previous summer, but had dropped in on impulse this night. When the last sibet had descended, the newcomer was ushered upstairs to see Mrs. Keech. Her consultation lasted between twenty and thirty minutes, or roughly twice as long as that of most of the members, and correspondingly delayed the beginning of the meeting. About 9:30, the unexpected caller left on a personal errand, saying she would return in ten or fifteen minutes. Shortly after she had gone, Mrs. Keech came downstairs, and the formal meeting got under way.

The prolonged delay in starting the meeting apparently produced extreme irritation in Bertha. During the intervening week, Bertha had become accustomed to her new position of power. Having tasted and relished the satisfactions of leadership, she was clearly prepared to accept the mantle which, in the beginning, she had worn so uneasily. It seems probable that her resultant irritation accounts for a great deal of what she subsequently said during the evening.

We shall not describe in detail the content of this meeting, which began at 9:45 Friday night, recessed at 3 A.M. on Saturday, began again at 9:30, and ended at about 6 P.M. on Saturday. Most of the occurrences of these two days were manifestations of Bertha's desire to reassert herself and to dominate the group. As such, they are irrelevant to our main theme, and the character of this meeting was different from anything before or after. It was essentially a stormy diversion that had little of lasting significance for the movement, and we shall give a relatively brief account of the sometimes exciting, sometimes stupefying events of these two days for the intrinsic interest they may have for the reader.

The meeting began with a number of petty assertions of Bertha's authority. She overruled Mrs. Keech on the decision as to where Bertha should sit, and on whether or not a particular light should remain burning. In subtle and gross ways, Bertha attacked much of the lore that Marian Keech had so carefully cultivated. Speaking with the voice of the Creator, she mocked the language that characterized Mrs. Keech's lessons: "I don't have to use fancy words like 'thee' and 'thou' and 'shalt.' We are talking cold turkey. You have had all the fancy words you need used on you before. There has been too much time wasted on this sort of stuff . . ." She ridiculed Sananda, belittling his knowledge: "Another in this room has been told that she was Mary but she was told that by Sananda, and Sananda did not know. Now you are getting it from the one who knows."

Bertha next ridiculed the idea of fasting or self-deprivation and asserted that caring for and nourishing the body was an important duty. As if to make her dominance all the more apparent, Bertha brought to the Saturday meeting a small roast of beef, her contribution to the luncheon. It was the first time that anyone had seen meat on Mrs. Keech's table, but Bertha ate it with zest and urged others to "have some protein." Mrs. Keech and the Armstrongs avoided the beef (as did the observers) but most of the other sibets followed Bertha's lead.

Bertha's most blatant act of domination, however, was to turn away the newcomer to whom Mrs. Keech had devoted so much attention during her individual consultations earlier in the evening. This lady had left the house before the Creator began speaking, but had announced her intention of returning. When she did come back, the Creator's voice peremptorily refused her admittance, even though Mrs. Keech half-protested. Marian later commented that the newcomer was a member of two flying saucer clubs and was "very important to us," adding: "It broke my heart to see her turned away."

The climax of the Friday evening meeting occurred near eleven o'clock, when Bertha's voice announced the miracle that had been visited upon her. She worked up to the climax gradually, over about half an hour, describing through the Creator's voice the shocking and bewildering information that He had instilled into her during the early part of the week — how she couldn't accept it at first, how she feared she was going mad. She had been told, the Creator asserted, that she was to be the mother of Christ!

As the clock began to strike eleven, with dramatic suddenness Bertha began to moan and cry for help: "The Christ has not been born in spite of what the Bible says . . . but the baby will be born right now! I need help! Oh, doctor, help me! A bed must be prepared, I have pain. Something is happening in my abdominal area! A bed and a doctor . . . and a nurse. Upstairs . . . No one else must be in the room. Oh, help me!"

Mrs. Keech and Dr. Armstrong were at her side in a moment and she was assisted up to the attic. There, after ten or fifteen minutes of groaning and writhing, she seemed to regain possession of herself and calmed down. While Mrs. Keech and May Novick remained to help her dress, the rest of the company assembled, quietly, at loose ends, in the dining room.

The effect of Bertha's performance was numbing. Everyone confessed to complete bewilderment at what had happened, and asked his neighbor for interpretation which, of course, was not forthcoming. Edna Post, as mystified as anyone, perhaps best expressed the feeling of the group: "I don't know what it means. I guess we'll just have to wait and see."

When Bertha finally did descend, with Mrs. Keech, she was almost girlishly naive in her protestations that it was "all a mystery to me." She kept assuring the group that she had not expected anything like the actual birth pangs and seemed quite concerned that no one believe that she had planned the "show" (as she called it, herself) in advance. She finally remarked, "Perhaps we'll find out what it means when I go back in [to the trance]."

And find out she did. The whole incident, the Creator asserted, had been a lesson, a demonstration of His originality and His intention to "run this show" His own way. Finally, it was a joke too, a joke played on all of the group to jolt them out of their "preconceived ideas" and show them that anything could happen.

The remainder of the Friday night meeting was anticlimactic, being taken up with lessons and discussion about such topics as absorbing learning without thinking; the technique of not thinking; souls, their division and reunion as soulmates; and further assertions of the Creator's power and wisdom.

A large portion of the Saturday meeting was devoted to attempts to demonstrate the Creator's power to heal. He attempted to remove a tiny blemish from the skin just under Bertha's right eye, and, when the audience seemed unconvinced that the mark was disappearing, the Creator announced somewhat peevishly that the demonstration had been a test of the audience's honesty in reporting what they saw. The Creator's major attempt at healing took up more than an hour which He spent on curing May Novick of her long-standing fear of walking alone outdoors.

The response of the various members of the group to Bertha's performance during these two sessions varied somewhat, but was, on the whole, accepting, almost as if they had been beaten into submission. Only Dr. Armstrong showed enthusiasm, when he remarked, late Friday night, that he had never seen such effective teaching in his life — "the pounding and pounding we're getting." Mrs. Keech's response was to incorporate the happenings in her scheme of things: "They're getting us ready for something big." Her explanation of the attacks on her cherished beliefs was that the Creator was demonstrating the principle that each person should "follow his inner knowing."

Among her closing acts on Saturday afternoon Bertha reemphasized the doctrine of "inner knowing." In the Creator's voice she pronounced everyone in the group now capable of receiving messages themselves. Such messages, she emphasized, were to be used only for personal guidance and enlightenment, and not for the instruction of others. The Creator did not prohibit "spreading the light" to people outside the movement, but emphasized that the task of instruction was limited to Bertha and Mrs. Keech.

Bertha also spoke for the Creator in the matter of "the brotherhood." All the members present were brothers of the "Brotherhood of Sananda" and the "Order of the Light." She demonstrated the secret sign by which one brother might recognize another — the left hand palm down on the right shoulder, and the head bowed — and cautioned the group to use the sign unostentatiously and only to make sure of the identity of someone who claimed to be a brother.

These last acts of Bertha's emphasize once more the general attitude toward proselyting. Attempting to convince others was not specifically prohibited, but it was certainly not encouraged, and the task of instructing neophytes was limited to Bertha and Mrs. Keech. The introduction of the sign of the Brotherhood marks the first clear-cut distinction between "chosen" and "heathen," and further points up the extreme discretion in talking about the ideology that was being imposed on the members.

Except for these remarks on proselyting, only one occurrence during the entire two days of meetings has relevance for our interest in the movement. During a "private consultation" with the Creator, one observer, asking what the future held for him, was strongly advised to quit his job as a schoolteacher because it was not as important as his duty in the Brotherhood. He was assured that he could manage to get along without a job because there was so little time left before the end. Here, as far as we know, is the first time Bertha joined Mrs. Keech in urging members to make major changes in their lives and to commit themselves to belief in the flood.

In the main, the events of December 3 and 4 were diversionary. Although powerfully disconcerting, the impact of these meetings was short-lived, for the members of the group soon returned to their major preoccupation — preparation for the cataclysm. One clear result of the meetings was that there were now two "independent channels" of information from the Guardians. There had been some conflict between these two channels, but, in the ensuing weeks they began to work in harmony, "validating" each other's messages. Before long, too, Mrs. Keech had regained her position of leadership.

As matters stood on Sunday, December 5, however, Bertha's behavior had created a perplexing situation, for she had challenged some of Mrs. Keech's most dearly held tenets, but she had not produced the orders that everyone was waiting for. Most of the members had to tolerate this uncertainty, but not so the Armstrongs. Typically, they went to a third source. They returned to Collegeville on Sunday night, and on Monday morning set out for Steel City to consult Ella Lowell.

In the séance that took place that morning, Dr. Armstrong heard many things that must have gratified him as well as settled doubts in his mind. Dr. Browning, Mrs. Lowell's familiar spirit, discoursed for more than an hour and made a number of flattering references to Armstrong's future importance in the coming crisis of the world. Dr. Browning never once mentioned December 21 as the specific date, or in any other way directly confirmed Mrs. Keech's prediction, but he did give a good many details connected with the coming cataclysm. He supplied a lavish and vivid picture of how the chosen would be "taken up" in space ships, given a "spiritual anesthetic" so there would be no fear or pain, and assured his listeners that there would be no panic for them: "We'll put you to sleep and reborn you." He instructed the group not to tell their families what they knew: "You don't *need* to tell them. You know they will go to the same area as you . . . You and your immediate ones will be saved."

Among the many items that Dr. Browning covered in his talk, there were a number that were consistent with the Armstrongs' previous beliefs and their picture of the cataclysm. These they remembered well, and, in the coming weeks, often quoted — for example, Dr. Browning's assurance that they "would know about the calamity. You will know the exact hour," and his statement that they might be picked up at any time, anywhere.

The last part of Dr. Browning's talk urged his audience to "continue doing exactly as you have been doing in your daily routine until called upon to do otherwise." In answer to Daisy

Armstrong's question "At this eleventh hour, would it be a good idea to inform other people that they should become interested?" Dr. Browning was brief and decisive: "It is too late. We have them all chosen anyway. It would be useless to try to change their minds." At another point in his talk, however, Dr. Browning said that if anyone came asking questions, it was the members' duty to inform the inquirer about the disaster and answer all his questions, since not everyone who had been chosen had been "beamed in" yet. Like Sananda and the Creator, Dr. Browning was preaching cautious and selective proselyting. In general, the Armstrongs seem to have been reassured by what they heard from Dr. Browning.

Despite the fact that they had already disbanded the Seekers, on Wednesday, December 8, the Armstrongs planned another meeting of the group for the following day. Since Daisy Armstrong had destroyed her list of members' names, and could not remember them all, she called on Susan Heath and Kitty O'Donnell to assist her. They did well, for, although a heavy snow was being driven down by a bitter wind, a total of eighteen people showed up at the Armstrong home. Among them were all the heavily committed members and most of the moderately committed.

Dr. Armstrong began the meeting with a very brief account of the recent meeting in Lake City, and explained that a new "source," Bertha, had appeared in the group there. He went on to inform those present that he expected to get his own orders soon, and that he thought they would be receiving individual orders. He described his latest meeting with Ella Lowell, and added that he felt it would be best for them to hear, for themselves, just what Dr. Browning had said. He thereupon played an hour and a half of tape-recorded séance, containing the material we have already mentioned above, and, of course, much more.

Some of the listeners were entranced by the description of how they would be picked up and returned the next day to hear it again. Others were simply confused or left at loose ends as to what they should do personally to prepare for the flood. Bob

116

Eastman and Kitty O'Donnell, who were practically members of the Armstrong household, accepted the barrage of instructions calmly. The only notable reaction came from Hal Fischer, the chief skeptic of the Seekers, who seemed to become more convinced of the flood prediction: "This," he remarked, "is independent evidence."

The remainder of the week was without incident in Collegeville, until Sunday rolled around and things began to happen. Dr. Armstrong made a phone call to Mrs. Keech on Sunday afternoon, during which he learned that there was to be a meeting in Lake City on Tuesday night, the 14th, and he informed her that Ella Lowell would be paying a visit to his home on Sunday evening. Whether he invited Mrs. Keech or she volunteered to come is unclear, but, at nine that night she arrived, with Mark and Edna Post; and the two women whose messages from the spiritual world had been guiding Dr. Armstrong's beliefs for so long finally met face to face. Dr. Browning had given many details about the modes of saucer pickup to be enjoyed by the chosen while being vague about the date; whereas Sananda had been firm in the matter of the 21st, although he had been unclear in specifying how the elect were to be saved. Meanwhile, Dr. Armstrong had been serving as the vital link of communication between these two ladies, and each knew rather well what the other had been "given."

One of Ella Lowell's first questions to Mrs. Keech raised the question of the latter's age. Recalling that Dr. Browning had once instructed her never to accept an earthly teacher who had been born before 1900, Ella asked directly for Marian's birthdate. When the answer came back May 6, 1900, the possibility of dispute seemed to vanish. For reasons best known to herself, Ella Lowell accepted Mrs. Keech as her teacher on earth, and then proceeded to go into a trance and speak with Dr. Browning's voice.

The details of this séance, while fascinating, would only encumber our report here. It is sufficient to say that Mrs. Lowell, through Dr. Browning, clearly and emphatically confirmed the validity of December 21 as the day of catastrophe, and in several references to the "source" or "teacher" in Lake City, showed a very deferential attitude. Furthermore, Dr. Browning acknowledged that the orders he gave to the Armstrongs and to other members of the group were subject to overrule, presumably from Mrs. Keech's writings. Dr. Browning's orders to Thomas Armstrong, for example, were that he go to Lake City the following Tuesday and return to Collegeville on Friday, "unless other orders intervene." Mrs. Keech seemed entirely satisfied at the cooperative relationship that grew up between her and Mrs. Lowell, and not the slightest sign of tension showed between the two women.

On Monday afternoon, and again in the evening, Mrs. Lowell and Mrs. Keech continued to discuss their beliefs, feeling each other out on technical points and, apparently, storing up considerable information. It seems probable that their discussion resulted in the quiet, but final, abandonment of the very early plans to go to one of the "safe places" in the mountains. Instead, Dr. Browning's suggestion that the chosen would be picked up individually by flying saucers came to be accepted.

The audience for these sessions included several Seekers who were meeting Ella Lowell face to face for the first time. She seems to have made a strong impression on Bob Eastman, Kitty O'Donnell, Hal Fischer, and Cleo Armstrong, and, through them, she continued to exercise a considerable influence on the Collegeville group in the weeks to come. But the main immediate effect of Mrs. Lowell's séances and her discussions with Mrs. Keech was to clear up a number of points on which Dr. Armstrong felt Sananda's messages had been ambiguous or vague. From that time on, he was sure he knew just what was going to happen.

On Tuesday morning, the Posts and Mrs. Keech set out for Lake City, followed shortly by Thomas and Daisy Armstrong. The Armstrongs left behind them a disorganized and somewhat confused group of college students, most of whom would shortly be leaving for their homes, since the Christmas vacation was beginning. They left three children, putting the youngest in the joint charge of Kitty O'Donnell and our female observer. And they left a vacuum of information about their future plans.

With the departure of the adult Armstrongs to Lake City, the center of interest shifted there, and remained there until after December 21, for the Armstrongs did not return to Collegeville until well after that date. There were several developments of importance in Collegeville, however, and we shall summarize them briefly at this point, before we return to the major line of our narrative — the events in Lake City.

On Tuesday morning, just one week before the 21st of December, Kitty O'Donnell drove Mrs. Lowell back to Steel City. Bob Eastman and Cleo followed later that afternoon and all four attended a séance that evening at which Dr. Browning addressed his remarks both to the Collegeville contingent and to some of the regular members of Ella Lowell's circle in Steel City.

Exactly what Dr. Browning had to say on this occasion is obscure (to us), but when the three disciples returned on Wednesday, they were moderately unhappy. They had found that Mrs. Lowell's "group" in Steel City had not been told about the December 21 prediction by Dr. Browning and did not believe in it. They noticed that Mrs. Lowell's spirit did not tell a consistent story; the strong affirmation of the date that Dr. Browning had given Mrs. Keech was not repeated in Steel City two days later. Rather, the ethereal doctor seemed to dismiss the whole question as rather trivial and turn his attention to problems of previous incarnation. In subtle ways too, Mrs. Lowell seemed to be trying to weaken the conviction of Bob Eastman and Kitty O'Donnell. Mrs. Lowell expressed to Kitty her fear that Bob was "so deeply involved" that if the flood didn't occur he would surely "crack up"; and she seemed also to be preparing Kitty for nonoccurrence of the flood. At first Cleo had been upset by what she heard, but later on Wednesday she rallied her convictions, telling our observer that the Steel City group didn't believe in the date because they "weren't meant to" believe in it.

By Wednesday afternoon, most of the college students had drifted off on their separate ways for vacation. It was a relatively quiet day until about 6 P.M. when pandemonium broke loose.

At a routine meeting of the college administration, the news of Dr. Armstrong's dismissal and the circumstances surrounding it were made public. An enterprising reporter from the Steel City evening paper picked up the story and put it on the press association wires. Within a few hours, the peace of the Armstrong home was shattered as telephone calls began to pour in from major newspapers, news magazines, and the wire services all across the country.

It was fortunate that Cleo had regained some of her poise, for the burden of answering reporters' questions fell on her. Far from seizing this opportunity to propagandize for the belief system, she tried mightily to minimize the forecast of cataclysm. Her father was in Lake City, she told them, and not available for comment; he was looking for work there. She denied flatly that her father had predicted the end of the world, asserting that he simply believed there would be some changes in the earth's surface on December 21. Beyond this she refused to be pressed. She and her brother and sister were simply living their ordinary daily lives, she told the newsmen, and they would like to be left alone to do so.

The barrage of phone calls persisted through Wednesday night and began again on Thursday morning, interspersed with calls from student members of the Seekers wanting to discuss the news break. By Thursday afternoon the newspapermen had located Dr. Armstrong in Lake City and turned their attention to him, but new distractions arose as practical jokers began telephoning the house, and telegrams and calls from sincere opponents or supporters of Dr. Armstrong's beliefs began to come in. For two days or more, life in the Armstrong home was a bedlam from early morning till very late at night.

Cleo lost some of her composure when she saw the news stories in the Thursday editions. Angrily she denounced the papers that ridiculed her father, expressing the hope that the flood would come and show up the unbelievers. She and Kitty fabricated fantasies of violent destruction, with their having the last laugh as the waters swept over the multitudes who were mocking today. The two girls also took defensive measures against further penetration of their privacy, burning all remaining documents that related to the belief system and even destroying Mrs. Keech's address and telephone number in Lake City after memorizing it. Cleo's anxiety was real, though irrational. She pointed out that William Dudley Pelley had been "put in jail for his beliefs," and expressed the fear that those currently in the Armstrong house might suffer the same fate if any "evidence" were found by (unnamed) investigators.

In the middle of this chaos, Ella Lowell continued to sow the seeds of doubt. Bob Eastman went to a séance in Steel City on Thursday and returned with a tape recording of it which he played for Kitty, Cleo, George Scherr, and our observer. At the very beginning of the tape, Dr. Browning repudiated December 21 as the date of the cataclysm, and then confusingly proceeded to "take back" that repudiation in part, through ambiguous statements and instructions. For example, Dr. Browning seemed to admit that the sky would be black on the 20th, and a flood would occur in Lake City on the 21st. But it would be days or weeks before the waters reached Collegeville, months before the country as a whole was inundated. Dr. Browning had advised Bob Eastman to plan to spend Christmas with his parents in Steel City, yet to "act as if the flood were going to happen." The spiritual mentor of Mrs. Lowell explained that the date prophesied by Mrs. Keech was "a cultural idea," with no necessary relation to the plans of the spacemen.

The effect of this tape on the four people in Collegeville was depressing and extremely upsetting. George Scherr expressed his bewilderment and seemed tense and restless. Kitty demanded angrily if this meant that she would have to go looking for a job now? Cleo said she would have to, since there was no money left to keep her in college. Bob was shaken, although he tried to explain his theory that the change in expectations had been necessary in order to shatter their preconceived ideas. It was a depressed and fretful group who received a telephone call from Dr. Armstrong that night, in which he announced that he would not be returning from Lake City. He explained how difficult and unpleasant his position was, besieged by the press, and praised Cleo for doing such a wonderful job at her end. The remainder of the conversation was largely of personal matters and, if Cleo did give any indication of what she had just heard on Ella Lowell's tape, it seemed to have no effect on Dr. Armstrong. He told Cleo that great things were about to happen in Lake City and encouraged her to keep her spirits up.

By the next morning, Saturday the 18th, Cleo and Kitty had recovered their spirits somewhat. Cleo pointed out again that the Steel City group hadn't been "meant to be given" the date, and this probably explained why Dr. Browning had talked the way he had. She even began to doubt Ella Lowell's skill somewhat. Bob Eastman, however, still had great faith in Mrs. Lowell. At 11:30 another phone call from Lake City brought orders from Dr. Armstrong for Cleo and Bob to leave at once for Lake City — Sananda had commanded it, and they were to get going quickly for "something might happen anytime." Kitty and the others were to follow their own judgment, the doctor continued, and wait for further orders. This burst of instructions from the other end seemed to have a cheering effect on all hands, and they began to speak confidently again about "being taken up" in space ships.

The remainder of Saturday and Sunday passed quietly, but there was evidence of mounting tension and fretfulness on the part of the disconsolate Kitty. Abandoned now by all except the two observers, the Armstrong's son (who spent most of his time out of the house with school friends), and the uneasy George Scherr, Kitty grew increasingly irritable. She tried to find tasks to occupy her time; she began to smoke heavily and to complain about being confined to the house, waiting for orders. Susan Heath called in, asked for reassurance, and found little. George Scherr sneaked out of his home and listened to tapes, trying to find some rock of certainty in the confusion around him. It was an agony of doubt and directionless drifting for the rest of the Seekers. Ella Lowell did nothing to relieve the tension when she dropped in at eight or nine o'clock on Sunday night and talked (in her "own" voice) of how the future would be glorious and the chosen would be engaged in happy, important work; of how this would be a new age, and a better earth — all the while skirting any question of the validity of the date.

Toward 11 P.M. Dr. Armstrong telephoned from Lake City to inquire whether the children were all right, and Mrs. Lowell betrayed a great desire to talk with him. She finally got an opportunity and, after some chitchat about beaming in Lake City, made a remark to the effect that the 21st of December was not a particularly significant date, strongly implying, in the context, that she did not expect the catastrophe to occur. Sharply, Dr. Armstrong fired back his question: "What do you mean by that?" The question seemed to unsettle Mrs. Lowell, for she fumbled for a moment before replying that, well, of course, if there had been other orders received in Lake City, they would, of course, supersede anything she had received from Dr. Browning. Some of this got across to Kitty who was not cheered by it, and was only further confused when Mrs. Lowell asked her to drive to Steel City on Tuesday night (i.e., well after the predicted occurrence of the cataclysm) for a special séance.

The rest of the waiting period was pure hell for Kitty. She vacillated between doubt that the flood would come at all and conviction that Lake City would be inundated on the 21st and the rest of the country would gradually go under. Once, in her most doubtful period, she comforted herself with the thought, inspired by Dr. Browning, that even if the flood did not come, the belief and the publicity connected with it would have done some good simply by "awakening people to God." She added that she herself had been made more religious and "a better person" by having undergone this experience and had abandoned many of her bad habits. Once, in a crisis of feeling, she burst out bitterly that she hoped the flood would come with a vengeance and wipe out mankind; but almost immediately she retracted her wrath and remarked that it was a pity so many people would have to die, but that was the only way God would be recognized. Her conviction that some sort of disaster would occur frequently faltered, but in the end remained strong. She insisted on sleeping right next to the telephone in Dr. Armstrong's bedroom, since, she felt, she would probably get her orders by phone.

George Scherr was virtually a resident of the house during the last two days. He too was restless and tense, and stuttered markedly, anxious lest his name be publicly associated with the movement, and anxious lest he miss any news or orders concerning the coming cataclysm. For him, as for Kitty, these were trying days.

Meanwhile, a number of interesting events had occurred in Lake City during the week between the last group meeting (at which removal of metal had been so much emphasized) and the visit of Mrs. Keech and the Posts to Collegeville. Among the most important were the change in Bertha's position to a secondary role; the decision to call a special group meeting for the instruction of "new sibets"; and finally, the invitation Mrs. Keech received to give a talk on her ideas in a nearby small city.

The events that brought about the change in Bertha's position began with a stormy scene between her and her husband. Before that Bertha had, by one means or another, prevented him from knowing of her participation in the group; he believed she was simply practicing dianetic therapy. Then a few nights after the "birth of Christ" episode, she burst forth with the whole story of her mediumship, her capacity to talk with the voice of the Creator, her election to bear the Christ child, and related matters. Going into a trance, she behaved toward her husband as she had toward the members at the recent meeting in Lake City. The Creator gave him various orders and threatened to strike him dead at the first sign of disobedience. This revelation to a shocked and disapproving husband was the most important commitment Bertha made to the movement, for he ordered her not to leave the house without his permission and she was forced to disobey him in order to attend meetings of the group. Furthermore, by continuing her participation in the movement, she risked an investigation of her sanity; her husband declared that, if she had not voluntarily given up all connection with the group by January 1, he was going to send her to a psychiatrist and destroy all the books and writings associated with the movement.

At the same time, Bertha's husband held a council with Frank Novick who, apparently, had been trying to keep May away from Bertha's influence, and the two men appear to have agreed on tactics for restraining their wives. At any rate, May refused to visit Bertha or to allow Bertha to visit her. May Novick also refused to go to Marian Keech's house.

These events committed Bertha heavily, and undermined her confidence in her ability to talk with the Creator's voice. Deprived of May's companionship, no longer free from her husband's surveillance, threatened by an inquiry into her sanity, she lacked her former sureness and poise. Having exposed her beliefs to an unaccepting audience, Bertha was psychologically deflated.

Because several new people had expressed interest in the group, Marian had decided the previous week to hold a meeting for new "sibets." Her decision was supported by messages from the Guardians. She sent out invitations to a few people, but steadfastly maintained a policy of high selectivity as to whom she would invite. For example, during this week, two groups of sincerely interested high school students had called on her. One group she abruptly turned away; the other she invited into the house and talked to them for an hour about their major interest — flying saucers. She did not invite either group to the coming meeting.

As the week drew toward a close, Marian Keech began to manifest expectations of imminence. One evening, when one of our observers called, she asked him if he had brought her a message. When he replied that his only message was "I am standing by you," she nodded. "Fine," she said. "This may be the night. It wouldn't surprise me in the least if we were taken up out of this house tonight." Concurrently, attempts were made to increase the involvement of some of the members. One of our observers felt a persistent pressure on her to quit her job, and the other, as we have mentioned, had been explicitly ordered by the Creator, in private session, to quit his post. When our female observer announced that her job would be terminated on December 17, Marian immediately invited the observer to move in with her.

The meeting on the evening of December 14 was attended by ten members of the group and a total of four observers — our two regulars in Lake City and the two authors who had not attended the previous meetings. In addition to Thomas and Daisy Armstrong, Edna and Mark Post, Marian Keech and her husband, and Bertha, there were three new faces: Kurt Freund, Arthur Bergen, and a woman from the neighborhood. This woman had always been interested in mysticism, and had, on her own initiative, called on Mrs. Keech the previous summer and had returned several times for lessons. She appeared at Mrs. Keech's house this evening by chance, to return a pamphlet she had borrowed; and Marian informed her that she had been "sent." Throughout the evening, this woman gave the impression of being uneasy, if not frightened, and somewhat incredulous, although clearly impressed by what she heard. She left the meeting early, though unobtrusively, and never returned.

Arthur Bergen, on the other hand, became a regular member of the group. Between fifteen and sixteen years old, he was a high school student who was active in one or two flying saucer clubs in Lake City. Through a member of one of these clubs who knew Marian Keech, Arthur had learned of her lessons and had attended her "readings" at the Metaphysical Bookstore in Lake City during the early fall. A pale, slim, bookish lad, he seemed anxious to appear older than he was. Wanting to please and be accepted, he was always serious, deferential, and rather unpoised. He experienced difficulty with his parents' apparent opposition to his membership in Mrs. Keech's circle, an opposition that stemmed at least partly from his father's bitter personal experience with some "doomsday preaching" in Sweden.

Mrs. Keech showed considerable interest in Arthur and paid a great deal of attention to him. On Tuesday night, he had obtained permission to attend the meeting, and been warned not to stay out late. Yet he could not bring himself to leave, whether out of embarrassment or interest, and hence was still at the house when his mother telephoned him at 2:30 A.M. and sternly ordered him to come home at once. Mrs. Keech sensed the powerful effect of this

126

command on the youth and helped him to get started for his home immediately. When he was leaving, Mrs. Keech tried to console him and increase his attachment to the movement. She urged him to be strong and have faith, and to remember that he was working to save his whole family — they would all be "taken up" because Arthur was one of the chosen. Perhaps this reassured him, for he returned to the house during the crucial days just before the crisis.

Kurt Freund was a publisher, who, Marian Keech asserted, was interested in issuing her lessons in book form. She had sent him some of her lessons during the summer (when the messages were urging her to publish) and he had shown much interest. His delay in acting, she told us, had been due to Freund's feeling that Marian's material, by itself, was "too theoretical," and that he wanted to look for a flying saucer expert to collaborate with her, so that "more concrete" material could accompany her writings. He had visited her during the previous week and Mrs. Keech, now totally indifferent to publication, felt he had been "sent" so that he, personally, would be "brought to the light."

Freund sat quietly through most of the Tuesday night meeting and appeared to be bored by much of what he heard. He yawned a great deal and slept part of the time. During the coffee breaks, he was usually engaged in conversation by Dr. Armstrong who seemed quite eager to convince the publisher of the validity of the belief system. Freund reacted equivocally to these attempts. He was interested principally in flying saucers and believed unhesitatingly in their interplanetary function. When Dr. Armstrong pressed him on more spiritual matters the publisher replied that he had read much modern physics and modern philosophy and had been thus persuaded to adopt a "Neoplatonic" position, disbelieving in material reality. Further, he added, his experiences in dianetics and scientology had added to this conviction.

Yet, when the conversation turned to questions of the flood, he remarked that he had often had feelings of approaching disaster, intimations of catastrophe, but that didn't prove anything. When one of the observers asked him what he was doing to prepare for the catastrophe, he smiled and said: "Nothing." Pressed as to whether he believed in the date, he gave an ambiguous reply: he had seen many strange things in his life, he said, and would not be surprised if a flood occurred. Finally, we noticed that, when Mrs. Keech was in the process of getting a "private lesson" for him, he was extremely inattentive — even leaving the room when she was writing — and seemed more puzzled than intrigued by what she produced. Although he returned to the group on subsequent occasions, it is our conclusion that he was at best suspending his judgment, and at worst a fairly skeptical person who maintained his interest for personal motives, best known to himself.

The content of the meeting itself need not occupy us long. It consisted largely of replaying, for the assembled audience, several tapes that Ella Lowell had recorded in Steel City and Collegeville. These were the tapes in which Dr. Browning stated emphatically that the flood was due on the 21st, gave details on saucer pickups, instructed everyone to wait at home for his own, personal orders, and urged no one to proselyte actively among nonbelievers, but to be helpful and informative toward those who came seeking.

At one point during the meeting, Mrs. Keech read a message instructing the group not to celebrate Christmas, not to buy presents or sing carols, for this would be "a black Christmas." Early in the session she took the precaution of pointing out to the audience that, while Dr. Browning spoke from the seventh level, Sananda, and he alone, was on the eighth level. The eighth was the highest from which any messages had been received, Mrs. Keech asserted, ignoring the question of the Creator's level. This assertion reinforced Ella Lowell's statements that any order she (i.e., Dr. Browning) might give could be superseded in Lake City. Mrs. Keech also made something of her acceptance as an earthly teacher by Ella Lowell — an incident we have already discussed.

Throughout the meeting of December 14, Bertha was a timid and ineffectual reflection of her earlier self. The last person to arrive on Tuesday night, she looked wan and tense. She was greeted with great surprise by Edna Post and Daisy Armstrong, who seemed not to have expected her, and their welcome was warm. Before the tapes were played, both Bertha and Mrs. Keech gave "private lessons" (in voice and in writing, respectively), and most members went to both sources. In her consultations with our observers, Bertha behaved quite differently from the way she had in previous such sessions. To most questions she simply replied: "Follow your inner knowing," and once went so far as to say: "Accept no authority, not even the authority of the Creator." During the group meetings, Bertha made three separate attempts to direct the activities, but failed each time. Once she gave up after a few fumbling sentences; once she failed utterly to gain the attention of the audience. Finally, when she tried to persuade Mrs. Keech to play a tape that she (Bertha) had made a few days earlier, Marian ignored her and Bertha withdrew her suggestion.

Although she had lost much of her earlier power, Bertha did not become a nonentity in the group. Rather, she and Mrs. Keech developed a close working relationship. The two women tended to "consult" each other's spiritual guides, and to ask each other to go to her "source" for "validation" of a message the other had received. This cumbersome apparatus was used on any occasion when the validity of a message was of crucial importance.

One of the most striking points made during the meeting was the supposed need for secrecy and restriction of information at this point in the movement. Mrs. Keech's concern for secrecy had grown markedly during the previous week. She had received "orders" to destroy all the extra copies of her lessons and certain other material relating to the movement; some was to be saved, sealed, and placed in a safe place, for Marian felt sure that her house was going to be searched by inimical though unspecified persons. Much material was burned and what Marian could not bring herself to part with was packed into two cardboard cartons and sealed.

Just before the Ella Lowell tapes were played, Mrs. Keech warned the group emphatically that no one was to breathe a word of what was said on the tapes to anyone outside the group.

Later, she repeated this warning, adding that if any information did leak out, the Guardians would see to it that the tape was erased.

When one of the observers (deliberately) suggested that he take notes on the contents for the benefit of one of the absent members, Mrs. Keech immediately and flatly rejected the suggestion. No notes were to be made; if anyone had made notes, he or she would have to burn them before leaving the house. At the same time, she acknowledged the legitimacy of carrying some word of the meeting back to the member. To her questioner she said that it would be all right to talk with the absent member about the meeting; he would no doubt give the sign (of the brotherhood) and that in itself would establish his right to hear the news. On several occasions, Mrs. Keech and the Armstrongs mentioned "the inner circle." These lessons were not for the public, Mrs. Keech said; they were to be restricted to the inner circle.

One further development of importance at this meeting was the first specific moves toward concrete preparation for the evacuation of the chosen before the cataclysm occurred. Early in the evening each member present was issued a "passport" (a piece of blank stationery and a three-cent stamped envelope) to be shown when boarding the flying saucer that would pick him up. During the private consultations with Marian Keech, members were also informed of the password ("I left my hat at home") to be used on the same occasion. Some members were even assigned a numbered seat on a specific saucer. Having equipped the sibets with passports and password, fortified their belief through Dr. Browning's words, and sworn them all to secrecy, Marian Keech brought the meeting to a close at 4:30 Wednesday morning.

Such detailed planning for the evacuation signaled the growing feeling of the imminence of the disaster. The convinced members now awaited evacuation hourly, expecting to be rescued, prepared to be picked up at any time. When their thoughts turned from preoccupation with the personal future, they felt their kinship with ideologically sympathetic groups in other parts of the country. Mrs. Keech and Dr. Armstrong occasionally made reference to such groups who, although they had not been "given the date," were nonetheless among the chosen. At the same time, the members were aware of the existence of some disbelief. Even some of the foremost authorities on flying saucers, men who were greatly respected in the group, were known to be skeptical about December 21.

The daylight hours following the meeting were quiet. Mark Post was ordered to give up the strict diet of nuts on which he had been placed several days before. He spent part of the day composing a letter to a girl friend in a distant city in which he told her their romance was ended as far as he was concerned. Since she did not believe in Sananda, Mark felt that he and she were not well matched.

Marian Keech may have spent part of Wednesday considering what she would say the following evening when she was scheduled to address an audience in a nearby small city. Certainly the engagement had been much on her mind since she had received the invitation a week earlier. On December 8 Mrs. Keech received a telephone call from the president of the "Northeastern Association on Unidentified Flying Objects" asking if she would consent to talk to this "saucer group." Her reaction to this invitation is of great interest to us, because it provides an excellent example of her feelings and behavior when presented with a splendid opportunity to proselyte an audience she herself had not selected.

Mrs. Keech's first response to the invitation was to ask the club president whether it was "an order" or simply a request, indicating her constant and unbounded expectation that her orders from the Guardians might appear in any guise and through any outlet. The president of the flying saucer club assured her that it was a request, and Marian replied that she would think the matter over. And think it over she did. During the following days she discussed the invitation with Edna, Mark, our two observers in Lake City, and the Armstrongs. She looked to each of these people at various times for guidance and often asked advice in the now standard language of the group: "Do you have any light on whether I should go to the Saucer Club?" On December 10, she also asked the question of Bertha — i.e., the Creator. The Creator hesitated a moment before replying, then turned the question back to Marian, asking what light she had on the invitation. Mrs. Keech's reply was that her "inner knowing" told her to accept and to read a lesson to the flying saucer club. She then repeated her question to the Creator and received the reply that Marian would know what to do, through her "inner knowing," when the time came.

In short, Mrs. Keech's reaction to this proselyting opportunity was to hesitate, debate, and ask for advice in making the decision about acceptance. Her dalliance with the invitation lasted several days, during which, it seemed, she either had no desire in the matter or was too timid to express it directly. Had the invitation been phrased as an "order," she would doubtless have complied at once. Phrased as an invitation, it became a matter of grave uncertainty. She finally accepted only after her visit to College-ville on December 12–13, when Dr. Browning suggested that she do so. Even though the time of the cataclysm was but a week or so away, Mrs. Keech showed great reluctance to proselyte for her beliefs and did so only when a spiritual mentor specifically instructed her to do so.

Of further interest, of course, is how Mrs. Keech used this opportunity. The meeting took place on the evening of December 16, the day on which the news stories of Dr. Armstrong's dismissal from the college had appeared. Both he and Mrs. Keech had been besieged at her home that morning by reporters from all the Lake City newspapers and the wire services. By that evening they were well aware that they were nationally known figures or, at least, would be when the news stories appeared the next morning.

The meeting got under way at 9 P.M. in the private dining room of a restaurant, where twenty-five or thirty people had assembled. After the chairman had made a few general comments that brought the group up to date on the latest saucer news, he introduced Mrs. Keech. Although she was expected to deliver a talk, she began by suggesting: "Well, why don't we start it out with questions? I can wrap it up in ten or fifteen minutes. I would rather have it that way."

For the next forty-five minutes Mrs. Keech answered questions from the audience, questions that were concerned mainly with how she received messages, the nature of the language in them, some of her early experiences. She spent a good deal of time explaining the meaning of such words as "sice," "Losolo," and "UN." Never once did she mention the prediction of the cataclysm, even though it was due in less than five days. Finally, the chairman asked her directly about the prediction. She replied by giving a long, detailed account of the circumstances under which she had worked with Dr. Armstrong during the late summer, but made absolutely no reference to the prophecy, the date, or any expectations she had about the future. She simply evaded the whole question.

The chairman excused her and called on Dr. Armstrong. He spoke, at most, for five minutes, giving an account of his early interest in flying saucers and asserting his belief in their interplanetary origin. In his closing words, Dr. Armstrong came as close to active, public proselyting as anyone had come since the September press releases. In order to convey the curious flavor of his style of "proselyting" we quote here the relevant parts of his talk:

"I'll say to you that all of you who are interested in saucers are in a special category. Now, you don't know that, but you are, because it seems that the people around the world who have been having a special interest in saucers are people who have had that interest because they had something within themselves that goes back to things they have forgotten. Therefore there is something within you that returned to life. So don't be surprised within the next weeks and months ahead, regardless of where you happen to find yourself, if you find that you have an unusual experience in relation to spacemen or saucers or something of the kind. Because I think I can say to you — and it's no secret — that spacemen have said that they are here for a purpose and one of those purposes is to remove certain of their own people from the earth.

"Now, you don't know who they are. Jack over here may be a spaceman for all I know. He probably is. You don't know it either. You don't know yourself. So I'll give you a little bit of the ancient wisdom that was given to me in an old book: 'Know thyself for in thee great secrets are hid.' Now we don't know who we really are. When we begin to discover and when we begin to have the book opened for us, and some of us have had that privilege, then we have discovered that we are much greater and much more than we think, as we have recently found.

" 'Know you not that ye are God?' You never thought of yourself that way, but that's what you are, Gods in the making. We are all in the making. We ourselves are destined to become a part of much greater things. So I will say to you, in view of the turn of events, begin to ask yourself, why saucers? Will you ask yourself why saucers? Why now? Why in my lifetime?"

The doctor sat down to applause and was thanked, never having referred to the cataclysm or the date on which it was expected, or having said anything specific about the future. This proselyting, if such it was, can perhaps be best termed "proselyting by decree": everyone in the audience was, willy-nilly, declared by implication to be among the chosen.

When the chairman attempted to question him directly about his "personal plans for the next hours and days," the doctor answered simply: "I can tell you right now, I don't know." And that was that. The meeting broke up shortly thereafter, at 10:30, and the two speakers returned to Mrs. Keech's home exhausted. They had spent almost the entire day fending off inquirers, coping with questions, and trying to shield their personal beliefs from the scrutiny of the world. They had need of rest, for the following day, December 17, was to prove just as tiring as the 16th had.

The excitement in Lake City had begun early on Thursday morning, the 16th, when a reporter and a photographer turned up on Mrs. Keech's doorstep shortly before nine o'clock. They represented the alert newspaper that had printed the interview with Mrs. Keech in September and was now following up the announcement of Dr. Armstrong's dismissal — a story that had broken the previous evening. The arrival of these newsmen signaled the start of one of the most frantically busy and chaotic days the house had ever seen. From then on, it was a steady babel of telephone calls and rings at the door, with people asking questions of Dr. Armstrong and Mrs. Keech. The major newspapers in Lake City and the representatives of the wire services sent men to the door; more distant newspapers phoned; local representatives of national news magazines came around; and finally came the newscasters and commentators from radio and television stations.

Some reporters were admitted to the house after prolonged and insistent effort, but for a long while got no further. Dr. Armstrong fought this intrusion on his privacy; he was a professional man, he said, a man concerned with accuracy; he was afraid they were too hurried and untrained to do justice to the ideas of the movement. He protested that he had wanted to avoid the limelight, but had involuntarily been made "the goat." Finally, he added, he didn't want to make a public show of himself. He was not a street-corner evangelist; he was not interested in saving the world; and he didn't want to persuade anybody to join anything —this was not a cult, not a religion.

He sincerely fought the newsmen for about an hour and some of this tenacious breed appeared almost discouraged. Finally, several reporters made remarks, almost threats to the effect that the newspaper would publish *something* about him, and wouldn't he rather have them publish the truth than inventions? At this, Dr. Armstrong appeared to capitulate. Repeating that he didn't seek publicity, he asserted that he felt an obligation toward accuracy and therefore would consent to make a statement. He and Mrs. Keech flatly refused to permit pictures of themselves or the interior of the house. They reacted violently when one photographer surreptitiously snapped a picture and hurried out of the house. They refused to travel downtown to make a live television broadcast and also refused to permit cameras to be brought to the house for that purpose.

Finally, after much persuasion, Dr. Armstrong agreed to record a few remarks for a national network, to be played that evening on the regular news broadcast. In all, he gave only one press interview and made one half-minute tape for broadcast on Thursday, both after extremely strong pressure from the newsmen. He was polite, and civil, did not lose his temper, but was firm, though greatly harassed. Mrs. Keech seemed to pattern her actions closely after Dr. Armstrong's. She too finally gave a brief interview to the newspapers, but did not make a broadcast tape.

The news stories on December 16 had been prominently displayed in most newspapers, but had been brief, containing only the bare facts of Armstrong's dismissal and the statement that he expected "the end of the world" on December 21. In the interview he gave at Mrs. Keech's home on the 16th, Dr. Armstrong tried to correct the erroneous impression that had been splashed on so many front pages. He denied that the world would end on the 21st, but said that he expected a tidal wave and a displacement of the earth's crust "extending from Hudson's Bay to the Gulf of Mexico which would seriously affect the center of the United States." He explained that the world was "in a mess." "But the Supreme Being is going to clean house by sinking all of the land masses as we know them now and raising the land masses now under the sea. There will be a washing of the world with water. Some will be saved by being taken off the earth in space craft." He declined to say what he was planning to do in preparation for the cataclysm and added: "What changes I am making in my life as a result of this prophecy are matters of my personal conviction — not for public explanation." Most stories also carried some details about Mrs. Keech's receiving messages from outer space, and stated that she had been given the prophecy from the planet Clarion.

Most of the news stories treated the subject straightforwardly, quoting or accurately paraphrasing statements by Dr. Armstrong or Mrs. Keech and refraining from comment. But the headline writers took full advantage of a golden opportunity for ridicule. Through their efforts the group of believers were impressed with the scoffing and mocking of a skeptical, if not hostile, world. One

136

newspaper, for example, headed their front-page story TUESDAY — THAT SINKING FEELING, while another called its readers' attention with WORLD WON'T END, BUT BOY IT SURE WILL SHAKE.

Columnists and editorial writers tried invariably to be funny at the expense of the group. One gossip columnist began his piece: "Had any messages from outer space lately?" while another wrote: "When that story first broke about Dr. Thomas Armstrong predicting the 'end of the world on Dec. 21' (later changed to a tidal wave engulfing Lake City), comedian Jimmy Edmonson put in a hurry-up call: 'Anybody want to buy two on the 50-yard line for the Rose Bowl cheap?'" An editorial writer, commenting on Mrs. Keech's method of communicating with outer space, took the opportunity to ask for a prediction: "For a starter (are you listening, Venus?) who is going to be the next mayor of Lake City? P.S. If the answer has fins on it, don't bother."

In succeeding days, the ridicule mounted. Dr. Armstrong and Mrs. Keech were both hurt and angry at the press notices that belittled them, and became even more reluctant to talk to reporters. They frequently referred to the "unfair" and "distorted" accounts of their beliefs.

Late on Friday morning, December 17, as the newspaper publicity began to have its effect, a trickle of callers, both in person and on the phone, asked for more information and explanation. High school students predominated, but there were several adults, too, mostly women. There were a small number of practical jokers, but a substantial proportion of the callers were sincere, although sometimes skeptical.

The treatment accorded these inquiring souls seemed confused, though it was consistent with the established policy of selective proselyting. Only the chosen were eligible for instruction, and mere curiosity seekers or those who came to jeer were to be turned away. How to discriminate between chosen and heathen was a matter for one's inner knowing. Whoever answered the telephone or the doorbell (usually Mark Post or Dr. Armstrong) made a preliminary judgment as to the visitor's sincerity. If they "passed" they were sometimes brought in and treated to a brief lecture or had their questions answered. Whoever happened to be on deck handled the case, and, if the only available instructor was busy with a previous caller, the potential proselytes were often left to twiddle their thumbs. There was no plan, no systematic indoctrination, but simply huge, indifferent chaos. Toward the middle of the afternoon, when all hands were fatigued, even sincere inquirers were sometimes turned away, especially over the phone, and told there was nothing to say beyond what had appeared in the newspapers.

Such was the state of the group on Friday afternoon, when the first of a series of disconfirmations began. Exposed to a tremendous burst of publicity, they had made every attempt to dodge fame; given dozens of opportunities to proselyte, they had remained evasive and secretive, and behaved with an almost superior indifference. In Dr. Armstrong's words, they "were not trying to get anybody into anything."

For Marian Keech and the group around her in Lake City there was not just one disconfirmation but a series of them occurring over several days. The great flood was due to engulf the city at dawn on December 21, but the believers thought that they would be rescued before the cataclysm took place. They expected flying saucers to land, pick up the chosen ones, and transport them either to other planets or to some "safe places" designated by the Guardians. The first disconfirmation occurred on December 17, and the series came to an end at 5 A.M. on the morning of December 21. During this time there were three specific and unequivocal disconfirmations and a strong attack against the key points in the ideology. We shall narrate the events of this crucial period in some detail.

Many of the Lake City group had been holding themselves in readiness for the pickup for some time now. As far back as December 4, it will be recalled, they had gone through the procedure of removing all metal from their persons — an act considered essential before one might safely board a saucer. Thomas Armstrong had repeatedly told both the Seekers and the believers in Lake City that he was prepared to be picked up at any time, that he was on "twenty-four-hour alert" in the service of the Guardians. The atmosphere in the group was one of eager expectation. By the time they had seen the morning papers on December 17, and read the scoffing comments in the columns, Mrs. Keech and Dr. Armstrong were even more ready to be picked up and must have wished their rescuers to come as soon as possible and remove them from a hostile world.

Sometime before noon on Friday, December 17, Marian Keech received a phone call from a man who told her he was Captain Video from outer space. He informed her that a saucer would land in her back yard to pick her up at four o'clock that afternoon. That, at least, is the message Marian relayed to the others in the house — the two Armstrongs, Edna and Mark Post, and a new recruit named Manya Glassbaum. The telephone message was undoubtedly the work of a practical joker, but the believers took it seriously and began to make preparations for the pickup. Daisy Armstrong seemed inclined to question the message at first, asking her husband and Marian if they were sure someone wasn't pulling their legs, but she was immediately and firmly quelled. All telephone messages had to be taken seriously, she was told; the people of outer space could communicate with the group by phone, but often had to use coded messages.

There is no doubt that the believers really expected a saucer to land in the back yard at four o'clock. By noon, all five of the regular members of the group had removed every scrap of metal from their persons — including zippers, metal clasps, buttons with metal backing, bobby pins, and belt buckles. As soon as she arrived, our observer was put through the metal-removing process so that she too would be ready to board the saucer. By 1 P.M. only Manya Glassbaum was wearing or carrying any metal object, for it had not yet been determined whether she was truly among the chosen and would be picked up with the others.

The newest member of the Lake City group, Manya was a girl of about eighteen years of age who had been interested in flying saucers for some time and was convinced they came from outer space. Sometime during the summer she had called on Mrs. Keech and learned of her messages and beliefs, but had not seen Mrs. Keech again until the latter addressed the meeting of the flying saucer club on the previous evening. Manya's interest and belief seem to have been aroused by Mrs. Keech's talk on that occasion, for she returned to the Keech home and spent the night there.

On Friday morning, under "orders" from the Guardians, Manya telephoned the newspaper where she was employed and quit her job. She also gave up smoking and drinking coffee and seemed prepared to accept the further orders that she take up residence with Mrs. Keech. In other words, she took the belief system seriously and was beginning to commit herself to it. It is equally clear that Mrs. Keech considered her a promising disciple and Manya's status in regard to the expected saucer pickup at four o'clock did not long remain in doubt. Toward 2 P.M. Marian sat for a message and received instructions that Manya too was among the chosen, and must immediately remove all metal. She had to cut her slip apart in order to remove the metal clasps from it, and she ripped the zipper out of her skirt.

From then on the group waited restlessly for four o'clock, while they coped almost absent-mindedly with some jobs that were fast becoming routine. The press was still eager for more information and telephoned frequently. Mark Post, who had been deputized to handle such inquiries, gave newsmen a standard "No comment," and shut off further questions by hanging up. The lone reporter (from a national news magazine) who braved this refusal and called at the house personally did finally gain entrance, but could not prod any information out of any of the members. In a short while she left, discouraged and rather angry at being ignored so positively. A truck with television cameras waited in the street outside but the prohibition against any pictures was still in force, and no cameramen were allowed in the house. The believers were still angry at the photographer who had surreptitiously snapped a picture of Mrs. Keech the day before.

Mrs. Keech's home address had been printed in the morning editions and there were other callers besides the press. Those who telephoned to ask questions were told by Mark Post that all the available information was in the newspaper stories. If the caller persisted and was, in Mark's judgment, sincere, he was told he could call at the house in person if he felt he needed to know more. A large number of people, half of them in their teens or very early twenties, came directly to the house, where they were screened at the doorstep by Mark or Thomas Armstrong. Many were turned away, but between ten and fifteen were admitted, among them two adult women to whom most of Mrs. Keech's time was devoted. The others got scant attention from anyone, many being ignored while they sat almost begging to be proselyted. The relatively slight interest that most members had in making converts at this point had been even further reduced by their preoccupation with their four o'clock appointment.

Four o'clock finally came and the chosen ones gathered in the kitchen with their coats, simply walking out on whatever visitors there happened to be in the living room at the time. Mrs. Keech was ecstatic. Hardly able to stand still, she ran between the back porch and the kitchen window, her eyes turned up to the sky. The others caught her excitement and joined in the scanning. For ten minutes they continued their search while the tension mounted. Then, abruptly, Marian removed her coat and, instructing the others to keep watch, returned to the living room. After a brief interval, the Armstrongs abandoned their stations too — Daisy to go out for a walk, Dr. Armstrong to retire to the attic. Only the Posts and Manya Glassbaum remained on duty.

By 5:30 they too gave up and returned to the living room. There was almost no discussion of the matter among the believers. Our observer waited until the house was empty of visitors to ask Mrs. Keech why the saucers had not come. But Marian refused to discuss the topic, and none of the others in the living room seemed interested in the question either. Instead, Marian sat for a message and received one that made her weep because it bore such glad tidings. Sananda informed her that when the group was picked up she would return to "the Father's house" and need not come back to earth again. The rest of the group expressed their happiness for her and began to discuss questions of their joint future in higher density space.

The message had the effect of reaffirming Marian's importance and the validity of her messages, as well as diverting thinking from the disconfirmation that had just occurred, but the diversion succeeded only temporarily. By the time the group had eaten dinner the disconfirmation was clearly on their minds again. Mrs. Keech turned the television set to the Captain Video program and instructed the company to watch carefully for coded messages intended for them — she was sure there would be one on the program. But no one detected any such message and the problem once again disappeared into uneasy silence.

The group could not abandon the matter completely, however, and soon various members were suggesting explanations for the failure of the saucers to appear that afternoon. One suggestion was that the presence of strangers, nonmembers of the group, in the house had caused the spacemen to veer off. This possibility was discussed with interest for a time but was clearly unsatisfying. A few other suggestions were advanced, but the one the group agreed upon in the end was that the afternoon incident had been an alert. The saucers would indeed land when the time was ripe, but everyone had to be well trained, "well-drilled actors," so that when the real time arrived, things would go smoothly. The spacemen were not testing their faithfulness, but were simply unwilling to leave any possibility that their human allies would make a mistake. The four o'clock watch had been a practice session.

This explanation was more satisfying to the members but did not completely eliminate their disappointment. When another of the observers arrived at the house about 9 P.M., he found Mrs. Keech still quite upset. She told him about the events of the afternoon and concluded with a complaint: while she and the rest of the group were trying to do their best, it almost seemed as if the spacemen were deliberately trying to mix them up. She said she had almost called on the Clarionites to come on down and straighten things out.

The disconfirmation was sufficient to disillusion one person, however. Until it happened, Manya Glassbaum had been planning to stay on at the Keech house. But that evening she received a phone call from a boy friend and, without consulting anyone, asked him to come out to see her. Marian was quite disturbed by Manya's action, but she could not prevent the visit. The boy came to the house, and about eleven o'clock he and Manya left, presumably to get a coke. Manya never returned. The newest convert with the least commitment had been lost, shaken loose by the first disconfirmation.

That evening there were more visitors, people who came out of curiosity, interest, or belief — drawn there by the newspaper stories. One of them provided strong support for the beliefs of the group. He was a seventeen-year-old boy who had driven over from his home several miles away, arriving late in the evening. In an excited manner he said that he wanted to speak alone to Dr. Armstrong. The doctor had a private conversation with the boy for a while and then summoned Marian to join them.

After the boy left, Marian and Thomas told the others what tidings the boy had brought. They said he had been sitting in the bathroom reading about the prophecy in the newspaper when suddenly a voice said to him, "You don't believe that, do you?" He had looked up to find a strange man in a gray jacket standing in front of him. The man had continued: "Well, it's true and you don't have to worry. You will be picked up."

Whether this boy was deluded or was playing a practical joke, the fact remains that his story was received as "independent" verification of their beliefs. It probably helped the group to recover from the four o'clock disconfirmation and perhaps precipitated the next prediction, a matter we shall get to shortly.

From about 10 that evening until 11:30, between twenty and twenty-five people visited the Keech house. They were mostly high school teen-agers, with a sprinkling of boys from a nearby junior college and three university students home on vacation. The visitors arrived intermittently, usually in groups of three or four, and were seated in the living room where Dr. Armstrong and Mrs. Keech expounded at length on their beliefs and on the prophecy. Some of the inquirers offered counter-arguments and the discussion of controversial points was very lively.

The change in the attitude of the two protagonists toward inquirers was noticeable: no longer were they indifferent or preoccupied with other matters. Rather they made pointed and deliberate attempts to persuade and convince. This change may have been a reaction to the four o'clock disconfirmation, although it is difficult to judge because the only comparable period *before* the disconfirmation was the few hours that very morning and early afternoon when similar callers had been attracted by newspaper stories. In any case Dr. Armstrong and Mrs. Keech engaged in proselyting until the last visitors left at about 11:30. The house became relatively quiet again, but the believers were not allowed to rest, for the Guardians, it shortly became apparent, had further plans for them.

Toward 11:30 our observers had to leave the house on an errand. One of them returned about an hour later to find that at midnight Mrs. Keech had received a message of the greatest importance: that a flying saucer was even then on its way to her back yard to pick up the chosen, and it would not wait for anyone who was not ready. There must have been an intense flurry of preparation as the group struggled to meet this sudden deadline. The story is best told in the words of the observer:

"I came back to the house about 12:30. The front door was unlocked. The lights were on. The house was empty. I went upstairs and looked around. There was no sign of a soul in the house. When I returned downstairs Mark Post came in the back door and said, 'Do you have any metal on you?' I said I did not and he then told me to come with him.

"We went out in the back yard. It was cold and snowing and the ground was very wet. Marian, Daisy, Thomas, and Edna were all there. Marian told me about the message and asked me again about metal. She wanted to know about my shoes and Edna said I would have to take my shoes off because they had nails in them.

"Mark came back in the house with me. I took my shoes off and Mark started to rip the heels from the shoes. I stopped him and said, 'Don't do that. Just get me a couple of pairs of wool socks and some bedroom slippers.' He did this and then pointed out that the buttons on my suit did have metal on them. I ripped the buttons off my coat.

"We got back outside again and Edna took me aside and said, 'How about your brassière? It has metal clasps, doesn't it?' I went back in the house and took my brassière off. The only metal on

145

me was the fillings in my teeth and I was afraid someone would mention those. We all proceeded to wait, standing at the side of the garage. Marian told us to keep our voices down and be quiet so the reporters wouldn't come around. I said that they were too lazy to be up at this hour of the night. Marian replied that was not so. If they heard about this they would be out there with spotlights to take pictures for movies and television. We had to avoid that at all costs. Mark supported her by telling me that reporters had, for example, awakened Cleo at 5 A.M. one morning.

"At about 1 A.M. Marian started saying that she was very cold. She added that if they all wanted her to go into the house and get a message, she would do it. She emphasized that she would do it only if they all wanted her to. She was getting very cold and tired but did not want to herself take the responsibility for going indoors. Everyone urged her to go in and get a message. She then said, 'All right. I'll go in and get a message. If I blink the light that means you're to come back in, that it's a test.' I firmly expected her to go in, blink the lights, and we'd all go back indoors. But she came back in fifteen minutes and told us we were to stay out in the back yard. The flying saucer would arrive to pick us up within the hour.

"We waited outdoors until 2 A.M. The group was quite gay and elated with anticipation. There was quite a bit of lightning in the sky, and Thomas kept saying that these were signals. Then Marian said that she saw a bright spot of light hovering around the chimney. The light, she said, would come and go.

"There was great anticipation and also a great deal of cold. We were shivering and pounding our feet. Dr. Armstrong was doing calisthenics. At two o'clock we couldn't stand the cold any longer and Mark suggested that we open the garage doors, turn on the motor of the car and sit in the car until we warmed up a bit. The four women got in the car while Mark and Dr. Armstrong continued to stand watch out in the yard.

"In the car Marian started to write another message. It was exceedingly long. The first half of the message consisted of repeated blessings to those who are patient and disciplined. Those who

146

were patient and disciplined would be rewarded. The rest of the message boiled down to saying that we were to go back and rest and that, at the proper time (unspecified) a man would come to lead us to the place where we would be picked up.

"We got back into the house at about twenty minutes past three in the morning. Marian talked a lot about whether we were or were not well-drilled actors and referred to the experiences of the day as drills and basic training."

So much for the events of the night. Three hours of uncomfortable but hopeful waiting had ended in just another disappointment, although outward signs of disturbance over the failure of the saucers to come were not obvious. The watchers made only a sketchy attempt to explain the disconfirmation that night. Exhausted and nearly frozen, they went to bed at once, and the matter was not fully discussed until several hours later, after breakfast. Even then they were unable to devise a more satisfying explanation of the events of the night. It had been a drill, a rehearsal, an exercise in discipline, they decided. But this rationalization did not suffice, for they had been too convinced, too eager to believe beforehand that the midnight alert was "the real thing." They found no way of adequately handling this uncomfortable disappointment—instead they kept it a secret.

Sometime during the morning, Mrs. Keech received orders instructing all those who had been present on the midnight vigil to be extremely cautious and discreet in talking about what had happened. When the observer who had been present returned to the house after a brief absence, she was immediately informed of these orders and warned to be careful to whom she talked. When one of the authors, who had theretofore been able to obtain information from Mrs. Keech and Dr. Armstrong quite readily, arrived at the house in the early afternoon and asked to be brought up to date on recent events, no one in the group volunteered even the slightest reference to the midnight vigil. It was only after extensive probing and pointed inquiry about what had happened the night before that he was told they had been on a saucer watch from midnight to 3:30 A.M. The matter was passed off casually as "just a drill." Except for this reluctant and belittling account, the watch party kept secrecy well. The other two authors were not told anything voluntarily, and when one of them attempted to quiz Mark Post, the latter replied simply that he was under orders not to talk. Even Bertha, the voice of the Creator, was told nothing. The whole affair was hushed up.

Secrecy was not the only reaction to the disconfirmation following the vigil of Friday night, for there was also an apparent need for group support. On Saturday morning Marian Keech received messages ordering her to gather together all the members of the group, and Mark spent a great deal of the morning at the telephone. He called all the believers in the local area, and put through long-distance calls to summon Clyde Wilton from his home, Cleo Armstrong and Bob Eastman from Collegeville, and the three authors from Minneapolis. By noon his task was done and there was promise of a good gathering for the meeting that night.

By Saturday afternoon, the influx of visitors to the house had not only grown in size, but also in importance and significance in the eyes of the believers. The general attitude of the group toward the newspapers was still negative. They tried to discourage reporters from coming to the house and "No comment" was still the answer to newsmen over the phone. But the believers were beginning to see the advantages of publicity in bringing people to the house whom they could attempt to persuade and convert. Edna and Daisy pointed out that the newspaper stories had had one good effect at any rate — they had alerted people. Thomas Armstrong, who had probably suffered most from his publicity, seemed cheerier than he had been about the matter: "Just imagine," he exclaimed, "if a guy had a million dollars he couldn't buy this kind of publicity." Dr. Armstrong even began to take an optimistic view of his success in proselyting. He told one of the observers that at least one of the young people who had been there the previous evening had walked out because the truth he was told had offended his prejudices but had returned in the morning — a significant change of heart, the doctor felt.

On Saturday afternoon, the members of the group began lecturing to visitors in a more serious and organized way. The instruction of teen-agers was turned over to Mark Post, who spent most of his afternoon with groups of four to six of them. Thomas Armstrong and Marian Keech devoted most of their energies to the adults who called and would often spend a long time in private consultation with those whom they considered "special cases." Their technique of proselyting is well illustrated by one of these, a thirty-five-year-old technical sergeant in the United States Air Force, who arrived at the house about 4:30 in the afternoon after having telephoned for an appointment.

Marian took him and one of the authors up to the attic with her, where she proceeded to describe the history of her messages, the prediction of the cataclysm, and the reasons it was being visited on the world. For more than an hour and a half she lectured to the sergeant, then told him to go home and meditate, pray, and wait for "awakening." She told him he could come back later if he wanted to and if he thought he needed "more light." The sergeant departed, somewhat baffled, with many of his questions unanswered, and never did return. It was ineffective proselyting, but the incident illustrates the time and energy being devoted to such activity at this time.

Not all callers got the same amount of attention, of course, and there was still some selectivity in admitting people to the house, though a smaller proportion were turned away on Saturday than had been the case on previous days. At one point Marian even instructed Mark and Dr. Armstrong not to send away anyone who was really interested. The need for social support following the disconfirmation on Friday was very strong.

By six o'clock the stream of visitors had dwindled, the phone rang less frequently, and the household settled down somewhat. More members began arriving for the evening meeting — Bertha, Kurt Freund, and Arthur Bergen from their homes in the area, Cleo Armstrong and Bob Eastman from Collegeville. Clyde Wilton telephoned to say that he had been unable to get a plane, but would arrive by train the following morning, and by 7:30, everyone who was coming had arrived. The meeting did not get under way at once, however. Marian Keech seemed preoccupied and expectant; she was called to the phone several times and after these conversations would sometimes talk privately to Dr. Armstrong, while the rest of the members stood about in small clusters making desultory conversation and wondering what the evening would bring. All were aware of the atmosphere of expectancy and there was considerable restlessness. Both Arthur Bergen and Mark Post were very tense, and several times remarked that they wished they knew what everyone was waiting for. No one knew, except Marian and perhaps Dr. Armstrong and they were not telling. All through that day Marian had been receiving a series of telephone calls which were a prelude to an important visit that night — a visit that turned out to be a major attack on the belief system.

The meeting finally got under way, but there was nothing to meet about, and it proceeded haltingly. The Creator started to speak but soon ran out of inspiration and instructed Marian to write. Marian wrote and asked the Creator to validate messages. The phone rang frequently, interrupting the meeting, because Mrs. Keech frequently took these calls in the privacy of her bedroom. While she was out of the room, the rest of the group sat in uneasy silence, waiting her return, waiting for the unknown event that would make that night unlike any other night.

Between telephone calls, Mrs. Keech received one message that needs detailed description, in view of what we know about the events of the preceding night and the secrecy in which they had been shrouded. At about 10:30, she received a rather long communique from Sananda that repeatedly emphasized one point: "I [Sananda] have never been tardy; I have never kept you waiting; I have never disappointed you in anything." Marian read the message aloud and further emphasized it by holding it up for everyone to see — a highly unusual procedure. Looking around the room she stated solemnly: "They assure me that so far not a single part of the plan has gone wrong, not a plan has gone astray."

Edna Post made the perfect response: "That's because we have such good planners."

Marian Keech was trying to bolster her belief. The disconfirmation following the midnight vigil still bothered her. In spite of the influx of visitors that afternoon and the requests for information over the phone; in spite of the ready response of the absent members to her invitation for that evening; in spite of the explanation, in which she concurred, that the midnight watch had been a drill, she still felt the gnawing discomfort of a prediction not fulfilled. It had been difficult to reinforce her beliefs while maintaining close secrecy about the events of the night before. The message from Sananda reassured her as it probably did some of the others who had watched with her, and raised her hopes again —high hopes that events later this very night would verify her expectation that the group of believers would be picked up by saucers. For that very night she was expecting spacemen, and perhaps Sananda himself, to visit her house.

Late that evening, Saturday, December 18, while the group was killing time in the living room listening to an old Ella Lowell tape, five young men in their late teens sought admission to the house. They spent more than two hours in the house that night and their visit had so great an impact on the group of believers that it merits a full description. Why these young men called at the house, what their purpose was, and who they were—these are things we do not know; they may have been practical jokers, or they may have had a serious purpose. Whatever their intention, they launched a vigorous attack against the ideology and the prophecy of cataclysm, bringing to a climax that night what was evidently a fairly systematic plan to shake Mrs. Keech's convictions. To tell the story coherently, we must go back in time, and begin with the day that Dr. Armstrong's dismissal from his job was headlined in the newspapers.

That day, December 16, saw the beginning of a series of telephone calls to Mrs. Keech from two young men who told her that they were from the planet Clarion. That night, when Mrs. Keech returned from her talk to the flying saucer club, she found on her television set a note: "We were here but you were not." It was signed "The Boys from Clarion." The telephone calls from these same two "spacemen" continued throughout Friday, the 17th, while Mrs. Keech's conviction grew that her callers really were from outer space and really had visited her home the previous evening. Her excitement over this evidence was matched only by her willingness to accept the orders that her callers began to issue.

On Saturday, the 18th, the calls became more frequent as well as more authoritative. Early that afternoon, one of the "boys from Clarion," intimating that he was Sananda himself, commanded Marian to sit for messages every hour on the hour — messages that he would later "verify" by phone, he said. She followed these instructions to the letter, even asking one of the observers to be sure to remind her every hour, so she would be ready to write at exactly the specified times. Between three and four o'clock she received a particularly long telephone call which she took privately in the bedroom. She emerged with tears in her eyes, sobbing joyously: "He is coming. He is coming."

And come he did that night with four companions. There was a momentary confusion over whether or not this band should be turned away, but as soon as Marian recognized their leader and heard his voice, her hesitation vanished. She swept them into the room and stood ready for their commands. Their leader, a twenty-year-old youth, asked to talk with Dr. Armstrong privately, and did so for nearly half an hour. Then it was Marian's turn, and she spent almost twice as long closeted with the five "spacemen."

The reactions of the rest of the members, milling about the living room, were mixed. Thomas Armstrong had emerged from his interview smiling, almost grinning with admiration. They were spacemen, all right, or as he put it, "some of the boys from upstairs." They had really put him through a quiz; he had never dealt with such brilliant minds, he said. He had penetrated their disguise as earthlings as soon as they walked in the door, he explained, but their superhuman minds were something to behold. Their visit was in the nature of a test, the doctor said, a check on whether he and Marian could give them the right answers. At that very moment, he added, the spacemen were "trying to get Marian to retract. They're trying to get her to take back all the things she's been saying. They say it's all mixed up and false. It's a check all right."

Edna Post was equally sure the visitors had come from outer space. Almost ecstatically she informed one of the observers that, while she had missed seeing the sice at Lyons field, tonight she had been alert enough to recognize Sananda. Edna's joy was unbounded. Daisy Armstrong and Mark Post also seemed excited and pleased, and it was clear they recognized these boys as spacemen. May and Frank Novick, on the other hand, were simply confused, as were Kurt Freund and Arthur Bergen. They did not know who the boys were or what was going on. Cleo Armstrong and Bob Eastman were highly skeptical — to them the fivesome looked like "a bunch of kids trying to put on a front."

Before she had gone into the adjoining room for her private talk with the "spacemen," Marian Keech had made clear her conviction of their identity. She pointed out to an observer that "the Guest" had arrived, and when the observer reminded her of the hour, as he had been doing since early afternoon, she turned to him almost in amazement: "We don't need that any more," she said; "we've made the contact now." As she waited expectantly for her turn to talk to these boys, her joy almost matched Edna's.

But when she reappeared in the living room after nearly an hour of being "checked," she was visibly shaken. She stood weeping near the door of the room where the boys were getting ready to leave the house, her frail body turned to the wall and her fists clenched at her sides. The visitors started to go out, but Marian would not let them go. Deeply shaken but unable to give up, she shepherded the boys back into the bedroom where all six remained in consultation for another half-hour.

When they had finished, and the boys had departed, Marian stood silently in the living room, wrapped in thought but apparently having recovered from her shock. To the group of believers who gathered around her she began to describe the conversations she had had with the "boys from Clarion":

"They kept forcing me to take back things. He kept trying to pressure me into saying they were not true. They kept telling me that what I had said was all false and mixed up. And they told me that they were in contact with outer space too and all the writings I had were wrong and that everything I was predicting was wrong."

She described how shocked she had been by this attack, how they had mixed her up till she scarcely knew what to say. She had been on the point of walking out on her tormentors, but then she had become angry and counterattacked in these words: "You can't make me do that. I'm not going to take any of it back. There is a Judas here. There is a Judas in this room. You have been sent here to try to confuse me and upset me. I *was* upset but I'm not any more. I know what you're trying to do."

Their reply to this outburst, Mrs. Keech asserted, was conciliatory. They had told her that they had indeed come to test her and, if she passed the test, then to reassure her and support her, which they proceeded to do. The trial had ended on a note of triumph for Marian.

We know the details of Mrs. Keech's conversations with the spacemen only through her own recital of what happened. How much of what she reported actually took place is hard to say, although one of our observers was told independently by one of the visitors that he and his friends had been in contact with people from outer space for three years and he was sure that ninety per cent of Marian's writings were wrong. Thus we have independent evidence of the attack on her beliefs, but we have only Marian's word about the subsequent reassurance. In any event, Marian seemed to need more reassurance than she had got from the visitors, and she proceeded to stimulate support from the group of believers.

She began to reiterate her reasons for believing that the boys really had come from outer space. As soon as they had entered the house she had felt the force of their superhuman personalities, their strength, their intelligence. She pointed out that they had known things about her messages and about recent events in the group that only spacemen would know. She was sure they were saucer pilots. Dr. Armstrong, his wife, and Edna joined the chorus of assent, agreeing fully with Marian and adding observations and inferences of their own. Edna and Daisy pointed out that three of the visitors looked exactly alike, while Mark and Edna said that the spacemen had refused earthly nourishment.

Cleo seemed rather skeptical of their conclusions and Bob Eastman said nothing, but it was Kurt Freund who most clearly sounded a note of dissent. In a rather low voice he remarked: "I must say I saw nothing." No one paid the slightest attention to him (except an observer) and he repeated his statement in a loud voice. Marian asked him what he meant and he replied: "They just looked like college kids to me. It looked as though they just came here for a lark." Marian smiled pityingly at him and no one paid him further heed. The flood of confirming and supporting detail continued. The interpretation of the visit was rapidly becoming a settled question and the group was waxing enthusiastic about it. The representatives from outer space had come, and subjected them to the supreme test and they had passed.

Whereupon Marian, with sparkling eyes, exclaimed excitedly, "At this point I think I deserve a standing vote of confidence." At this almost everyone stood up and several cried that Marian had their full confidence. Kurt Freund, Cleo Armstrong, and Bob Eastman were conspicuously slow to join in this standing vote, but the others were enthusiastic. The overt support of most of the group brought discussion of the episode to a close. A challenging attack on the ideology had been turned into confirmatory support. Later in the evening the group was reminded of that by Marian: "Remember," she said, "we have passed an important test tonight. Don't forget it."

The net result of this attack on the belief system and the prophecy was to strengthen conviction. Furthermore, it seems probable that this episode finally enabled the group to recover from the effects of the Friday night disconfirmation. In effect, the spacemen *had* come. It was simply that they had come Saturday night instead of Friday night.

On Sunday morning, in contrast to the secrecy of the day before, those who had been on the midnight vigil on Friday spoke freely about the period of waiting in the yard for the saucer. But they spoke about it briefly and as a prelude to the wonderful and exciting events of Saturday night. When one of the observers reached the house at about 9 A.M. on Sunday, and again when Clyde Wilton arrived later that morning, Mrs. Keech narrated the happenings of the previous two days in some detail. She explained that she had received a number of phone calls from "the boys from Clarion" and reported the message she had received about the promised visit of the saucer on Friday night. Laughingly, she described how the watchers had stood out in the yard, almost frozen, for two or three hours, adding about the Guardians: "I'm not laughing at them, I'm laughing with them." She gave a glowing account of the Saturday night visitation, emphasizing how the spacemen had tried to force her to retract her teachings and how, when she refused to do so, they told her they had been testing her faith. They had been sent to see whether or not she would "sell her belief," she said; at this point she felt she had been tested as much as Christ had been.

Although the visit of the "spacemen" bolstered the faith of most members, two people were disaffected. May and Frank Novick, who had come to the house that night at Marian's urging, left shortly before the boys from Clarion departed. Neither of them ever returned. Their connection with the group had been growing weaker; they did not attend the December 13 meeting, for example, and May had broken off contact with Bertha. Frank had probably never been much of a believer and his appearance on Saturday night was undoubtedly out of deference to May's wishes. It seems highly likely that the events they witnessed on Saturday night, as interpreted by the skeptical Frank, helped persuade May to sever her connection completely.

The next day, Sunday, was a day of waiting. The believers marked time while the stream of visitors continued and the constant ringing of the phone brought more requests for information about the flood, about how the inquirer could save himself and his family from disaster, about why Mrs. Keech was so sure there would be a cataclysm and how she had received the warning. From late in the morning till ten or eleven o'clock that night, the house was never empty of visitors and rarely was a believer unoccupied in expounding doctrine, attempting to persuade a skeptic, or defending the belief system against a challenger.

There was still selectivity about who was admitted to the house: those who were considered sincere were allowed to enter while obvious jokers and scoffers were turned away. But one new feature appeared in the proselyting approach: a marked tendency to assume that everyone who got into the house was one of the chosen and would be saved. Whether he asked for reassurance or not, the caller who gained the living room was informed that he was probably among the elect, and it was pointed out that the very fact he had come to "seek the light" was the best evidence of his having been "chosen" by the Guardians. This appeal was often the basis for trying to convince people that they ought to believe.

The other fact worth noting about the atmosphere on Sunday afternoon was the growing concern about holding the group together, especially on the part of Marian Keech. Several times during the afternoon she mentioned the absence of certain members — Bertha, Kurt Freund, Arthur Bergen, and several of the observers (who were getting some much-needed rest) and commented that now was the time to stick together, now, above all, there ought to be a "strong group." The group and the support it offered were evidently very important, and the slightest sign of disintegration or defection was painful to those who remained behind. Clyde Wilton had made plans to return to his home on Monday and this fact bothered Mrs. Keech a great deal. She finally received a message sanctioning his departure and telling him to gather together three families with his own on the fateful night that was so near at hand. The need to hold the group together may have been intensified by the knowledge of several probable defectors: Manya, who had not been heard from for two days, and Frank and May Novick, who had shown no intention of returning. Throughout the afternoon Marian's concern over the absentees increased and she finally became rather annoyed at them —a mood that passed instantly when several turned up in the early evening.

Some group members did not share Marian's concern. Cleo continued to contest her father's view that telephone calls from "Captain Video" or from unnamed "Martians" should be taken seriously. At one point she complained that a message Marian had received for her was "nonsense" and "asinine." Bob moped about the house, taking occasional part in the proselyting, but usually preserving a disgruntled silence. Between the doubts planted in them by Ella Lowell before they left Collegeville and their reluctance to swallow many of the interpretations of events they had witnessed in Lake City, Cleo and Bob were not in a convinced frame of mind.

Kurt Freund too showed signs that he was not fully convinced, though he was not outspokenly doubtful. He sat around much of the time in an almost aloof silence, and seemed to prefer talking about general issues of space travel, or psychic communication, rather than specific items in the belief system of the group such as the flood itself. From his occasionally questioning, occasionally skeptical remarks one got the impression that he was not convinced that the cataclysm would take place.

The rest of the group, however, showed no lack of conviction. They worked at proselyting or at household chores, or they simply waited for the hours to pass until they would be rescued. But they did not torture themselves with doubt that the flood might not come.

At about ten o'clock on the morning of December 20, Marian Keech received a message for the whole group. It read:

"At the hour of midnight you shall be put into parked cars and taken to a place where ye shall be put aboard a porch [flying saucer] and ye shall be purposed by the time you are there. At that time you shall have the fortuned ones forget the few who have not come—and at no time are they to be called for, they are but enacting a scene and not a person who should be there will fail to be there and at the time you are to say 'What is your question?' . . . and at no time are you to ask what is what and not a plan shall go astray and for the time being be glad and be fortuned to be among the favored. And be ye ready for further instructions . . . Beleis."

This was the message everyone had been waiting for and it had come none too soon, for before another dawn the whole of Lake City was to be flooded. But the chosen would be safe. In just fourteen hours they would at last be picked up by flying saucers and whisked away. All the arrangements had been made and specific further instructions would be forthcoming.

This message brought a great release of tension to the believers. This was it. Now they knew what was to happen and when. Now they could wait easily and comfortably for midnight. They relaxed, and spent the day in peaceful idleness. Marian rested a great deal, while Thomas and Daisy Armstrong spent most of the day simply sitting — not tensely as they had done, but calmly. Some of the others read or played cards. When Arthur Bergen arrived late in the afternoon and told the group his mother had threatened to call the police if he were not home by two o'clock the following morning, the believers smilingly assured him that he need not worry — by that time they would all be aboard a saucer.

The believers treated their visitors calmly too. As on the previous day, most callers were assured that they were among the chosen and had nothing to worry about. They were simply to go back home and, wherever they might be, they would be picked up. But today the believers seemed more certain of what they said — and less frantic in saying it. Now that they had specific orders their proselyting too had become calmer.

The day passed uneventfully while the believers gathered for their final earthly session. Bertha Blatsky had arrived early in the morning, Arthur Bergen in the afternoon. Two observers were present during most of the day and three more joined them in the early evening. Kurt Freund arrived shortly after 9 P.M. Together with the seven people who were currently living in the house — the three Armstrongs, Bob Eastman, the two Posts, and Marian, there were fifteen people in the living room when preparations for departure began to be made. Only Mrs. Keech's husband was missing. He had apparently decided the vigil was not for him and had retired early to his bedroom in the rear of the house.

Shortly after 9:30 there began a meeting conducted jointly by Marian (writing messages from Sananda) and Bertha (speaking with the voice of the Creator). The proceedings were extremely formal and were executed with painstaking correctness. Marian would write a message, read it off, and ask the Creator to verify it — or the Creator would speak and request verification in writing from Sananda. Verification was usually forthcoming, but, clearly, both Bertha and Marian felt a trifle uncertain of themselves and were extremely anxious that there be no mistakes or misinterpretations this night.

The telephone rang sporadically as reporters tried to learn how the believers were spending the eve of the flood, but such calls were terminated very quickly: "No comment. We have nothing for you now. Leave your number and if we have anything for you later we will call you." Other callers were equally quickly silenced, no matter what their inquiry was. Clearly, the believers had their orders now and nothing was allowed to interfere with the meticulous "verification" of each step of preparation for the midnight departure.

During the day Mrs. Keech had received additional instructions and, one by one, these too were "verified" and "clarified." The most important of these was the information that precisely at midnight a spaceman would come to the door and escort them to the place where the saucer [tola] was parked. Everyone was instructed to be perfectly silent while en route to the saucer. When their escort knocked on the door at midnight, Thomas Armstrong was to act as the sentry and ask the caller: "What is your question?" There was a thorough rehearsal of the passwords the believers would have to use in boarding the saucer. Marian Keech temporarily took the role of the Guard at the portal of the spaceship and delivered the specific challenges he would use: "I am the porter," "I am the pointer," and so on, while the group in the living room responded aloud in unison "I am my own porter," "I am my own pointer," after each one. The group went through the drill with intense care.

The next step in preparation was the removal of metal. The Creator and Sananda went over the matter thoroughly and left no doubt in anyone's mind that to leave any metal on one's person or in one's clothes would be a very dangerous error. All the believers complied painstakingly with this order. Arthur Bergen, for·example, carefully unwrapped the tinfoil from each stick of chewing gum in his pocket. Coins and keys were removed from pockets and watches from wrists. Many of the group had already checked their clothes and shoes carefully but now they went over them again and consulted each other about possible omissions. It was agreed that those who wore glasses with metal frames could simply discard them immediately before entering the saucer. For some reason, never specified, identification of any kind was also to be removed from one's person — it could be destroyed on the spot or simply left behind, but not taken to the saucer. Since this was a new order and an unanticipated one, it produced a flurry of excitement as the members sought to recall what items of identification they might be carrying. Finally, the "secret books" of Marian's messages were ordered packed into a large shopping bag and given to Mark Post to carry aboard the saucer. These preparations consumed a great deal of time, for each one was carefully reviewed and cross-checked. There was no margin for error.

At about 11:15, Mrs. Keech received a message ordering the group to get their overcoats and stand by. There were a few minutes of milling about and the group reassembled in the living room, where Marian instructed everyone to be seated quietly and to "act as if this were just an ordinary gathering of friends" in an ordinary house. She particularly warned the members not to stand in front of the living room window, lest they attract the notice of the police, newspapermen, or neighbors who might be watching and might attempt to follow the group when it left. She was especially concerned about the police and made a careful check to see whether a patrol car was outside the house. Her suspicions of being watched were reinforced when twice the phone rang but there was no answering voice on the other end of the line. These calls, Marian asserted, were from reporters checking to see whether the group was still at the house.

By 11:30 all was in readiness and there was nothing to do but wait and think of things that had been overlooked. The few details that did come up were disposed of hurriedly, for everything had to be in order by midnight. When Arthur Bergen suddenly remembered that his shoes had metal toecaps, it was too late to cut them out. From the ensuing excitement emerged the suggestion that he should simply loosen the laces and step out of his shoes before entering the saucer. At about 11:35, one of the authors let it be known that he had not removed the zipper from his trousers. This knowledge produced a near panic reaction. He was rushed into the bedroom where Dr. Armstrong, his hands trembling and his eyes darting to the clock every few seconds, slashed out the zipper with a razor blade and wrenched its clasps free with wire-cutters. By the time the operation was complete it was 11:50, too late to do more than sew up the rent with a few rough stitches. Midnight was almost at hand and everyone must be ready on the dot.

The last ten minutes were tense ones for the group in the living room. They had nothing to do but sit and wait, their coats in their laps. In the tense silence two clocks ticked loudly, one about ten minutes faster than the other. When the faster of the two pointed to 12:05, one of the observers remarked aloud on the fact. A chorus of people replied that midnight had not yet come. Bob Eastman affirmed that the slower clock was correct; he had set it himself only that afternoon. It showed only four minutes before midnight.

These four minutes passed in complete silence except for a single utterance. When the (slower) clock on the mantel showed only one minute remaining before the guide to the saucer was due, Marian exclaimed in a strained, high-pitched voice: "And not a plan has gone astray!" The clock chimed twelve, each stroke painfully clear in the expectant hush. The believers sat motionless.

One might have expected some visible reaction. Midnight had passed and nothing had happened. The cataclysm itself was less than seven hours away. But there was little to see in the reactions of the people in that room. There was no talking, no sound. People sat stock still, their faces seemingly frozen and expressionless. Mark Post was the only person who even moved. He lay down on the sofa and closed his eyes, but did not sleep. Later, when spoken to, he answered monosyllabically, but otherwise lay immobile. The others showed nothing on the surface, although it became clear later that they had been hit hard. The next morning both Bertha Blatsky and Dr. Armstrong, for example, admitted that the shock had been overwhelming. Having lived through that trial, Dr. Armstrong felt, he could now stand anything.

At about five minutes past midnight, the Creator announced that the plan still held: there had been a slight delay, that was all, a slight delay. The silence settled in again, and the minutes ticked by. Occasionally someone shifted in his chair or coughed but no one made a comment or asked a question. The Creator began to talk again, haltingly and disconnectedly. The attention of the group began to focus on Bertha's words and a stir of life passed through them. The phone rang two or three times, as reporters pursued their search of news, but the answers were brief: "No comment. We have nothing to tell you."

By 12:30 the talk of the Creator began to crystallize into the promise of a miracle, a miracle that would be wrought that very night, when a loud bang on the door cut short His talk and brought another expectant hush to the room. It was momentary, however, for Thomas Armstrong leaped to his feet and made for the door. Marian half-rose from her seat, calling: "Remember, 'What is your question'?" and quickly dispatched Bob Eastman and one of the observers to remind the doctor of the watchword. But the excitement was short-lived, for the doctor returned to the living room without even having asked the question. The callers were just some boys, he said, just ordinary boys, not the man we were waiting for. The tension seeped back out of the room, and only the disappointment remained. The Creator resumed speaking.

The next two hours were consumed by what amounted to a diversion. As the Creator droned on, occasionally asking to have something "verified in writing" by Mrs. Keech, He gradually developed the point that the group had been gathered this night to witness a miracle, namely, the death and resurrection of Marian's husband. The appearance of such a curious matter on the agenda is perhaps best understood as a reaction to the failure of the expected midnight visitor to appear. If the attention of the group could focus on so spectacular a matter as the promised miracle, they could forget, at least temporarily, the terrible disappointment they had suffered. The Creator had once before predicted the demise of the nonbelieving Mr. Keech and perhaps the idea came quickly to mind. But this time, for a real miracle, his death was to be followed by a resurrection.

The elaborate exposition of the nature of miracles which accompanied the Creator's attempt to perform this one may have succeeded in making the believers forget temporarily the saucer, the cataclysm, and the midnight failure. Mr. Keech had retired to his bed before nine o'clock and the miracle required first finding him dead and then returned to life. Three times that early morning Thomas Armstrong and one of the observers were sent to Mr. Keech's room to see if he had died yet. Three times they returned, reporting that he was still alive and breathing normally. The miracle did not seem to be forthcoming, and finally the Creator, floundering for a solution, announced that the miracle had already occurred — Mr. Keech had died earlier that evening but had been resurrected and was once again alive. This solution was so inadequate, however, that even the authority of the Creator could not gain acceptance for it. It was quickly buried in silence.

At this point the miracle working was interrupted by a mundane matter that demanded immediate attention. Arthur Bergen, who had expected by that time to be far off in space, recalled that his mother was planning to notify the police of his whereabouts if he were not home by 2 A.M. His announcement created a flurry of down-to-earth concern. A visit from the police at this point would have been the final humiliating blow. Arthur was urged to telephone his mother at once that he was on his way home, and a cab was summoned for him. There was a brief parting ceremony in which Arthur was assured that his departure was a sacrifice to save the rest of the group, but that the spacemen would not overlook him, no matter where he might be.

After he had left, the Creator began reworking the miracle, telling the group that the death and resurrection of Mr. Keech referred to a purely spiritual matter and had indeed already occurred. During the previous weeks Mr. Keech had been spiritually dead, just a walking shell; but recently he had begun to take a new interest in the beliefs of the group and tonight in his sleep, the process had been completed. He was now spiritually resurrected. This interpretation seemed to be accepted by the group and the topic of the miracle was dropped. At about 2:30, Marian received a message from Sananda urging the group to take a break for coffee.

During this break, which lasted for about half an hour, everyone in the group was reluctant to talk about the failure of the midnight prediction — everyone, that is, except the five observers who wanted to talk about it very much. They kept asking the others in the house such questions as "What do you think happened to the man who was supposed to come at midnight?" "Why didn't he come?" "What did the miracle have to do with his not coming?" "Will the saucer still pick us up?" and so on.

Bob Eastman seemed disillusioned. The promised pickup at midnight had not materialized and he seemed inclined to write the whole thing off. The publisher seemed withdrawn and detached. He told an observer that time didn't mean anything; perhaps the saucer pickup happened a thousand years ago or perhaps it would happen a thousand years from now. The others, however, were neither willing to accept the disillusionment nor tranquil about the failure of the escort to appear at midnight. Dr. Armstrong, when questioned, responded, "Have no fear, don't ever not believe, he'll show up, he'll come." The doctor felt the group might have misinterpreted the message, but he was sure that the plan was working out the way the "boys upstairs" intended. Edna Post's answer was that the message from Sananda had not specifically stated that a man was to come at midnight, but she didn't want to discuss the actual message. When one of the authors offered to check the message with her she ignored the opportunity. Nor could Bertha think of any explanation other than possible misinterpretation of the message.

The observers were pressing Dr. Armstrong and Mrs. Keech in particular to face the fact that midnight had passed and nothing had happened. The doctor seemed unable to offer an explanation that satisfied even himself. Marian refused to give any new interpretation of the message. Instead, she gave a rather long reply that carried the seeds of what was to be the eventual rationalization of the failure of the saucer pickup to occur:

"Well, all right. Suppose they gave us a wrong date. Well, this only got into the newspapers on Thursday and people had only 72 hours to get ready to meet their maker. Now suppose it doesn't happen tonight. Let's suppose it happens next year or two years or three or four years from now. I'm not going to change one bit. I'm going to sit here and write and maybe people will say it was this little group spreading light here that prevented the flood. Or maybe if it's delayed for a couple of years there'll be time to get people together. I don't know. All I know is that the plan has never gone astray. We have never had a plan changed. And you'll see tomorrow the house will be full of them and we'll have an open house and I'll need every one of you to answer the phone and maybe they'll ask us to go on television. I'm not sorry a bit. I won't be sorry no matter what happens."

Shortly after 3 A.M. the coffee break was called to a halt and the group reconvened in the living room. It is highly likely that, by this time, most of the believers knew that no man would come, no saucer would pick them up, and perhaps also that no cataclysm would occur. The questioning by the observers during the previous half-hour probably hastened their realization of these things and made it difficult to push the disappointments out of their minds any longer. At any rate, in the next hour and a half, the group began to come to grips with the fact that no caller had

166

arrived at midnight to take them to the saucer. The problem from here on was to reassure themselves and to find an adequate, satisfying way to reconcile the disconfirmation with their beliefs.

They began by re-examining the original message which had stated that at midnight the group would be put into parked cars and taken to the saucer. In response to some of the observers' prodding about that message during the coffee break, the Creator stated that anyone who wished might look up that message. It had been buried away among many others in a large envelope and none of the believers seemed inclined to look for it, but one of the observers volunteered. He found it and read it aloud to the group. The first attempt at reinterpretation came quickly. Daisy Armstrong pointed out that the message must, of course, be symbolic, because it said we were to be put into parked cars; but parked cars do not move and hence could not take the group anywhere. The Creator then announced that the message was indeed symbolic, but the "parked cars" referred to their own physical bodies, which had obviously been there at midnight. The "porch" (flying saucer), He went on, symbolized in this message the inner strength, the inner knowing, and inner light which each member of the group had. So eager was the group for an explanation of any kind that many actually began to accept this one.

Curiously enough, it was Marian Keech herself who refused to agree with this interpretation. To her, she said, it did not ring true; it didn't sound right; she didn't believe it was the correct interpretation. Bertha, with some hostility, asked Marian whether she had a more valid interpretation whereupon Marian replied, "No, I don't have a more valid one. I don't think we have to interpret it, we don't have to understand everything. The plan has never gone astray. We don't know what the plan is but it has never gone astray."

But this position too, was unsatisfactory. The shock and disappointment had been too great and the predicted cataclysm was too close (if it were still to occur) for the believers to be content with no explanation, so the discussion went on with various alternative suggestions being made. When 4 A.M. came without a sat-

167

isfactory resolution having been achieved, another break was taken. One of the authors walked out the front door to get some air and Dr. Armstrong, thinking he was becoming disaffected and needed bolstering, dashed out after him. The doctor proceeded to deliver an inspirational talk, an important part of which was a statement about his own situation and his own belief. This is presented below as nearly verbatim as his listener could record it immediately after Dr. Armstrong left him alone "to meditate":

"I've had to go a long way. I've given up just about everything. I've cut every tie: I've burned every bridge. I've turned my back on the world. I can't afford to doubt. I have to believe. And there isn't any other truth. The preachers and priests don't have it and you have to look closely to find it even in the Bible. I've taken an awful beating in the last few months, just an awful beating. But I do know who I am and I know what I've got to do. I know I've got to teach just as Jesus knew, and I don't care what happens tonight. I can't afford to doubt. I won't doubt even if we have to make an announcement to the press tomorrow and admit we were wrong. You're having your period of doubt now, but hang on, boy, hang on. This is a tough time but we know that the boys upstairs are taking care of us. They've given us their promise. These are tough times and the way is not easy. We all have to take a beating. I've taken a terrific one, but I have no doubt."

While Dr. Armstrong was outdoors counseling the observer, Mrs. Keech broke down and cried bitterly. She knew, she sobbed, there were some who were beginning to doubt but we must beam light on those who needed it most and we must hold the group together. The rest of the group lost their composure too. They were all, now, visibly shaken and many were close to tears. It was a bad quarter of an hour.

Soon afterward, however, the observer re-entered the house and announced that Dr. Armstrong had helped him a lot. His return cheered the group considerably and brought visible relief to Mrs. Keech. But the fundamental problem of the group remained; it was now almost 4:30 A.M. and still no way of handling the disconfirmation had been found. By now, too, most of the group were talking openly about the failure of the man to come at midnight. They milled about the living room or stood in small groups discussing their feelings. Both Edna and Mark Post, for example, compared the events of this night to the disappointment they had suffered three days earlier when they stood for hours in the icy back yard waiting for a saucer to land.

But this atmosphere did not remain long. At about 4:45 A.M. Marian once more summoned everyone to the living room, announcing that she had just received a message which she read aloud. She then read these momentous words:

"For this day is it established that there is but one God of Earth, and He is in thy midst, and from his hand thou has written these words. And mighty is the word of God — and by his word have ye been saved — for from the mouth of death have ye been delivered and at no time has there been such a force loosed upon the Earth. Not since the beginning of time upon this Earth has there been such a force of Good and light as now floods this room and that which has been loosed within this room now floods the entire Earth. As thy God has spoken through the two who sit within these walls has he manifested that which he has given thee to do."

This message was received with enthusiasm by the group. It was an adequate, even an elegant, explanation of the disconfirmation. The cataclysm had been called off. The little group, sitting all night long, had spread so much light that God had saved the world from destruction. As soon as the full acceptability of the message was clear, Marian had two more messages in rapid succession, the first of which was to be used as an introduction to the main message: It read: "Such are the facts as stated that the group has sat for the Father's message the night through and God has spoken and that is every word to be said." The second message was to the effect that the main message and the introduction were to be headed "The Christmas Message to the People of Earth"; this "Christmas Message" together with the fact that it had been received at 4:45 A.M. was to be released immediately to the newspapers.

Soon after this second message had been read Kurt Freund got up from his chair, put on his hat and coat, and departed. The group had lost another member as a result of the disconfirmation.

But the rest of the believers were jubilant, for they had a satisfying explanation of the disconfirmation. The whole atmosphere of the group changed abruptly and, with it, their behavior changed too. From this point on their behavior toward the newspapers showed an almost violent contrast to what it had been. Instead of avoiding newspaper reporters and feeling that the attention they were getting in the press was painful, they almost instantly became avid seekers of publicity.

Marian insisted that the first reporter to be informed should be one who had been sympathetic toward the group in the past and had written stories she felt were fair. As she reached for the phone, Mark asked whether she wouldn't like someone else to make the call as she must be tired. Mrs. Keech vigorously rejected the suggestion; she wanted to do it herself, she said. She called the newspaper, but had some difficulty finding the reporter of her choice since he was at home asleep at that hour. Marian insisted that she had something exclusive for him, and while the newspaper tried to rouse their man, she sat holding the line open for some fifteen minutes.

During her wait one of the observers asked: "Marian, is this the first time you have called the newspaper yourself?" Her reply was immediate: "Oh, yes, this is the first time I've ever called them. I've never had anything to tell them before, but now I feel it's urgent." The whole group could have echoed her feelings, for they all felt a sense of urgency. The message was to be given to the newspapers as soon as possible, with emphasis on the fact that this group had saved the world and on the fact that the message had been received several hours before the cataclysm itself was to have begun.

Mrs. Keech finally spoke to the newsman, read the message to him, and took pains to see that he had got it all exactly right. No sooner had she hung up than the rest of the group began to make suggestions about calling other newspapers. Dr. Armstrong urged calling the Associated Press and the United Press, for "this thing is pretty important — it's a very big thing, bigger than one newspaper." Bertha Blatsky supported his view, saying she didn't think the Creator would want this to be an exclusive story. Mark Post said he wanted to call a local reporter who had been friendly to him, and so it went.

While Bertha and Dr. Armstrong were probably most insistent, the rest of the group seemed to agree with their desire to spread the word as widely and as quickly as possible. One of the observers pointed out that if the group wanted to give a news beat to the paper Mrs. Keech had called, they ought not to phone any others; anyway, the observer added, the other papers could pick it up from the first one to publish it. These remarks were completely ignored and the matter was finally settled by deciding to give the one newspaper a five-minute head start. Their sense of urgency was enormous.

There were further suggestions about publicity. Bertha asked if perhaps *Life* magazine should be given the news, but Mrs. Keech got a message saying that no photographs were to be permitted, or photostats of the actual message. "They shall have the word only," she announced.

At this point, apparently overcome with fatigue or relief, Marian loosed her grip on the phone and dragged herself over to the couch. In a matter of moments, Mark was dialing the number of another newspaper and asking for his favorite reporter. Dr. Armstrong succeeded him and, in rapid fire order, called the major wire services. For the next hour and a half he kept control of the phone, making and answering calls in a brisk, self-assured manner, explaining at length the significance of the message. Daisy Armstrong began typing out copies of the "Christmas Message" to give the reporters when they came to the house, occasionally "correcting" it or making emendations. The machinery of publicity was rolling at a furious rate.

By 6:30 A.M. all the local newspapers and the national wire services had been called, and some of the initial jubilation had abated. Not only were the members of the group utterly exhausted from the fatigue and tension of their vigil, but some were beginning to face the hard facts of life in an unflooded world. Edna Post, for example, withdrew to the kitchen where she began to cry very softly. She explained that she was completely at a loss as to what to do now. In anticipation of being picked up by a saucer both she and her son had given up their jobs and now had little income. Their savings would last for a bit, but what had she to look forward to? Who would help her? What could she do? Daisy and Cleo Armstrong fell to discussing a similar problem a little later. Their family too faced an uncertain economic future and Dr. Armstrong would have to get a job, but where? They could not return to Collegeville and face a scornful town, they felt, and Cleo would probably have to give up college. They did not know where they would go or how they would live.

Bob Eastman was exhausted and somewhat bitter: "Right now, I don't know how to feel. I just — it's not clear. The way it is around here, your right hand doesn't know what your left hand is doing. I think I'll go to bed." Marian, Bertha, and Dr. Armstrong seemed less depressed than the others, although they too were less elated than they had been an hour earlier. The disconfirmation had been rationalized but it still left an uncomfortable situation.

It was Bertha who revived their spirits somewhat by turning their attention to new outlets for publicity. In a session lasting almost an hour, the voice of the Creator made two important pronouncements; first, all the hitherto private, in fact secret, tape recordings were to be made available to the public — anyone could obtain a copy; and, second, the Creator Himself would make special new tapes for anyone who wanted one. All the interested person had to do was to provide new tapes and he could have a private session in which the Creator answered his questions and recorded the answers. All this, furthermore, was to be free of charge. When Dr. Armstrong asked whether any of the tapes should be released to television and radio networks, the Creator assured him that such a move would be advisable, and the major networks ought to be informed soon of the availability of the recordings. The purpose of releasing the tapes, the Creator said, was to spread the light as far and wide as possible. It is hardly necessary to stress the complete about-face that had occurred with regard to the tape recordings — from being sworn secrets they were catapulted into the full glare of national news.

Finally, the Creator assured all the members there that they need not worry about the future. They must continue to learn, to study, and to teach and spread the light to others, but they themselves would be taken care of.

At about eight that morning the group tuned in a network television program to hear the tape which they had recorded for it that morning over the phone. They were as ready as they would ever be for the day ahead of them, for the reporters, and for the world.

CHAPTER VI ⁓ *An Unfulfilled Prophecy and an Elated Prophet*

CHAOTIC though they may seem, the days immediately preceding December 21 were at least loosely organized around a dominant theme — cataclysm and salvation. By dawn on the 21st, however, this semblance of organization had vanished as the members of the group sought frantically to convince the world of their beliefs. In succeeding days, they also made a series of desperate attempts to erase their rankling dissonance by making prediction after prediction in the hope that one would come true, and they conducted a vain search for guidance from the Guardians.

The first reporter to appear in response to their calls on the morning of December 21 was from a newspaper that had treated the whole story rather flippantly. Before Marian Keech would say even a word to him, she examined the clippings from his paper. Then she turned on him with "The answer is no, we have nothing to give you. We have nothing at all for you. What we have won't go in a scandal sheet like this." The reporter began to protest but before he could finish his sentence she interrupted: "We can't give you anything; we have no news." So saying, she shoved the press release into his hand with these words: "Look at this — see if *that* isn't news. Read it, read it, read it."

While the reporter was reading the release the telephone rang and Mrs. Keech answered. Her conversation seemed to be interminable and finally the reporter left the house even though Marian called to him to "Sit down, sit down and wait while I finish with this call." When she had finished, long after the reporter's departure, Marian looked about the room for him and seemed quite concerned over his leaving. She asked everyone in

174

the room what had become of him, what he had said when he walked out, and whether he would be coming back. When informed that he had said he would be back later she seemed relieved.

The long telephone call had been from a glib local newscaster. On the morning of the 20th, he had phoned to invite Marian to an end-of-the-world cocktail party to begin at midnight and last until the end of the world. During this earlier call, the commentator had apparently been impertinent and irreverent and when Marian refused to join his party, he accused Sananda of being narrow-minded. Marian had terminated that call in heat and anger.

In his call on the morning of the 21st the commentator apparently continued his baiting tactics, for Marian argued vigorously with him and refused to let a point go by. Finally, he asked if he could come out and see her. Marian responded, "Only if you're serious," and added, "I will ask for a message but you must abide by it. If the message says 'no,' then you will abide by it. If it says 'yes' then you are to come right out." She took paper and pencil and wrote an enormous "YES." Returning to the phone she said with elation, "The message said 'yes.' Come right out, come right out this minute."

When the commentator arrived, he asked Mrs. Keech to record a tape for his evening program. She indicated that she would consent to record only the message that had come through at 4:45 A.M. and asked, "If I read the message to you and record it for you, will you give it in its entirety without deleting a word?" He agreed; Marian read the message; and then, while still recording, the commentator proceeded to question her. She eagerly answered all his questions in great detail, and succeeded in making an exceedingly long tape with a full exposition of her beliefs, the background of the movement, and some explication of the messages.

This interview concluded, another broadcaster who had accompanied the newscaster to the house asked Mrs. Keech: "I have a program concerned with women's views on various important problems. I wonder if you would make a transcription for me?" He seemed prepared to persuade her, but there was no persuading to be done. Eagerly seizing another opportunity to proselyte she grabbed his microphone saying,"I think one of the most important problems is the difficulty of education. Our educational system is all wrong." And for some ten minutes, she talked into the microphone on what the messages from Sananda and colleagues had revealed about the problem of education.

And so the day continued. Till evening, the house was crowded with the now-welcome horde of newspaper, radio, and television representatives; the phone rang incessantly; and visitors, mostly leather-jacketed high school boys, streamed in and out the door.

The press and the broadcasters got what they wanted and more. The initial pretense of dealing only with reporters who had been sympathetic in the past quickly vanished and all newsmen were received cordially, offered coffee and food, and granted extensive interviews. Not only were all their questions answered freely but much information was volunteered. In some cases, interviews with the press lasted more than two hours.

Though the newspaper people were, of course, interested in speaking chiefly to Mrs. Keech and Dr. Armstrong, other members of the group inserted themselves at various times into these interviews. Bertha Blatsky, who had previously made a point of avoiding publicity out of fear of her husband, now talked at length to at least one reporter; Daisy Armstrong took part in several interviews; Mark Post had taken pains to invite a particular reporter to the house and saw to it that the man's every question was answered. Mrs. Keech and Dr. Armstrong made a total of five tape recordings for radio broadcast. Only one prohibition remained in force: pictures were still forbidden.

The vivid contrast between all this activity and the earlier behavior of the group toward the press is, of course, dramatic. During the five days preceding disconfirmation, the believers had flatly refused to have anything to do with the press and the newsmen had been able to extract only one interview from Mrs. Keech and Dr. Armstrong and a single, thirty-second recording of the doctor's views. Furthermore, the reporters had almost been forced to beat down the door to talk to the two principals and had been granted their interview only after hinting the threat to publish their own versions of the group's beliefs.

The barrage of telephone calls that day came from newspapers, from seriously interested or idly curious private citizens, and from jokers. Those reporters who did not trouble to visit the house were nevertheless given extensive interviews over the phone and subjected to detailed exposition of the events of the past several days and the beliefs of the group. Serious individuals who called received similar treatment and were usually invited to the house. Even the most absurd jokers were treated cordially and answered with good-humored banter; in some cases badinage with them continued for ten or fifteen minutes, ending with an invitation to come to the house.

Visitors to the house were indiscriminately admitted, and, in contrast to earlier days, no attempt was made to sort the chosen from the heathen. Both Dr. Armstrong and Mrs. Keech made an effort to see their visitors, to answer their questions, and, if the situation permitted, to engage in prolonged explanations or arguments. But they were so often interrupted by telephone calls, questions from the press, and the arrival of new groups of visitors that their attempts to carry on discussions were disjointed and fragmentary. Although Mrs. Armstrong and the Posts tried to fill in when the two principals were busy elsewhere, they were simply not colorful or newsworthy enough to hold their listeners' attention and occasionally the visitors wandered off in boredom. Anxious though all the members were to proselyte, they were inept and ineffective. Still without a plan for carrying on instruction, without any written material to hand out, without any duties or rituals to prescribe for potential converts, they concentrated their efforts on explaining their system of beliefs, relating the rationale for the failure of the flood to occur, and trying to answer whatever questions the visitor might bring up.

Although no one in the house had slept for more than three or four of the past thirty-six hours, the amiable, manic uproar continued till early evening. By then the last member of the press had gone, and the group in the house took time out for dinner.

By this time, too, the believers had become concerned about the possibility that some of the telephone calls coming into the house might be coded messages from the Guardians. In order to be sure that they would not miss any important information or orders, they hooked up a tape recorder to the telephone and recorded all incoming calls. This hookup was maintained for a week, during which the recordings were occasionally reviewed in an effort to sift out any orders they might contain.

At about 8:30, nine high school students trooped in to converse with Mrs. Keech. They found her at the telephone deep in a discussion of flying saucers with a caller whom, it later turned out, she believed to be a spaceman. Eager to continue talking to him and at the same time anxious to keep her new guests, Marian simply included them in the conversation and, for more than an hour, chatted alternately with her guests in the living room and the "spaceman" on the other end of the telephone. So intent was she on proselyting that she seemed unable to let any opportunity go by. At the same time, however, she wanted to entice the "spaceman" to pay her a visit. Her solution was to adopt a strategy that accomplished both ends; she quizzed her guests on their attitude toward spacemen, and steered the conversation in such a way as to reassure the telephoner that he would meet a friendly reception. Thus her questions to the visiting high school students ran: "Do you think that the spacemen could teach you anything? How many? Show me hands, quick. At least you're willing to learn. Would you be willing to work with them? How much would you sacrifice to work with them? If a spaceman came and he had to have a place to hide to keep from being persecuted, would you take him into your home? Who would? All right, everybody would take a spaceman in. Well, that's a good showing."

This three-way conversation continued until the telephone caller indicated that he would like to come to the house for a visit. Some of the high school boys volunteered to drive over and pick him up. When these boys had left, Mrs. Keech explained to one of the observers why she had been so intent on prolonging the phone call: "As soon as I heard his voice," she said, "I felt a sympathetic communication and I knew that this was one of the boys from upstairs." Her pleasure at the way the incident was working out could hardly be missed.

Shortly afterward the telephone rang again and a young boy's voice told Mrs. Keech: "We have a flood in our bathroom and we're going to have a party. Would you like to come over?" Marian hesitated not a moment; she took down the address, and, very excitedly, called to the other believers: "Everybody get your coats. Let's go." The entire ménage trooped out to a nearby address and returned, in disappointment, fifteen minutes later.

None of the observers went on this brief excursion, but Edna Post described the incident the next day. They had all walked over to the address, marched up to the door, and knocked. A woman answered and Mrs. Keech asked, by name, for a boy who had visited earlier in the day and whom Marian suspected of being a spaceman. But the woman turned them away, and everyone returned to the house. Clearly, Mrs. Keech was grasping at anything, even so obvious a joke as this, in an attempt to find some confirmation of her beliefs, for she was sure that spacemen were trying to communicate to the group in code. One clue as to how this incident was rationalized comes in a further remark of Edna's: "As we got there a car that had been parked in front of the house drove away. We missed our cue. We were too late there; we didn't get what we expected."

Soon after the group returned to the Keech house, the high school boys who had gone to fetch the alleged "spaceman" came back with him. He was a teen-age *aficionado* of flying saucers and had brought along quantities of literature on the subject. He passed it out among the group and the rest of the evening was spent in a discussion of saucers. By 11 P.M. all the visitors had left except the suspected spaceman, and Dr. Armstrong and Mrs. Keech took him aside for a private conversation. We do not know what they talked about, but it is a reasonable guess that this "spaceman" was plagued for orders. If this was the case, it is an early instance of behavior that was to become more marked later on. All the members, but especially the leaders, were floundering. Still fast in their beliefs, but more and more directionless as each succeeding prediction failed, they searched desperately for guidance, for some sign or some person to tell them what to do next.

One further trend was noticeable on December 21. As the day wore on, Mrs. Keech began to make more and more of the importance of some recent news items. The morning newspapers contained an article about an earthquake in Nevada that had occurred about five days earlier, pointing out that if the quake had happened in a populated area, the destruction would have been enormous. Mrs. Keech showed the story excitedly to the members of the group, emphasizing the fact that, indeed, cataclysms *were* happening; though the Lake City area had been spared because of the light shed by this little group, upheavals were taking place elsewhere. Here, she declared, was evidence for the validity of the prediction. This theme did not play a prominent part in the press interviews she gave during the morning and early afternoon, but it grew in importance in response to further disaster news.

At about 2 P.M. both the Associated Press and the United Press called Marian to inform her of earthquakes that had occurred that very day in Italy and in California. She took this news in stride, telling the inquiring editors that "It all ties in with what I believe." During the remainder of the afternoon she made frequent reference to these earthquakes when she was talking to outsiders, pointing out that cataclysms were taking place just as her messages from Sananda warned her, and describing dramatically the vastness of the destruction wrought by these disasters. Mrs. Keech continued to play on this theme and incorporated it into her views of recent events. She and the others in the group probably found in the earthquake reports support for their beliefs. In spite of the elegance of the "Christmas Message" as a rationalization, there was still a clear need for some kind of confirmation. The dissonance created by the major disconfirmation still rankled.

In the early morning of December 22, Mrs. Keech's pencil recorded a message that the group seized upon as a new reason for calling in the press. This message revoked the firm prohibition against pictures, and even instructed them to make special efforts to please photographers. The message read in part:

"Be on your toes and give it to the papers at the time they come to you. You are to give it together and you are to be as a unit and you are to pose together and you are to put the best foot forward and you are to give them the very best care and at no time are they to be angered or unduly gored. Be you at the door to receive them . . . and give the proper selling for the people who come and be in the middle of the confusion and give them what they are after . . . For the time being say it is the prophet who has given his concern to the pictures and for the first one who called give him the first picture and not a one is to be denied. So gladly ye shall pose and give them the sign and no one shall know who is not a brother and not a potter shall be among them. Be ye wise and give the sign to each reporter and that is essential and for that matter there is not one who shall be admitted to this room who is not to be used for the good of all. And not a person shall say who is who or what is what and go into the place wherein is the new dress put it on and give them a show put upon thy face the smear [lipstick] and give them the works and put thy furbish on."

Dr. Armstrong and Mrs. Keech, with the occasional participation of other members of the group, prepared a new press release before calling the newspapers. This is a particularly interesting document, for it highlights once more the extent to which the disconfirmation still pained the believers. The major portion of the release has no connection whatever with the contents of the message that stimulated it, but rather is concerned with "faults in the earth's surface" and with recent geophysical disturbances. The relationship between concern with such matters and Marian Keech's reaction to the news about the Italian and Californian earthquakes is obvious, and it is also clear that the group considered these recent events to be consistent with portions of the cataclysmic prediction and the beliefs on which it was based. The press release, in its entirety, reads:

"Due to the confusion which has arisen from the prophecy we have decided to unite forces to complete the prophecy.

"It was reported on the 21st that the cataclysm was stayed by the hand of the God of Earth. The date was given in order to alert the people to the possibilities in case of a disturbance so that we could avoid panic.

"It has come to our attention that the Flying Saucers, or more correctly, the 'Guardians of Earth,' are here for a definite purpose. They have been surveying the earth where there are faults in the earth's surface and they are prepared to land in case of an impending emergency and evacuate some of the people before the disturbance occurs.

"It is necessary for the people to be prepared and alert to the possibilities in order to avoid panic.

"It is now commonly known and has been reported in the press that the surface of the earth is in an unstable condition. This very year on Oct. 4, the News Press said in part: 'As for the earth skin slipping, Dr. Robert R. Revelle of the U.S. National Research Council and Dr. Walter H. Munk of the Scripps Institute of Oceanography, say, in Rome, that there is a slip of about 75 ft. per year between the earth's outer skin and her inner core. To make matters worse, the AP reports that these scientists confirm an increasing tip in the earth's axis.'

"We wish to call the people's attention to the fact that there have been a number of violent disturbances in the past few years, particularly the one several years ago in Assam and Tibet, and more recently in the Mediterranean area and Western United States."

Besides indicating the leaders' need to incorporate "confirming evidence," the press release well documents their desire to proselyte. It is also interesting to note that the ostensible reason for giving out the release was the necessity for warning the public of probable upheavals "in order to avoid panic," precisely the reason employed before December 21 to justify the opposite — extreme secrecy about the forecast cataclysm "in order to prevent panic."

182

The press release completed, there began a new surge of publicity seeking. The press services and the local newspapers were once again phoned and, for the first time, calls were made to the picture magazines, newsreel companies, and television stations. Once again, the press responded enthusiastically, this time to receive an even more cordial reception than they had on the previous day. Members of the group posed in any arrangement the photographers wished. Interviews were prolonged, gracious affairs and for the first time Marian Keech consented to demonstrate for the press her mode of receiving communications from the Guardians.

During four separate interviews, with little urging, she took pencil in hand and received messages — some directed to herself and some apparently addressed to the reporters, but all concerned with spreading the word of truth. One such message advised her to treat the reporters well: "Give them of thy love and be ye glad for they but champion thy cause. So bless them and give them the peach which they seek." Another admonished the reporters: "Because ye have a responsibility to the poor people who have not learned to be their own communicators have ye been sent to communicate for them so shall it be done with dignity." A third message was lengthy but contained only two main instructions to the newsmen about how to treat Mrs. Keech: "Do not belittle her" and "Be her sibet." When Marian had finished writing this message she read it aloud and then spent several minutes discussing and explaining it. She discussed *only* the meaning of the word "sibet" and made it crystal clear that the message instructed the reporters to be her students.

By late afternoon of December 22, the flow of visitors had declined and, on Marian's suggestion, Dr. Armstrong took advantage of this hiatus to start on a hurried overnight automobile trip to Collegeville. His sister had initiated court action to have the two Armstrongs declared legally insane and to have a guardian appointed for their children and their estate. The purpose of this trip was to get the little girl and her older brother out of Collegeville that night and to bring them back to Lake City.

Following Dr. Armstrong's departure and still during the late afternoon lull, Mrs. Keech received a message which made a new, though minor, prediction. The most interesting portions of the message are the following:

"So shall ye be at the altar at the time of the evening when there is a tola [flying saucer] directly over you. So by your own tape shall ye play a song and dance your own time. Use the mike and put it on the altar and sit where you are and put the hand to the mike not too close and be the first to get the direct taped posy word. And give thyself the pleasure of a pretty song which has been sung by the boys' glee club of the Losoloes. Be in the altar at the time of eight o'clock and at that time ye shall give the boy the job of recording but stay where you are."

Following these orders, the group gathered at the altar (the sun porch) promptly at eight o'clock. Marian resting in an armchair, extended her right arm with fingers pointed to within a few inches of the microphone and uttered not a sound. The tape recorder was turned on to the recording position and for almost an hour the group waited in complete, devotional silence while the writing hand of Marian Keech presumably transmitted the songs of Losolo University to the tape.

Before the reel of tape had run its length, there was a knock on the door and a cluster of four reporters and photographers entered the house. The machine was turned off, and Marian devoted her full attention for the next two hours to the press. While this interview was going on, Bob Eastman walked over to the recording machine, rewound it, and, at medium volume, started to play back the tape. He listened, for some ten minutes of silent concentration, to nothing, and then he was joined by Mark and Edna Post, who turned the volume control all the way up. Together they listened to tube hum and finally turned off the machine and walked away. Bob took out the message instructing them to record and studied it carefully. When Bob was asked, "Why do you think nothing happened?" he shrugged and said simply, "I don't know." To the same question, Mark Post replied, "Well, so many things that we've received messages on haven't come out. I don't know."

Mrs. Keech had also noted that the tape was still completely blank, and admitted that she had heard nothing when it was played back. When she was asked "What do you think is the reason?" she replied, "Well, the reason was, I'm afraid, that I was thinking while the machine was turned on to record." And that is all we know of the rationalization of this disconfirmation.

One further incident of that evening illustrates again the extent to which these successive disconfirmations of her predictions were pushing Mrs. Keech, her belief still intact, to hunt in every direction for guidance. When two of the authors prepared to take their final leave of the group, they asked Marian for a last message. Her response, by implication and innuendo, as well as in the words she wrote, made it perfectly clear that she had decided that the two either "had their own channels" to the Guardians or perhaps were spacemen themselves, and she therefore considered their request a huge, though private, joke. With a knowing smile, she picked up her pencil and wrote two messages, interrupting her task from time to time with such comments as "Why don't you let us in on your secrets? When will you tell us everything?" Because the tenor of the two messages is the same, we quote the relevant portion of only one of them: "So shall ye put your cards on the table and call an ace an ace and a spade a spade and ye shall also say who is who and what is what. And now do your duty as a Brother. Beleis." The desperation of her search for direction was growing rapidly.

On the next day, December 23, Dr. Armstrong returned from Collegeville with his two younger children, and found group headquarters in a relatively quiet state. There were occasional calls from reporters, but the press had begun to lose interest in what might be happening at the Keech home, and stories about the group were no longer front-page news. Other inquiries, whether by phone or in person, had also become less frequent and only a few bands of teen-agers came to the house. In spite of all the publicity they had received, in spite of their vigorous proselyting, the group had failed to attract a single new adherent and even the supply of *potential* converts appeared to be dwindling.

Perhaps this complete failure to obtain even a trace of support for their ideology precipitated another prediction and a last-ditch frantic effort to stimulate public interest — an effort that followed a now familiar pattern. On the afternoon of the 23rd, Mrs. Keech received a very long message that forecast momentous events to take place on Christmas Eve. The message commanded the group to assemble at 6 P.M. on the 24th on the sidewalk in front of the Keech home and to sing Christmas carols. The group would be visited there by spacemen, the message continued, who would land in a flying saucer. Finally, in marked contrast to the secrecy attending the preparations for the saucer landing on December 17 and 21, they not only were to notify the press of the expected event but also were to invite the public to be present.

The receipt of this message renewed the activity of the believers in the Keech house. The leaders set about preparing another press release and, once more, they alerted newspapers and press associations. The exact contents of this press release are unknown to us, and the evidence we have about it is equivocal at two points: first, it is not clear whether the visiting spacemen were to be visible to everyone or only to the chosen few; second, the release may have stated that the believers definitely would be picked up by the saucer, or it may have only alleged that such a pickup was possible. If, for both of these cloudy points, the second alternatives are correct, then this press release marks the first time that Mrs. Keech's messages make a prediction that cannot be disconfirmed. If the first alternatives are correct, then the ensuing hubbub was one more disconfirmation in a long series.

Faithfully at six o'clock on Christmas Eve, Mrs. Keech, the two Armstrongs and their children, Edna and Mark Post, and Bob Eastman gathered on the street in front of the house. The invitation issued through the newspapers had attracted about two hundred people, who milled about in a somewhat unruly fashion while the little band sang their carols. They sang and waited for the spacemen for perhaps twenty minutes before they retreated to the living room.

The clearest description of this event and the explanation of what the believers felt had happened can be found in excerpts from a verbatim transcription of one interview that a reporter had with Dr. Armstrong over the phone. This interview took place shortly after the group had re-entered the house and is typical of several other such interviews that evening. It lasted almost an hour, but we shall reproduce here only those parts of it that are most enlightening:

NEWSMAN: Dr. Armstrong, I wanted to talk to you with reference to this business about — you know — your calling the paper to say you were going to be picked up at six o'clock this evening. Ahh, I just wanted to find out exactly what happened. . . . Didn't you say they sent a message that you should be packed and waiting at 6 P.M. Christmas Eve?

DR. ARMSTRONG: No.

NEWSMAN: No? No, I'm sorry, sir. Weren't the spacemen supposed to pick you up at 6 P.M.?

DR. ARMSTRONG: Well, there was a spaceman in the crowd with a helmet on and a white gown and what not.

NEWSMAN: There was a spaceman in the crowd?

DR. ARMSTRONG: Well, it was a little hard to tell, but of course at the last when we broke up, why there was very evidently a spaceman there because he had his space helmet on and he had a big white gown on.

NEWSMAN: Oh, the spacemen were there?

DR. ARMSTRONG: Well, there was one there.

NEWSMAN: One spaceman there. And what did he say? Did you talk to him?

DR. ARMSTRONG: No, I didn't talk to him.

NEWSMAN: Didn't you say you were going to be picked up by the spacemen?

DR. ARMSTRONG: No.

NEWSMAN: Well, what were you waiting out in the street for singing carols?

187

DR. ARMSTRONG: Well, we went out to sing Christmas carols.

NEWSMAN: Oh, you just went out to sing Christmas carols?

DR. ARMSTRONG: Well, and if anything happened, well, that's all right, you know. We live from one minute to another. Some very strange things have happened to us and —

NEWSMAN: But didn't you hope to be picked up by the spacemen? As I understand it —

DR. ARMSTRONG: We were willing.

NEWSMAN: You were willing to be picked up the spacemen. But didn't you expect them to pick you up? As I understand it, you said that you expected them to come but they might change their minds, that they're unpredictable. Is that correct?

DR. ARMSTRONG: Well, ahh, I didn't see the paper, what was actually printed in the paper.

NEWSMAN: Well, no, but isn't that what you said?

DR. ARMSTRONG: We had some instructions to pass on the news, ya, that the spacemen possibly would pick us up.

NEWSMAN: Who gave you these instructions?

DR. ARMSTRONG: Well, they came through our channel from Sananda —

NEWSMAN: Oh, but now, didn't he [Sananda] tell you you were going to be picked up by the spacemen?

DR. ARMSTRONG: Ahh, well now, let's see. I don't think he made a promise to that effect, no.

NEWSMAN: Didn't he say maybe they'd pick you up at 6 P.M. Christmas Eve?

DR. ARMSTRONG: No, we were told to tell the press that.

NEWSMAN: Oh, you were told to tell the press that? But you didn't really believe it yourself?

DR. ARMSTRONG: Well, I said it could happen.

NEWSMAN: Uhuh. Well, how do you account for the fact that they didn't pick you up?

DR. ARMSTRONG: Well, as I told one of the other news boys, I didn't think a spaceman would feel very welcome there in that crowd.

NEWSMAN: Oh, a spaceman wouldn't have felt welcome there.

DR. ARMSTRONG: No, I don't think so. Of course, there may have been some spacemen there in disguise, you know. We couldn't see. I think — I think that's quite possible.

NEWSMAN: There might have been some in the crowd?

DR. ARMSTRONG: Ya, that's right.

NEWSMAN: Uhuh. Ahh — so you think the reason the spacemen didn't pick you up was that they were scared away by the crowd?

DR. ARMSTRONG: Well, I wouldn't say they were scared, but then, I guess the general has the right to change his plans if he wants to.

NEWSMAN: Uhuh, but do you think it's conceivable that they were scared away by the crowd?

DR. ARMSTRONG: Oh no, they weren't scared away, but a thing like that, it's, shall we say, expedient?

NEWSMAN: Expedient?

DR. ARMSTRONG: Ya —

NEWSMAN: In what way?

DR. ARMSTRONG: Well, I mean to get the mob reaction to that kind of a setup before they actually decide to do anything.

NEWSMAN: In other words, so they wouldn't start a riot or something, if they picked you up then.

DR. ARMSTRONG: Well, heavens, they've had riots over less than that, you know.

This mélange of incompatible and halfhearted denial, excuse, and reaffirmation was typical of the untidy fashion in which the members of the group attempted to explain this happening of Christmas Eve. In interviews with the press and discussions among themselves, the believers made two major points. First, they asserted that the spacemen had appeared at the carol-singing but were invisible or unknown to the mob of nonbelievers. Edna Post in a phone conversation with Bertha Blatsky enthused, "We could see them surrounding us last night, some of his foot helpers — it was real thrilling. I could spot very serious faces in the crowd, just forming a ring around us. Marian says to tell you it was as if we had the Notre Dame football team surrounding us." Secondly, they said that the spacemen had restrained themselves from landing their saucers for fear of creating a panic in the rowdy mob of onlookers.

On December 25 a new participant observer was introduced into the group. We shall describe his reception in some detail, for it stands in vivid contrast to the treatment accorded the Lake City observers who first called in October and November. They were received politely, but somewhat distantly. The new observer was dined, wooed, and made the center of attention. As the reader will see, the warmth of his welcome is attributable in good measure to the hope and expectation that he, at last, would bring the group their orders, would give them a plan for their future. Had he done so, it would also have provided independent verification of their beliefs.

The new observer knocked at the door at about 1 P.M. on Christmas Day, and asked to speak to Mrs. Keech. He was ushered inside where he immediately became the center of attention. Let him tell the story in his own words:

"Mrs. Keech asked me why I had called and I told her I had read about her in the papers and wanted to know more. Mrs. Armstrong, Bob, and Edna picked up pads of paper and with pencils poised were apparently ready to record our conversation.

"The significance of this didn't immediately occur to me although I realized quite soon that what they were looking for was a sign of some kind, and they thought I had a special kind of message to deliver. . . . I said that one of my courses had dealt with a little astronomy and that this had aroused my interest in space travel and that I wanted to learn more about this if I could and that I would be interested in anything that she could tell me about her experiences. At about this point she looked at me and suggested that there were perhaps some things that I could tell *her* and this increased my feeling of being on the spot and having to give her some kind of answers. I, of course, said that I had nothing to tell her and that I knew nothing, but wanted to learn.

"At this point, Mrs. Keech asked someone to call Tom. He

came in and we were introduced and he looked at me with what I took to be a certain look of expectation. He too began to question me. . . . I felt my dilemma steadily increasing but I couldn't see what else to do other than to play it as straight as possible because it seemed that no matter what I did or what I said, it was going to be significant. . . .

"The role that I assumed in keeping with Dr. Armstrong's questioning of my interest in the group was that of a person who was somewhat confused by the times and was lonely and sought guidance and understanding of many of the things that are happening today. In connection with my feeling lonely, Dr. Armstrong asked me if I had ever felt as if I didn't belong on this planet, if I had been born on some other planet. I answered, of course, that I had no knowledge of my having been born on any other planet, but simply that I thought that I had been born in the same way that everyone else is born. This brought a smile from Mrs. Keech who looked at me again with a very knowing look. . . .

"Sometimes when the attention shifted back to me, Mrs. Keech would make some reference to the fact that she was impressed by my presence on Christmas day — statements like, 'This is the happiest Christmas we've had because YOU have come.' And such other statements."

Exhausted, the new observer left at 4:30 P.M. That evening in a phone conversation with a sympathetic friend, Marian said, "And we had a very, very, very, very, very special guest for dinner. He came in and dined with us today, so it has been the most joyous, the most joyous Christmas that any of us have ever known."

The same observer returned the next day to face a similar reception. He reports:

"They seated me in a position of some prominence in the room again, in terms of chair arrangements, and turned their attention to me again. . . . Dr. Armstrong looked at me expectantly and the others in the group seemed to look at me expectantly and Dr. Armstrong said, 'I'd like to hear from you. Haven't you something to tell us?' And I said, 'Why no, I don't know of anything

I have to tell you.' And he said, 'Well, can't you sing us a song?' and I said, 'Why no, if you knew what kind of a singing voice I have, you wouldn't want me to sing a song.' And he said, 'Well, can't you tell us a story?' and he kept pressing me, and Mrs. Keech concurred with him in this and kind of wanted to urge me and other members of the group also said this."

The next day Mrs. Keech had her first chance to converse with the observer alone. He describes their talk:

"She said in a very, kind of last-straw voice — that's the only way I can describe it — she seemed sort of at the end of her rope and she said, 'Are you sure that you have no message for me? Now that we are alone, we can talk.' And I said, 'Gee, I'm sorry, I just don't know of any message that I have.' She said, 'Do you feel that there are any disturbing influences around? Anything that's disrupting your giving me a message?' I, of course, answered that I wasn't aware of anything of this sort."

This observer continued to visit the group approximately every other day for the next two weeks. All through this period those who remained in the Lake City group persisted in viewing him as someone special — a space brother who was not telling all he knew.

The experiences of this observer well characterize the state of affairs following the Christmas caroling episode—a persistent, frustrating search for orders. At this time too, an array of forces extrinsic to the group began to scatter the members widely. Marian Keech and the Armstrong family left Lake City and the Post household became the center of what little activity there was thereafter. It became impossible for us to remain well informed of their activities and beliefs, although some of the members continued to write us occasionally during the next couple of months and thus kept us abreast of at least the major developments in their lives. We shall describe the breakup of the Lake City group and the reasons for it later. In the next chapter we shall interrupt our narrative in order to take a closer look at how the events we have just described affected individual members of the group, and to draw together the evidence bearing on the main theoretical point of this book.

I<small>N PRESENTING</small> the sequence of events immediately before and after December 21, we have focused on those events that were of significance to the entire group in Lake City, and, with the exception of Mrs. Keech and Dr. Armstrong, we have not detailed the impact of these events on the behavior and beliefs of the individual members. We shall try to remedy this omission by describing in the first part of this chapter the immediate and long-term effects of the series of disconfirmations on each member. The last part of the chapter is, from a theoretical point of view, the heart of the study, for there we shall summarize and integrate the evidence relevant to an evaluation of our hypothesis.

*Mrs. Keech and Dr. Armstrong.* Throughout the period of disconfirmation Mrs. Keech and Dr. Armstrong remained unwaveringly firm in their conviction. Though they searched desperately for messages that might guide them, never during this entire time did either of them utter a serious word of doubt or indicate in any way that they might have been wrong. Indeed, their sublime faith remained firm long after the Lake City group had dispersed. Even after Mrs. Keech had left Lake City, she continued to receive messages from Sananda which she relayed to her flock by mail.

Dr. Armstrong and his family returned to Collegeville where they sold their house and prepared to leave town. On January 12, their last afternoon in Collegeville, one of our observers talked with them and reports: "Dr. Armstrong seemed highly confident as to the future; he was in as good spirits as I can remember. Mrs. Armstrong, too, was in fine spirits, bubbling over with the plan.

Everything was still going according to the plan, the plan imposed on them as messengers of the supernatural." As to the future, Dr. Armstrong said, "Being an M.D. is a lot of work and I kind of enjoy lecturing and talking to people." He intimated that he would not be looking for a job or trying to practice the medical profession but would go out lecturing and attending meetings in order to propagate the faith. Their immediate destination was a meeting of the Casey Foundation in Virginia, an institution named for the man who, Dr. Armstrong commented, had done so much of the basic work in reincarnation.

This impression of the doctor's intention to go out to preach is confirmed in a letter from Clyde Wilton to one of the observers in which, on February 8, he commented: "I wrote Tom recently and suggested that he apply at one of the plants here if he was now looking for a job. He replied that he would not be accepting permanent employment in the foreseeable future as he was touring around the country contacting people interested in the teachings we have received, etc. He said he was traveling with Daisy and people who had sources of contact." Quite evidently, the doctor had given up medicine for the role of itinerant proselyter.

We have only one additional item of information concerning Armstrong's persistent conviction. In early May, some five months after the prediction of catastrophe, Dr. Armstrong reappeared briefly in Collegeville. During his travels he had received a message through Ella Lowell that he would be picked up by flying saucer at the garage ramp of the largest hotel in Collegeville. All through one night, the doctor, his wife, his daughter Cleo, and Ella Lowell waited. Indeed their faith was boundless and their resistance to disconfirmation sublime.

*Daisy Armstrong and Edna Post.* Mrs. Armstrong and Mrs. Post had served as handmaidens of the group. All through the period from December 17 to the 26th, they had acted as servants, cooks, dishwashers, and secretaries. They were loyal, devoted disciples who beamed when Mrs. Keech or Dr. Armstrong praised them and were distraught if criticized. For example, early in the evening of December 20, Marian spoke to Daisy Armstrong about a recent lesson that Daisy had received; Daisy reported that she had burned it and Marian replied that she should not have done so. Daisy seemed quite upset at learning she had made a mistake. Jokingly, Marian commented: "Well, I guess you're just not going to get a seat [on the saucer] then." The doctor laughed too, adding: "I guess we'll have to leave you out." Daisy broke down completely and cried for almost half an hour, sobbing over and over that the lessons were precious to her — as precious to her as they were to anybody else and she hadn't wanted to burn the lesson; she had wanted to keep the lesson but she had thought it should be burned.

Both women were greatly upset by the disconfirmation of the morning of December 21, Edna Post being hit especially hard. Nevertheless, throughout the period of disconfirmation both these women unquestioningly accepted the messages, predictions, and rationalizations that Mrs. Keech and Dr. Armstrong worked out for the group. Both of them simply repeated the rationalizations of disconfirmation that the leaders elaborated and glowed over the wonder and beauty of the plan. Their faith, too, remained firm all through the time that we maintained contact with them. On January 24, Daisy while en route to Virginia wrote to one of the authors, saying, "Believe me, we certainly have had divine guidance all along the way. We get orders from 'upstairs' en route." And "Give our 'best' to the other two from Minneapolis. Tell them we know the future is 'rosy.' We've been promised many wonderful things and we still know who our *Director* is. We go as his guests — his representatives."

And Edna, too, remained faithful. In a letter dated January 30, she reported that she had been writing to Marian for messages; and she evidently continued in her self-appointed secretarial role, for she also wrote, "I have typed up many of the tapes that I thought might be helpful to members of the group and am trying to serve as a sort of 'clearing house' or communications center, to the best of my ability."

*Mark Post.* Of the younger disciples, Mark was, on all counts, the most ardent. He subjected himself completely to the discipline

Marian Keech imposed on him. For several days he adhered to a diet prescribed by Marian and lived solely on nuts. He received orders from the Guardians not to leave the house for any reason, and, until the orders were rescinded several days later, he stayed indoors all the time. Between the 17th and the 20th of December he took a modest part in the affairs of the group but obediently and faithfully handled such chores as answering the telephone, receiving callers, and, when instructed to do so, lecturing to teen-agers about the beliefs of the group. The rest of his time he spent studying the lessons, playing cards with Cleo Armstrong, or simply sitting, waiting with mounting tension for the 21st to roll around.

Mark may have had a period of doubt following the midnight saucer vigil on the 17th of December, although his immediate reactions to this can only be surmised since he had been sworn to secrecy about it; but shortly after the rationalization of the December 21 disconfirmation, Mark mentioned that for the past few days he had had some doubts about the truth of the prophecy. These doubts seem to have been laid to rest by what happened on the morning of the 21st, however, and Mark was one of the first to telephone the newspapers to inform them of the "Christmas Message." On December 22, Mark busied himself as never before in removing all metal from his person; he threw away the metal band of his watch and made himself a leather one; he replaced his belt buckle by a leather thong; and he discarded a cigarette lighter that he dearly loved. It is not clear whether these actions betokened his intentions to be ever ready for a pick-up by saucer, or whether by this time he had come to share with Mrs. Keech and Daisy and Thomas Armstrong a general aversion to the presence of metal.

Mark's zeal continued and, when we last heard of him, it was still high. When Marian, on December 26, was preparing to leave her house, a large quantity of lessons, notebooks, and messages were rather hastily dumped into a cardboard carton and given to the Posts for safekeeping. Mrs. Keech considered the contents of this box as the "secret books" and asked one of the observers to put a seal of protection on the carton. He meticulously tied the carton together and sealed it with the note "Seal of Protection — Do Not Open." In the letter from Edna Post on January 30, she wrote, "Mark said to tell you that his lessons were put in the box that is sealed shut and if it is ever convenient for him to get them back, he would appreciate it." Despite the fact that the box was in Mark's possession, he refused to open it without explicit permission. He still believed.

*Cleo Armstrong and Bob Eastman.* Cleo and Bob arrived in Lake City on the night of December 18. During the previous week they had spent much of their time with Ella Lowell, who had begun to undermine their belief in Mrs. Keech's prediction of disaster and salvation on the 21st. Ella Lowell never quite dared to renounce this date unequivocally, but she had strongly hinted that the flood might not occur. Though both Cleo and Bob were heavily committed to the December 21 prediction, they arrived in Lake City in a somewhat doubtful frame of mind.

Between the 18th and the 20th, Cleo was an unhappy girl. She was upset and felt guilty at having left her brother and sister in Collegeville. She did not feel at home in the Lake City group, most of whom were strangers and older than she, and were, she felt, gloomily unable to talk of anything else but the cataclysm. She was uncomfortable in this strained atmosphere and precipitated scene after scene with her parents in the course of which she attacked some aspect of their belief. For example, in a private lesson with Mrs. Keech, Cleo had received a number of messages, which she showed to her father. He attempted to discuss them with her but she broke out crying, repeating again and again, "But this is nonsense, it's nonsense, it doesn't mean a thing, it's nonsense." At another time, she and her father were discussing whether the phone calls made to the house were simply from jokers or were genuine messages and tests from the boys from outer space. Dr. Armstrong insisted that they were coded messages and were part of the discipline. To this, with acid in her voice, Cleo retorted: "That's asinine!" These incidents, however, must be viewed against the background of her general acceptance of the belief system. Nor was her behavior at this time all one-sided, for she did engage in such activities as ripping the metal out of her clothes.

Bob Eastman, too, was surly and moody during the days before the 21st. He amused himself chiefly by listening to tapes made by Ella Lowell and discussing her views with his mentor, Dr. Armstrong. He was so sullenly quiet during the days preceding the 21st that it was impossible for the observers to assess his beliefs properly. His reactions to the December 21 disconfirmation, however, were unique in the group. In the early hours of this crucial day, before the message resolving the disconfirmation had arrived, one member of the group asked, "What are the lessons of tonight?" Bob volunteered, "Impatient boredom." When asked, "Boredom with what?" he replied, "Waiting, waiting, always waiting — so many meetings, I've been to so many meetings and I no longer can figure out what is real information; what is true information."

Shortly after the "resolution" message arrived, one of the observers commented to Bob, "Well, it's been an interesting evening, hasn't it?" To which Bob replied, "Yeah, I'll say, interesting. The way it is around here your right hand doesn't know what your left hand is doing. Or if it does, it's a preconceived idea. I'm going to bed."

Though both Cleo and Bob had been convinced believers earlier in the fall, they clearly seemed, at this time, somewhat more doubtful about the beliefs of the group.

In the days following the 21st, their behavior took an astonishing turn. Though it might be most plausible to expect that they would give up their beliefs following disconfirmation, quite the reverse happened. On December 22, Cleo busied herself helping her father and Mark Post rid themselves of metal. She replaced buttons, made leather thong replacements for belt buckles, and so on. That evening, Marian Keech was called away for approximately three quarters of an hour from an interview with two newspaper reporters. Cleo immediately stepped into the breach and took over completely. For this entire time, she presented the beliefs of the group and vigorously argued with the newspapermen. This was the very first time that Cleo had done any such thing. In Collegeville, previous to the 21st, she had either avoided reporters completely or told lies in order to rid herself of them.

A similar event took place on December 25 when again Cleo took a particularly active part in an interview a reporter was conducting with her father and Mrs. Keech. Events such as these would certainly seem to indicate not only markedly increased proselyting on her part but new-found confidence in her beliefs. Cleo's increased conviction seems to have persisted long after she returned to her classes in Collegeville. On January 17, one of the observers had a discussion with Hal Fischer, the chief skeptic of the Collegeville group. Hal reported that he had had an argument with Cleo and that Cleo was still firmly convinced about the prediction and Mrs. Keech's messages. The observer (who had lived in the Armstrong house for several days before Cleo left for Lake City) remarked, "Well, that's interesting. Before she went to Lake City she was a trifle skeptical." Hal replied, "Well, she's firmly convinced now."

Further evidence of the permanency of her change of heart is, of course, to be found in the incident in May when Cleo, then living in a college dormitory, joined her parents in waiting for the saucer. Possibly under the impression that it would be pointless, Cleo failed to get permission for an overnight absence. Her dormitory counselor, Susan Heath, formerly a devoted and convinced member of Dr. Armstrong's group, described the incident and commented, "I no longer believe this stuff, but Cleo sure does."

Bob Eastman, at least temporarily, had a similar reaction. On the evening of December 22, one of the observers asked Bob how he felt about things now, to which Bob replied: "Well, I was really skeptical last night but since then we've had lessons, we've had messages, and I think I'm beginning to understand it and see the meaning of it all." When asked what he was planning to do next, Bob's answer was "Well, it depends on my orders. My parents think I'm crazy to be here over Christmas, but it depends on my orders. If my orders tell me to go back to Steel City, I will. If they tell me to stay in Lake City, I'll stay in Lake City."

Apparently Bob also found new confidence in the beliefs of the group after the major disconfirmation, although the disconfirmation following the Christmas Eve caroling seems to have put some strain on his faith in Mrs. Keech. His mood at that time is perhaps best indicated in a long-distance call he made to Kitty O'Donnell on December 25. Early in the call he sounds skeptical, but as he talks to the unbelieving Kitty he revises his stand and reaffirms his faith.

BOB: I don't know, maybe I'm wrong, but since I've been around here I don't have much faith in Marian.

KITTY: You didn't get picked up, huh?

BOB: No, we haven't had any positive action like that.

KITTY: Well, I thought they were supposed to be out there — it said in the paper they were supposed to be out there singing Christmas carols at seven o'clock in the morning, or at night.

BOB: No, no, six o'clock last night. There's a lot behind all that though, it's hard to explain it, especially over the phone, but it's just a part of a whole big picture, that it's training for us.

KITTY: I'm glad you believe in it then, I don't — I'm all done with them, I'll tell you that much.

BOB: You really got into a negative environment.

KITTY: I don't think it's negative at all — I just have more faith in Ella Lowell, that's all.

BOB: Oh, she's a very fine woman, I enjoyed my three days with her very much, but I don't find that much difference between her and Marian.

KITTY: Well, I don't know.

BOB: It's interesting to hear your viewpoint on this now.

KITTY: Well, I don't know, but I just regret in a way, Bob — course I learned a lesson, but I just regret that I made such an ass of myself of giving up my money and stuff and I don't know —

BOB: You mean the disappointment of the 21st.

KITTY: No, not necessarily, 'cause I never believed in it a whole lot anyway. I did to an extent, but I mean it was no surprise that it didn't come off.

BOB: Oh. Well it was cooked for us until after we got an explanation of it.

KITTY: Well, I am thankful for one thing, that I kept my name out of the papers, anyway.

BOB: Well, you know none of us wanted to, that's part of our training too; we were told to get into the papers. That's part of our humiliation process, I think . . . Everything that happens is with the sanction of the brothers. . . .

KITTY: I wish you would tell me what you are doing.

BOB: I'm just waiting. I'm completely in their hands.

KITTY: Don't you believe anything that Ella Lowell has told you?

BOB: Sure, I believe everything that she told me — none of it contradicts anything I've learned at this end since then.

How long Bob maintained his renewed confidence we do not know. Late in December, he returned to Steel City where he enrolled in an electronics school and resumed his attendance at the séances of Ella Lowell.

*Bertha Blatsky and Clyde Wilton.* Both Bertha and Clyde, though strongly committed and deeply involved, were unable to take as active a part in the affairs of the group between December 17 and 21 as were the other central members. Fear of her husband restrained Bertha from regular attendance at Mrs. Keech's home during this period, while distance and concern for his family similarly handicapped Clyde. These same factors forced them to face the period following the major disconfirmation in isolation, separated from their fellow believers. This state of affairs probably prevented their full recovery from the disillusionment following disconfirmation.

Throughout the history of the group, Bertha's attendance at Mrs. Keech's house, while spectacular, had been sporadic. She was able to visit the house only through some stratagem or through open disobedience of her husband's orders — orders that, as we have seen, became quite clear and firm early in December. During the critical days between December 17 and 21, Bertha put in her first appearance the evening of the 18th. She spent the night, leaving in the early morning of December 19 and returned that evening for a few hours. She showed up again in the early morning of December 20, remaining until about 9 A.M. on December 21. After this she saw no member of the group again until January 7, when she came to Edna Post's home in Highvale. Between December 21 and January 7 she had only two contacts with any members of the group: a telephone conversation with Marian and Edna on the night of December 24 and another call to Marian the following week. Her absence during this period was nonvoluntary, forced on her by her husband. On January 7, he left town on private business and Bertha took advantage of this chance to rejoin the group.

Bertha's state of mind during the critical pre-cataclysm days was one of inner turmoil and doubt, insecurity about her own powers and uncertainty about the prediction. On December 18, the following conversation, as described by the observer involved, took place:

"Bertha talked a little about her husband and said that she had promised him to get out of this business after the 21st, that he was being very patient with her and letting her do pretty much as she pleased until the 21st and then she'd promised him to get out of this movement. She said, 'It's these doubts that are the worst.' When she mentioned the 21st, I sort of cocked an eyebrow at her and said, 'Well, you probably won't have to worry then about anything after that.' And she said, 'Oh, it's the doubting that's the worst.' I said, 'Yes, I imagine it is pretty difficult,' and she confessed that she had been having a lot of doubts about the date and the prophecy and about her own role and I said, 'Yes, you mentioned on Tuesday that you were having trouble validating your messages. Has that cleared up at all?' And she said, 'No, it's the responsibility, you know. I have to make sure that what I'm saying is right and I just don't know. In this house it's easy not to have doubts, but when I get home alone or when I'm with my husband, I'm full of doubt, and I just don't know what to do.' And I said, 'Well, the only thing you can do is just stick with it and your doubts will resolve themselves one way or the other.'

She said, 'Yes, by the 21st I won't have any more doubts left, I'm sure.' "

Bertha's immediate reaction to the events of December 21 was one of exultation. Instead of trying to avoid publicity, she released the secret tapes, volunteered to make new tapes for anyone, and, for the first time, spoke to a newspaperman. Her moment of exhilaration, however, was apparently soon over, for when she was once more able to see the group on January 7 she was a worn and distraught woman who reported that ever since she had left the group on December 21 she had been going through pure hell and her life had been a misery. She had spent the past weeks alone thinking through what had happened and re-examining her own role in the group. Her doubts had returned and multiplied.

On the morning of December 18, Clyde Wilton had received a long-distance call from Marian Keech who urged him to come to Lake City at once. At first he seems to have been reluctant to leave his home, but he ended by obeying orders. Unable to get a plane that day, he did not arrive in Lake City until two o'clock the following afternoon. He stayed just one day, for Mrs. Keech received orders for him to return to his family on December 20.

Although Clyde's commitment was less than that of other central members of the group, his investment in the ideology was still quite heavy. He had made the five-hundred mile trip to Lake City three times in the space of a month, always on orders received through Mrs. Keech and for the sole purpose of meeting with the group. He not only bore the expenses of these trips himself, but lost pay for each day he was absent from his job, and these absences from work had begun to involve him in difficulties with his supervisors. His conviction about the ideology can perhaps be described best as sympathetic open-mindedness. He was the scholar of the group, intimately familiar with the lessons and teachings transmitted by Mrs. Keech. The beliefs seemed generally acceptable to him, though he frequently demonstrated a need to relate these beliefs to his scientific knowledge, remarking on one occasion: "I guess we'd all like to have more evidence. We're being asked to take a lot on faith."

Clyde returned home on December 20. The only evidence we have about his reaction to the disconfirmation of the 21st is contained in two letters. In the first one, dated February 8, he describes his own behavior on the crucial night:

"On the night of December 20, I stayed up most of the night — dozing now and then. About 5 or 6 A.M. on December 21, I telephoned Marian and she had Tom read to me the message for the newspapers which had just been received. I wondered why we had been led to believe that a flood would occur if it were avoidable or if it wasn't going to happen! Was there a good reason? Had the sources been having some fun with us? I don't know."

Though it is difficult to say very much about Clyde's attitudes from this note, a subsequent letter indicates more clearly that his reaction to disconfirmation was disillusionment and confusion. On March 12, he writes:

"I shall be reluctant to go out of my way for purposes which aren't clearer to me than the trips to Lake City were. I do have a feeling that important events or happenings are imminent — within the next few years or decades. Just what — I do not know.

"Yes, I was disappointed in the outcome of events. I had been led to believe that perhaps the teachings were all true. Then when things turned out as they did, it left me wondering what part, if any, of the teachings might be true. The only one here to whom I could talk about the prediction, etc., was the wife of a friend of ours — she felt as confused as I did.

"I think there is something to the teaching: strive for one's own knowingness. This is difficult and one never feels really sure except on relatively rare occasions."

In many ways, Clyde's reaction was similar to that of Bertha. Both responded to disconfirmation with increased doubt, though neither was willing to give up altogether the beliefs of the group. Their reaction, then, was quite different from that of other central group members who responded to disconfirmation by remaining firm in their belief, and, in some cases, actually increasing in conviction. There is perhaps a clue to understanding this difference in the fact that Bertha and Clyde alone were forced to spend the days after the 21st in isolation from other group members. It is reasonable to believe that dissonances created by unequivocal disconfirmation cannot be appreciably reduced unless one is in the constant presence of supporting members who can provide for one another the kind of social reality that will make the rationalization of disconfirmation acceptable. The extent to which even a brief contact with fellow believers helped to strengthen Bertha's beliefs and diminish her doubts is well illustrated by excerpts from a letter that Bertha wrote to one of the observers shortly after seeing him and several members of the group at Edna Post's home on January 7:

"Need I tell you what a comfort it was to have had you folks with me last evening. It was indeed an answer to a prayer which I had not really expected answered so soon.

"It was a real demonstration to me that when the need becomes as great as mine was and that when directed toward the Good it cannot help but bring Good. I must admit there is so much I still would like to know, but I do know that it most likely is not the time, and when the time comes — all will be revealed — and it was so wonderful to be assured by people whom one *can trust* even though one does not know why — that the forces of Light predominated — and that is saying a lot. . . .

"Well, I shall try to stand on my own two feet. The funny thing about it is that previously, I am the one that others leaned on — and now all of a sudden I am the one to need the help. And then I don't know what kind of help I need — there is just that longing — lost feeling, I guess. I suppose when I really get lost in doing things again and giving of myself that will be the answer. I had been holding myself in reserve, I guess and not putting enough in the Now as has been taught us."

*Kurt Freund.* As we have pointed out in earlier chapters, Kurt was a firm, though usually not an outspoken, skeptic. Usually, he posed as a philosopher of the cosmos, whom nothing could surprise. He was convinced of the existence of flying saucers and of life on other planets but he admitted his grave doubts about the prediction, the messages, and the visits of "spacemen" to Mrs.

Keech's home. He maintained these attitudes through the critical days before the 21st. For example, on December 18 when the five boys claiming they were from Clarion showed up, Kurt was the sole vocal skeptic in the group, maintaining stoutly that these were not spacemen. "I saw nothing. They just looked like college kids to me. It looked as though they just came here for a lark," he insisted.

His commitment to the group was correspondingly low. The sole indication of any sacrifice on his part was his assertion that he had given up a Christmas vacation trip to Arizona. When asked why he had done so, he said it was because he was too busy, although it is entirely possible that he simply wished to be present on December 21.

During the December 17–21 period, Kurt showed up three times: the evenings of December 18, 19, and 20. He stayed all night on December 20, leaving just before the newspapermen started coming to the house. He never came back.

His failure to reappear at Mrs. Keech's house would certainly seem to indicate that he had grown thoroughly disillusioned with this group and its specific beliefs, but in a conversation with one of the Lake City observers on February 24, Kurt praised Marian highly. Whether this reflects simple compassion or reveals something about his attitudes of which we were previously unaware, we do not know. Our best hunch is that Kurt was not a true believer before disconfirmation and certainly not afterwards. Perhaps he felt that movements such as this one have their place in cosmic history and saw himself as a distant but interested observer.

*Arthur Bergen.* Arthur, the young high school student, was convinced that flying saucers were real and that there was life on other planets, but he seemed also to have doubts about the prediction and associated beliefs of the group. He was generally shy, silent, and difficult to interview and our categorization of Arthur as having moderate conviction is based on far less information than for any of the people we have discussed so far. Symptomatic of his doubts is a conversation he had with an observer on December 18, in which the boy stated that he "didn't know what to believe." He was uncertain whether Mrs. Keech's writings contained the truth and whether the cataclysm would actually take place on December 21.

Much of his behavior, however, reflected greater conviction. He probably spent more time than any of the other group members listening to the tapes; during the frenzy of removing metal on December 20, he meticulously stripped tin foil from each stick of a package of gum he was carrying, and became quite upset when he discovered that he could not remove the metal tips from his shoes. His absorption with the question of the flood is demonstrated by the fact that he alone took the trouble to find out the exact time when dawn would break on the 21st and informed the group of it.

That his commitment was low seems unequivocal, for his sole sacrifice seems to have been his arguments with his parents about how late he could stay at Mrs. Keech's house and his description of these arguments make them seem not very serious affairs. When someone once asked Arthur if he had had any trouble with his parents, he said, "Oh, no, I have a very funny family. My mother worries and my father gets mad. I'm pretty much on my own but still I tell my mother not to worry and then she doesn't worry, and then my father gets mad because she doesn't worry, but I don't have too much trouble."

Even allowing for adolescent bravado and assuming more difficulty with his family than he admits, we are still faced with the fact that at every point during the December 17–21 period when Arthur was in conflict between staying at a meeting and getting home at approximately the hour he had promised his parents, he left for home. Clearly he was unwilling to face their possible anger in order to overstay his time at Mrs. Keech's house.

During the December 17–21 period, Arthur put in his first appearance on the afternoon of December 18, and returned daily after this until his departure at 2:30 A.M. the morning of December 21. This was his last visit. He telephoned once thereafter but never came to the house again.

He appears to have been disillusioned by the disconfirmation of

December 21. Early in February, an observer spoke with him again and Arthur indicated that he no longer had faith in Mrs. Keech. He still believed in flying saucers, still believed in the possibility of contact with outer space, but he had given up on Marian and her beliefs.

Summarizing the evidence on the effects that disconfirmation had on the conviction of group members, we find that, of the eleven members of the Lake City group who faced unequivocal disconfirmation, only two, Kurt Freund and Arthur Bergen, both of whom were lightly committed to begin with, completely gave up their belief in Mrs. Keech's writings. Five members of the group, the Posts, the Armstrongs, and Mrs. Keech, all of whom entered the pre-cataclysm period strongly convinced and heavily committed, passed through this period of disconfirmation and its aftermath with their faith firm, unshaken, and lasting. Cleo Armstrong and Bob Eastman, who had come to Lake City heavily committed but with their conviction shaken by Ella Lowell, emerged from the disconfirmation of December 21 more strongly convinced than before; Cleo's change of heart seems to have lasted while Bob's may have been temporary. Bertha Blatsky and Clyde Wilton started out with some doubts. They reacted to disconfirmation by persisting in their doubts and admitting their disillusionment and confusion, but still not completely disavowing Mrs. Keech and her particular beliefs. We have noted that both Clyde and Bertha were forced to face disconfirmation in isolation and have suggested that this factor may account for the sharp contrast between their reactions and those of Cleo and Bob.

We shall have an opportunity to examine the effects of isolation more closely in the next chapter, which is concerned with the effects of disconfirmation in the Collegeville group.

## Résumé of Proselyting Activities

At this point we return to the theoretical considerations that stimulated our interest in Marian Keech and her associates, and in the following section we summarize the evidence that bears on our hypothesis.

In Chapter I, we specified the conditions under which disconfirmation would lead to increased proselyting, and for most of the members of the Lake City group these specifications were satisfied. Most of the people in this group believed in Mrs. Keech's prediction and were heavily committed to this belief. Disconfirmation was unequivocal and the attempted rationalization was never completely successful in dispelling dissonance. Finally, with the exceptions we have noted, the members of the group faced disconfirmation and its aftermath together. Conditions were ideal for testing our hypothesis.

Undoubtedly, the reader has by now formed at least a rough impression of the extent to which the hypothesis is supported. With illustrative documentation we shall attempt to summarize the major differences before and after disconfirmation in publicity seeking, in personal proselyting, and in the extent to which the members of the group exposed their beliefs to outsiders. It should be noted now that with the possible exception of Dr. Armstrong the believers never did directly and indiscriminately go out to convert the world. Their techniques were gentler. Even at the height of proselyting their endeavors consisted largely of attempting to attract attention to their beliefs, then trying to convert those who came to the house or telephoned.

*Publicity Seeking.* Most dramatic, of course, was the precipitous change in attitudes toward the press. Had the group been interested in carrying their message to the world and securing new converts, they would have been presented with a priceless opportunity on December 16 when representatives of all the nation's major news reporting services converged on the Keech home, hungry for a story to follow up the news break on Dr. Armstrong's dismissal from the college. But the press got a cold, almost hostile, reception, and their most persistent efforts were resisted. In two days of constant vigil, the newspapermen succeeded in winning only one brief broadcast tape and one interview with Dr. Armstrong and Mrs. Keech—and that only after virtually forcing their demands on the leaders. A cameraman who surreptitiously violated the prohibition against taking photographs was threatened with a lawsuit. Between December 18 and the early morning of December 21 the numberless phone calls from reporters were almost invariably answered by a flat, unqualified "No comment."

This situation reversed itself with explosive immediacy within minutes after the group had developed the rationalization for the major disconfirmation on December 21. For the first time in her life, Marian Keech insisted on calling the newspapers to give them a story. No sooner had she put down the phone than Dr. Armstrong and Mark Post took turns phoning every one of the major news services and local papers, rejecting all suggestions that one paper be given an exclusive story. On December 21 alone, Dr. Armstrong and Mrs. Keech made five tape recordings for radio broadcast. Within the next three days, Marian's messages were used as reasons for drawing up new press releases and lifting the ban on photographers. Twice more the press was called in and their reception was warm and friendly. Reporters were granted extensive interviews and photographers welcomed. The once-rejected suitor was hotly pursued.

*Personal Proselyting.* Attitudes toward face-to-face attempts to proselyte had crystallized early in the history of the movement with the maxim "those who are ready will be sent" — a teaching shared by the Armstrongs, Mrs. Keech, Bertha Blatsky, and Ella Lowell. In effect, they preached and practiced caution: be discreet in talking about the beliefs, do not attempt to force people into belief. By early December an air of secrecy had enveloped the group and sentiments toward outsiders shifted to an even more extreme position — to almost an antiproselyting admonition: of those who come, speak only to the ones you are sure have been chosen.

Before December 17, the group did indeed practice a cautious policy toward outsiders. The best documented instances of this caution are, of course, the experiences of the four observers and the authors in attempting to win entree during the pre-cataclysm days. Only one observer had an easy time — the girl who came to the Armstrongs with a dramatic, invented dream. The remaining observers, who had more ordinary explanations of their interest, were treated well and their questions answered, but they were never exhorted, never on first contact invited back, and forced time and again to devise excuses themselves for coming back — treatment that would have discouraged a less purposeful outsider.

On December 16 and 17, large numbers of visitors were attracted to Mrs. Keech's house by the newspaper publicity. Many of them were simply turned away; those permitted to enter were treated in a fashion similar to that described for the observers. Following the two disconfirmations on December 17, conspicuously fewer people were turned away and those admitted were treated in a decidedly more exhortatory manner as the group members presented their beliefs in a genuine attempt to persuade. Many of the visitors were directly invited to return. By December 19, although there was still some selection at the door, almost everyone admitted to the house was declared to be among the chosen and vigorously exhorted. Finally, after December 21, almost every visitor was admitted. The reception given the observer introduced into the group on December 25 is, of course, in striking contrast to that received by the other observers. In part, his reception is attributable to their clear need for guidance; in part, to their hope of confirmation, so desperate that a complete stranger is nominated as one of the elect — a Guardian.

*Secrecy.* By late November, the group had begun to shroud itself in a veil of secrecy. The Armstrongs burned all copies of the lessons and, in effect, dissolved the Seekers. These actions made effective proselyting in Collegeville very difficult, for there was no longer a central group to which interested outsiders might come. In Lake City, a password and a secret sign were introduced, partially as devices for identifying the chosen. These devices, combined with the admonition "speak only to those who are chosen," if rigidly followed would have made it certain that no new persons would be admitted. Though such secrecy was not absolutely adhered to, it did clearly dominate the behavior and the attitudes of the group in the weeks preceding December 17. During this time even the prediction of cataclysm was considered secret and neither Mrs. Keech nor the Armstrongs mentioned it once when they addressed the flying saucer club. Clearly, their secrecy tended to shut them off from the outside world.

After December 21, this situation completely reversed itself as the group exposed its innermost secrets to the world, in effect saying, "See these wonderful things that have been given to us. Do you not wish to learn more?" Recorded tapes, which had been considered so secret that even members of long standing were forbidden to take notes on their contents, were released to anyone who might be interested and to network broadcasting companies. Mrs. Keech consented to receive messages for the reporters and posed for the photographers holding in her hand an open copy of the "secret books." Most dramatic of all, of course, is the contrast in the behavior of the group as they awaited the coming of the spacemen before the major disconfirmation and afterward. On December 17 and 21, they shielded themselves completely from outsiders, and the innermost circle alone watched for saucers in the privacy of Mrs. Keech's back yard or living room. On December 24 they not only informed the press, but invited the public to their Christmas carol vigil in the street in front of the Keech home. There is no doubt that, after disconfirmation, the members of the group made themselves far more available to outsiders, and thus to potential converts.

The evidence on publicity seeking, personal proselyting, and secrecy leave no doubt that, for this group, as for the millennial movements discussed in Chapter I, proselyting increased meteorically following disconfirmation.

Our comparison, so far, has involved contrasting proselyting in the weeks preceding disconfirmation with proselyting during the days following December 21. We must, of course, also be concerned with the level of this activity in the earlier days of the movement. For most of that period detailed consideration is unnecessary, since until the end of August proselyting was very slight. Between the end of September and the beginning of December, too, proselyting was relatively quiescent, for it was during those days that the twin principles of secrecy and "those who are ready will be sent" were taking root.

In the first half of September, there was a brief but marked spurt of proselyting closely following the receipt of the messages predicting cataclysm. Several activities were initiated to spread the word. Dr. Armstrong, impressed with the importance of the predicted catastrophe, prepared and sent out two press releases. At the request of a reporter whose interest had been stimulated by these releases, Marian Keech gave one interview to the press. Dr. Armstrong introduced the Seekers to the teachings and, at the suggestion of a friend, Mrs. Keech read from the lessons one or two times to small groups at the Metaphysical Bookstore. All this took place within a two- or three-week period and represents, of course, a considerable proselyting effort which we have attributed to the initial impulse to warn the world of impending disaster. It should be noted, however, that these activities were initiated chiefly by one man — Dr. Armstrong. All through this period of activity, Mrs. Keech played a relatively passive role, in all probability tacitly approving of Dr. Armstrong's activities but herself initiating few contacts with the larger world. Before the disconfirmation none of the other members of the Lake City group had ever engaged in large-scale proselyting.

In sharp contrast, intense proselyting activity characterized almost every member of the group following disconfirmation. For the first time in her prophetic career Marian Keech initiated telephone calls to the newspapers. Bertha Blatsky, in dread of her husband, had desperately avoided publicity before the 21st. On the morning of the 21st, she talked to reporters, released the secret tapes, and promised to record tapes for anyone who asked — including the National Broadcasting Company. Mark Post telephoned a number of the newspapers and was interviewed by several reporters. While she was still in Collegeville, Cleo Armstrong had done her utmost to avoid reporters and, when forced to speak with them, had, half-ashamedly, attempted to convince them that hers was a completely normal family preparing to celebrate

Christmas in the usual fashion. After disconfirmation Cleo lectured to reporters and boldly argued with them about the validity of the belief system. Even Edna Post and Daisy Armstrong, both painfully shy and eager to avoid the limelight, talked to many of the newsmen, posed for pictures, and took turns instructing some of the many visitors to the house. After disconfirmation, proselyting became the popular pastime.

*The Persistence of Prediction.* Though the focus of our study has been proselyting behavior, it is evident that proselyting alone does not exhaust the variety of reactions to disconfirmation or of mechanisms by which the dissonance consequent on disconfirmation may be resolved. We have noted that following the major disconfirmation, Mrs. Keech made additional predictions, and that with time there was a growing tendency on the part of the group to identify their visitors as spacemen. Though we did not anticipate these phenomena before starting the study, we believe that they are consistent with the theory from which our major hypothesis was derived. Proselyting, after all, is not the sole means by which support for a belief system can be won. If direct supporting evidence can be found, so much the better. It seems to us that these repeated predictions, in effect, represent a search for supporting evidence, for confirmation. Had the tape recorded "a pretty song by the boys' glee club of the Losolo," had a spaceman appeared on Christmas Eve, these events would indeed have been confirmation. It may be that further predictions were made in this group only because their proselyting activities were so lamentably unsuccessful, failing to win the social support of even one serious convert.

The notion of search for confirmation may also help us to understand the insistence of the group on designating so many of their visitors as spacemen. Though one or two visitors had been identified as spacemen in the months before the disconfirmation of December 17, after disconfirmation not a day passed without two or three telephoners or visitors being nominated for the position. In a way, such designations are similar to predictions. If a visitor had indeed been a spaceman, again there would have been confirmation.

Search for confirmation, however, is not a sufficient explanation to account for the passion the believers showed for labeling spacemen. Though in some cases they seemed content simply to identify a "Clarion boy," more frequently such identification was a prelude to a plea for orders and messages. The experience of the observer introduced into the group after the Christmas Eve disconfirmation is a particularly good example. For three successive days, the members employed every device they could think of to extract a message from him. It seems fairly clear that their intent on such occasions was to win guidance and direction. Floundering, increasingly disoriented as prediction after prediction failed, they cast about for clues, watching television for orders, recording phone calls the better to search for coded messages, pleading with spacemen to do their duty — all in a desperate attempt to discover a clearly defined next step on the path to salvation by saucer.

In the preceding pages of this book, and especially in the last chapter, we have fully documented one instance of a curious phenomenon — the increase of proselyting following unequivocal disconfirmation of a belief. But in Chapter I it was made clear that our intention was not simply to show that such a phenomenon can occur, but rather to go further and specify the conditions that will determine whether or not it will occur. The five conditions we listed were these:

1. There must be conviction.

2. There must be commitment to this conviction.

3. The conviction must be amenable to unequivocal disconfirmation.

4. Such unequivocal disconfirmation must occur.

5. Social support must be available subsequent to the disconfirmation.

These conditions were certainly present for most of the persons in the Lake City group. But simply showing, as we have done, that these five conditions were present and the phenomenon occurred is still not sufficient. We would also like to be able to show that if any of these conditions do not hold, the phenomenon will *not* occur. There were, indeed, some hints along these lines in the last chapter. For Arthur Bergen and for Kurt Freund, whose commitment was not very strong, disconfirmation led to discarding the belief rather than to increased proselyting. Thus there is a bit of evidence that conditions 1 and 2 are, indeed, necessary conditions.

There was also a hint, although a weak one, that condition 5 is a necessary one. Two people, Bertha Blatsky and Clyde Wilton, who faced all or most of the period following the disconfirmation in isolation began to lose faith and showed no desire to proselyte when apart from the group. For the purpose of further strengthening our evidence concerning the importance of condition 5 we will now turn to a consideration of the impact of the disconfirmation on the believers from Collegeville, most of whom also faced disconfirmation in isolation. If condition 5 is indeed necessary, their reaction should be quite different from the one we have observed in Lake City.

Early in December, Dr. Armstrong had instructed the student members of the Seekers simply to go about their own affairs and wait for whatever might happen on the day of the cataclysm. If they were among the chosen, they would be picked up wherever they were. Consequently most of the members scattered to their homes for the Christmas vacation. This dispersion, though fortunate in that it allowed us to test the importance of the isolation factor, did enormously complicate the problems of observation. Consequently, the data on the reactions of the Collegeville students to disconfirmation are scanty and, in large part, were obtained retrospectively when the students returned to college. Since most members faced disconfirmation in isolation, we shall describe the impact of December 21 separately for each member for whom data are available.

*Kitty O'Donnell.* Of those members of the Seekers who did not go to Lake City, Kitty was by all odds the most highly committed to the prediction. She had given up her job, left home, and, as the crucial date drew near, had spent and given away all her money.

Several days before the 21st, Kitty had moved into the Armstrongs' house, where she and an observer were caring for the two young Armstrong children. Kitty was an isolated believer in that house, for none of her companions provided a supportive social environment. On December 20, as she had on previous evenings, Kitty insisted on sleeping in the master bedroom so she would be close by the telephone in case her orders should come through. On the morning of the 21st she rose at 7:30 to listen to the news broadcast from Lake City. Her immediate reaction, our observer noted, was one sentence. She said simply, "Well, I guess nothing happened in Lake City," and lapsed into silence. At about nine o'clock the Armstrongs telephoned from Lake City and Mrs. Armstrong read to Kitty the "Christmas Message" which rationalized the disconfirmation, and it is clear that she understood its meaning. When the reporters started arriving at the house, Kitty ignored them and seemed greatly concerned about getting to Steel City to see Ella Lowell. She left the house remarking, "I'll be seeing you — maybe," and indicated that she would not be coming back. The remainder of that day she was part of a group at Mrs. Lowell's, surrounded by people who had always been skeptical of Marian Keech's prediction.

By December 26 she was declaring her own skepticism openly, as we have already seen in her telephone conversation with Bob Eastman, who was still with the group in Lake City. In the course of this conversation, portions of which we have already quoted, Kitty makes such statements as these: "I'm glad you believe in it then. I don't — I'm all done with them, I'll tell you that much." "I just regret that I made such an ass of myself giving away my money and stuff . . . " And, finally, "I'm not going to go on like I was before, because I just don't believe in it — I mean I've had passages in the Bible pointed out to me — not by Ella Lowell either, but by my folks, and I just don't go for it any more." We could not ask for a more unequivocal statement: Kitty admits that she was wrong, declares herself to have been an ass, and washes her hands of the Armstrongs and Marian Keech and her predictions.

*Fred Purden and Laura Brooks.* Both Fred and Laura were among Dr. Armstrong's most faithful disciples. They had attended almost every meeting of the Seekers, and had both quit studying for their courses — Fred had even failed an important examination. They were both in the bad graces of their parents because they maintained their faith in Mrs. Keech's beliefs and prediction in the face of angry parental opposition. In preparing for the coming flood Laura had thrown or given away a great deal of valued personal property. Fred and Laura left Collegeville together, but separated to go to their respective homes for the Christmas holiday, each to face disconfirmation in the company of their non-believing parents.

On the night of the 20th, Laura later told one of the observers, she had "concentrated on living in the present." She had eaten her dinner and enjoyed it, watched television, and gone to bed at eleven o'clock "sort of scared inside." The next morning she listened to every news broadcast she could find, read the newspapers, and waited for something to happen. When she learned that Dr. Armstrong had stated that God had intervened to prevent the cataclysm, she thought this "was kind of silly and just a way of trying to explain it all after it hadn't happened." Her immediate reaction, then, was skepticism and nonacceptance of the rationalization.

When she returned to Collegeville after vacation she visited the Armstrongs several times. On January 17 she discussed her beliefs and present attitude with one of the observers, saying that she felt her beliefs had not changed and that she had learned a great deal from the experience about human nature in general. She thought that everything that had happened was very important and had set people to thinking. On the other hand she flatly stated that she was no longer interested in the Seekers or in any other kind of meetings, and that she didn't want any more lessons. Moreover, she regretted having disposed of so many of her possessions.

Although Laura maintains that her beliefs have not changed, it would seem that she is referring more to her general outlook than to her specific interest in Mrs. Keech's teachings, for she rejects the rationalization, shows no further concrete interest, and regrets the actions that committed her. It would certainly seem that Laura's conviction had decreased markedly.

When Fred Purden later described his behavior on the 20th and 21st, he said that he had gone to bed rather late but convinced that if he were going to be picked up by a saucer the spacemen would wake him. When he awoke the next morning, he was very surprised to find that nothing had happened. He was unable to get a newspaper until the evening of the 21st and it was then that he read the message that rationalized the disconfirmation. Our first contact with him after the Christmas vacation came on January 26 when, our observer reports:

"Fred seemed more at ease with the world. His face was more relaxed. He kept saying he was glad the disaster hadn't happened because he was glad to be alive. He said that this term he is doing well in his studies; last term he didn't do well at all because he didn't study at all. He says his faith has not changed, but that he sees no need to go to meetings. He thinks now that the flood was not ever intended to occur; that is, the space people just told us that there would be a disaster as a test for us, a test of our faith to see if we could stand up under the crisis.

"He said that he did not believe as some believed that Mrs. Keech was a hoax; her messages were genuine, though she might not have been getting some of them right. He said: 'You know Dr. Armstrong believes there's going to be another disaster, the date only has been changed.' Then Fred went on to say that this disaster, according to Dr. Armstrong, would occur in maybe a thousand years or ten thousand years; it won't occur in our lifetime. Fred says that he doesn't believe that this disaster will ever occur. The way he put it was: 'When you stop and think of it, it seems rather cruel to drown all these people just to teach them a lesson, doesn't it? The way to teach people a lesson, or the way to educate people is to educate them slowly; you can't educate them with one big jolt. And it seems rather silly to drown people and hope to educate them in the astral life. It doesn't seem very logical, does it?'"

Purden seems considerably less disillusioned than does Laura Brooks. He perceives the nonoccurrence of the flood as a test rather than a disconfirmation, but he, like Laura, feels no need to meet with the group of former believers and, for the very first time, he is genuinely skeptical of some of Dr. Armstrong's beliefs.

*Susan Heath.* Susan was among the most active of the Seekers. Besides attending all the meetings, she was the most industrious proselyter in the student group, even working away at convincing others after Dr. Armstrong had formally banned such activity.

She had also made some sacrifices for the belief system. She had stopped participating in student religious activities because the adult counselors at the church were opposed to Dr. Armstrong's teachings; and she had given up a close friendship with her skeptical roommate rather than give up her belief.

Susan had gone home for Christmas, taking with her another member of the Seekers whose conviction and commitment paralleled her own. When our observers interviewed Susan on December 27 (we have no data at all concerning the reactions of her companion since the observers were unable to contact her), Susan described her actions on the fateful morning of the 21st as follows:

"When Tuesday morning rolled around, I just listened to the nine o'clock news and went back in the bedroom and waked my girl friend and told her all about it. Then we talked about it for about half an hour and then came out and had breakfast just as though nothing had happened. Then we continued on to sit down and pick this stuff apart."

Their discussion apparently centered around a comparison of the doctrine of the Seekers and that of Christianity, for Susan reports having discussed with her fellow Seeker such topics as the Apostles' Creed, the Trinity, and the celestial and terrestrial forms of Jesus Christ. The reconciliation they effected between Christian doctrine and the beliefs of the group appears to be largely a rehash of some of Dr. Armstrong's ideas. As Susan sums it up: "From what I gather, Christ has had several lives since He was here on earth as Jesus, and now it just so happens His name is Sananda and He is living on a different planet, probably a planet with more people of higher development but not as high as Sananda."

Although this flight into theology tells us almost nothing definite about Susan's immediate reaction to disconfirmation, it seems reasonable to conclude from the general nature of the discussion that Susan was still trying hard to maintain her belief. During her conversation with the observers, Susan volunteered that she had written to Dr. Armstrong a few days after the major disconfirmation:

"I asked him if we could possibly write a long article, perhaps a magazine article, explaining as well as we could what this was that we believe in, because people have the craziest ideas of it. Trying to piece things together—I mean, if it's all right with higher forces and so on. I'd also like to know if it's all right to talk to more people who know nothing about it but realize we're in the group. They have questions and just how much can we talk about it? Can we show them the lessons and things like that?"

When she was asked if she herself would like to talk to others, Susan indicated that she had already spoken to a few people. She said she had several times "tried to correct the crazy ideas" that outsiders had formed about the group from reading the newspaper stories, and she further described an encounter she had with an interested student nurse: "I asked her if I could come around this last night. We talked over a lot of things. It was all connected with flying saucers. I told her about exactly what had happened — I just made clear what the papers said. I cleared her up on a lot of that."

Although even before disconfirmation Susan had been an active proselyter, her desire to persuade others appears to have intensified after December 21. Not only does she talk to people, but, like the believers in Lake City, she shows an unprecedented urge to publish the views of the group to the world at large. She certainly appears to have maintained the firmness of her beliefs too, at least up through the end of December. Susan Heath's reaction to disconfirmation closely resembles that of most of the Lake City group. Like them, but unlike the other Seekers, she had the social support of a fellow believer on the crucial day following disconfirmation.

Just how long her conviction remained strong we do not know, but it finally dwindled. Our next contact with Susan was in May and by that time she had become an open skeptic. When Cleo Armstrong and her parents waited all night in Collegeville to be picked up by a flying saucer, it was Susan who informed our observers of this event, and who laughed at the whole affair, declaring that she now saw many contradictions in the belief system and that she definitely didn't accept the rationalization for the non-appearance of the flood. "Cleo believes this stuff," said Susan, "but I don't."

*George Scherr.* George was another faithful Seeker both in attending meetings and in paying calls at the Armstrong house at other times. He had committed himself to the extent of telling his skeptical friends and parents of the prediction and defending his beliefs publicly. In private, however, he had expressed some doubts to the observers.

George lived with his parents in Collegeville during the Christmas holiday and, in the days prior to the 21st, he was in continual contact with the residents of the Armstrong house — the observers, Kitty, the Armstrong children, and (until the 18th) Cleo and Bob Eastman. Ever since the story had broken in the papers, George had been in difficulties with his parents and felt it necessary to mislead them on the night of the 20th by telling them he had a date with a girl when actually he was going to the Armstrong home. That night again, as on several others, he listened to Ella Lowell's Dr. Browning talking on tape. On the night of the 20th he stayed at the Armstrong house till well after midnight, fluctuating between anxiety about the imminent catastrophe and plans to visit Mrs. Lowell in Steel City the next day. Finally, he went home.

In spite of going to bed late, George awoke in time to hear the earliest news broadcast on December 21. Unsatisfied by it and eager to talk to sympathetic people he telephoned one of the observers to ask whether there was further information to be had. Again that evening he dropped in at the Armstrong house to discuss the day's events and his views with our two observers who, with Kitty gone, were the only "group members" available to George. Obviously they could not give him the kind of support that a true group member might have, and, for all relevant purposes, George spent the day following disconfirmation in isolation.

Three days later, George called one of the observers, who reports the conversation as follows:

"George said he was beginning to wonder about the whole thing. When the sanity petition against Dr. Armstrong came up, he had just thought it wasn't the doctor who was crazy but the sister, who brought the action. But then when this latest business came up about singing Christmas carols out in front of the house in Lake City, George says he began to wonder. And he expressed the feeling that Armstrong had too blind a faith in Mrs. Keech. He said: 'I think the doctor is sincere. Maybe Mrs. Keech is misled by other spirits. I don't know what to think.' He said this several times."

It appears that George was beginning to doubt more and more and he began to shy away from his connection with the Seekers. In discussing a projected visit to some relatives in another state, George made it clear that he did not intend to disclose the fact that he had been close to Dr. Armstrong.

But George's faith seemed to return after a meeting with the Armstrongs on January 1, for he later reported his feelings to our observers, who set down the interview as follows:

"George Scherr said that he was present on the first of January when Ella Lowell was in Collegeville visiting the Armstrongs and had a séance. He said that Dr. Browning's talk was directed at the group but that he, George, felt it was directed personally to him. Before this he had been skeptical, although he had tried not to be. Now he was no longer skeptical. I asked him what he thought about the 21st and he said it was a test primarily for the Armstrongs but also for the rest of the group."

Thus, contact with the Armstrongs and with Ella Lowell, who may well have been supportive toward the Armstrongs on this occasion, seems to have bolstered George's faith. Whether this upsurge was permanent or temporary we do not know, for this is the last report on George.

*Hal Fischer.* A convinced mystic and savant of the occult, Hal had from the very beginning expressed doubts about Marian Keech's prediction. Although he claimed to have studied her lessons assiduously, he considered her a relatively inexperienced channel. He was the most challenging skeptic in the group.

Hal too had gone home for Christmas and we know nothing of his behavior on the 20th and 21st. The only indication of his attitude is the tenor of two Christmas cards he sent before the 21st: one to the Armstrongs bore the brief inscription "December 21?" while a card to Susan Heath carried the notation "Will see you *next* term."

The observers did not get in touch with Hal until January 17, the day following a gathering of a few of the former Seekers. Hal had attended and had some comments which the observers report:

"Hal said that five or six people had attended and that he had had an argument with Cleo Armstrong. He said: 'I think she was duped by her parents.' Hal said Mrs. Keech was an amateur at getting messages, that it takes a long time to become a medium, and a great deal of work. He said he had seen the Armstrongs since he got back from vacation and that Dr. Armstrong explains that everything that happened was part of a great plan. Hal rather laughed and said: 'You know very well that anything that would happen he would say was part of the plan.'"

It is almost certain that Hal had by this time given up whatever slight belief in Mrs. Keech's teachings and Dr. Armstrong's beliefs he might have had. To Hal, the leaders of the movement were amateurs.

Of the fifteen people who were central members of the Collegeville group, we have now presented evidence about how ten reacted to disconfirmation—six of whom we have just discussed and the four people who spent the crucial days in Lake City and whom we considered in the last chapter: Dr. and Mrs. Armstrong, Cleo, and Bob Eastman. For the remaining five members in Collegeville we shall have little to say since the data on their reactions are fragmentary at best and we cannot draw any conclusions about their conviction. The Armstrongs' son, who had never believed firmly but who was committed to the ideology by his parents' actions, awoke on the morning of the 21st to listen to the news and then returned to bed where he remained, face to the wall and uncommunicative for almost the rest of the day.

What he did have to say later attests to his fear of ridicule from his peers, and this seems to have been his chief reaction. About his conviction we have no evidence at all, for he effectively refused to discuss his beliefs with the observers. Of the four remaining members, we know too little to support even patent conjecture.

Whatever the inclinations of these four unknowns, however, it is clear that in short order the Collegeville group fell apart. Shortly after Dr. Armstrong had left town in January an abortive attempt was made to bring the group together again, the occasion mentioned above. The only ones to appear at this meeting were George Scherr, Cleo Armstrong, Hal Fischer, Susan Heath, and the friend with whom Susan had spent December 21. A good share of the meeting was devoted to an argument between Hal and Cleo, the former reading excerpts from an article by William Dudley Pelley that attacked Marian Keech, while Cleo defended her. As far as we can learn, this was the last meeting to be held. In the following months our observers occasionally ran into former members of the Seekers. They were usually greeted warmly but their attempts to talk about December 21 or the "old days" were usually unsuccessful. Dr. Armstrong's former disciples did not wish to talk about the whole affair and seemed to want to put all of it behind them.

It is clear that the effects of disconfirmation on the Collegeville members were quite different from those in Lake City. Reviewing the evidence on the six people for whom we have adequate information we find that Kitty O'Donnell unequivocally declared herself wrong; Hal Fischer, ambivalent before the 21st, afterward outwardly mocked Dr. Armstrong and said the prediction was wrong; Laura Brooks claimed that her general beliefs were unchanged but wanted no more to do with the group and rejected the rationalization of the major disconfirmation; Fred Purden retained his general belief but had grown skeptical of Dr. Armstrong's views on the flood; Susan Heath, who at first maintained her belief intact, by May was willing to admit that she no longer believed; and George Scherr, who at first reacted in a skeptical fashion, later, after a meeting with the Armstrongs and Mrs. Lowell, renewed his faith.

Eventually, then, three of these six people gave up their beliefs, two became more doubtful and only one, after a period of skepticism, maintained his faith. With the exception of Susan Heath, no one in the Collegeville group appears to have done any proselyting following the disconfirmation. Indeed, the reverse seems to have occurred when Kitty O'Donnell left the Armstrong house just as soon as reporters began arriving and when George Scherr decided to conceal his membership in the Seekers.

In summary, the effect of disconfirmation on the individuals from Collegeville about whom we have data was (with the exceptions noted) to decrease conviction and either to have no effect on proselyting or to inhibit it. This result is quite the opposite of the general pattern in Lake City, where proselyting surged up and there were only two defectors and two whose doubts increased. Thus, most of the Collegeville group reduced the dissonance created by disconfirmation through giving up belief, whereas in Lake City the members held fast and tried to create a supportive circle of believers.

Before we accept the differences between Lake City and Collegeville as demonstrating the importance of social support following disconfirmation, we must examine possible alternative explanations for these differences. We shall consider two such alternatives: differences in degree of commitment, and the effect of Ella Lowell's views on conviction.

The simplest alternative is that the Collegeville people were originally less committed than the Lake City people and could, therefore, more easily give up their beliefs in the face of hard reality. While degree of commitment is undoubtedly important, it certainly does not tell the whole story. Kitty O'Donnell was certainly as heavily committed as many in Lake City. Laura Brooks, who had given up studying, given away her possessions, and faced the scorn and criticism of her classmates and parents was probably as heavily committed as Bob Eastman. Yet Kitty's conviction vanished after disconfirmation, Laura's decreased, and neither showed the slightest inclination to proselyte.

During the last days before the cataclysm, Ella Lowell had strongly suggested that the predicted flood might not occur. We know that this weakened the conviction of Cleo Armstrong and Bob Eastman as well as Kitty and George Scherr. Though there is no evidence to this effect, it is possible that it may have affected other members of the Collegeville group the same way. Indeed the conviction and desire to proselyte of Kitty and George were seriously weakened immediately following disconfirmation. An explanation in terms of weakened conviction is not entirely satisfactory, however, for Cleo and Bob, who went to Lake City, increased markedly in strength of conviction and desire to proselyte after disconfirmation.

Although lesser commitment and weakened conviction may well have contributed to the differences between the Lake City and Collegeville believers, it is clear from the counter-examples we have cited that these variables alone cannot account for the differences. Let us, then, examine more carefully the implications of the view that differences between the Collegeville and the Lake City groups can best be explained by the factor of social isolation following disconfirmation. By isolation we mean simply the physical absence of any fellow believers. With the exception of one pair, each of the Seekers faced the morning of December 21 and the following days at best in the company of people who voiced neither agreement nor disagreement; at worst with people who were openly opposed to the views of the Seekers.

The effect of the news broadcast on December 21 was to establish a clear dissonance between the conviction relating to the cataclysm and the knowledge that Lake City had not been flooded. The degree to which such a dissonance can be reduced depends in good part upon the degree of outside support the individual can muster. Those Seekers who were surrounded by people with opinions openly opposed to their own heard arguments that could serve *only* to maintain or to increase their strong dissonance. It is scarcely surprising under such circumstances that doubts would increase and the beliefs would be discarded. Even those who did not face active opposition and were, in effect, alone in their belief could obviously not obtain the social support necessary to their acceptance of the rationalization as correct, a necessary condition for dissonance reduction to begin.

In Lake City, on the other hand, most of the members were in the constant presence of fellow believers during the period following disconfirmation. The Lake City people, who had social support, were able to accept the rationalization, thus reducing dissonance somewhat, and they regained confidence in their original beliefs. The presence of supporting co-believers would seem to be an indispensable requirement for recovery from such extreme disconfirmation.

Some of the deviations we have noted from the prevalent pattern of reaction in each of these two groups appear to be explained by the factor of isolation. In the Lake City group, both Clyde Wilton and Bertha became less convinced after disconfirmation and both of them, we note, had to spend the period after disconfirmation in isolation from fellow believers. In Collegeville, Susan Heath is the only person who, in the days immediately following December 21, appears to be relatively unshaken in her belief and the only person who gives any indication of proselyting activity. She is also the one person among the six on whom we have data who spent the whole of December 21 in the presence of a co-believer.

LATE in December, an unfriendly world finally forced the small band of Lake City believers into diaspora.

Trouble had been brewing for Mrs. Keech for quite a while. As we have seen, her beliefs in populated planets and interstellar spaceship travel had a strong appeal for school boys and all through the fall they flocked to her. As far back as October, their parents had lodged a complaint with the police who warned Mrs. Keech to cease and desist. This warning instilled in her a fear of police action that she never lost.

Then, on December 24, the episode of the Christmas Eve caroling brought the indignation of Mrs. Keech's neighbors to a climax. The band of believers, no longer shy, gathered in front of the Keech home to make their final bid for salvation. As they caroled and waited for a spaceman-to visit, they were ringed about by a crowd of some 200 unruly spectators, and police were called to control the mob. That evening the police were flooded with complaints against Mrs. Keech ranging from disturbing the peace to contributing to the delinquency of minors. Christmas was a day of peace but, on the morning of December 26, a warrant was sworn out making specific charges against Mrs. Keech and Dr. Armstrong.

The police themselves seem to have been reluctant to set the legal machinery into motion. They telephoned Mrs. Keech's husband to inform him of the warrant and warned him that, unless meetings and gatherings at his home were at once brought to an end, they would serve the warrant. Furthermore, they strongly hinted that, once legal action began, the community could try to commit Mrs. Keech to a mental hospital. Mr. Keech passed along the warning to the group remaining in the house — the Armstrongs and their three children, Edna and Mark Post, Bob Eastman, and Marian — and they prepared to flee at once.

Mrs. Keech and the Posts, accompanied by Cleo Armstrong and Bob Eastman, went into hiding at the Post home in suburban Highvale where Marian remained incommunicado for the next two weeks. Her alarm was so great that she not only shunned the press and outsiders, but even made it difficult for established members of the group, such as Bertha Blatsky, to talk to her. Within a few days of their flight, Marian was lonelier than she had been in weeks, for Cleo Armstrong left Highvale to rejoin her father, who was having legal difficulties of his own, and Bob Eastman went with her. The Lake City group had dwindled to three persons. Bertha could not join them, for her husband was still threatening to have her put through psychiatric examination and, even though she longed for the companionship of fellow believers, Bertha did not dare to disobey her husband and risk investigations of her sanity.

Even the small nucleus at the Post house did not remain undisturbed long. Early in January, Marian Keech, still apprehensive about the police, decided to leave the Lake City area entirely and to join a dianetics center in Arizona. She traveled alone, under an alias, taking elaborate precautions not to be detected at the airport. Exactly what has happened to her since we do not know. For some time she continued to receive messages from the Guardians which she transmitted to other believers by mail and, in the few ordinary letters she wrote us, she still seemed to be expecting some future action or orders from outer space.

By January 9, there was no group in Lake City. Edna Post continued to communicate with many of the believers and tried to act as a clearinghouse for information. By mid-summer she had about decided to move to Steel City in order to join the group around Ella Lowell. Of Mark's activities we know nothing.

Meanwhile, the Armstrongs had had their lives disrupted too. Within minutes of receiving the warning from the police in Lake City on December 26, the Armstrongs had packed their bags, tumbled their two younger children into the car, and were on the road back to Collegeville. Their departure was hasty but not unplanned, for trouble had been gathering for them too. As indicated earlier, Dr. Armstrong's sister had been outraged at what she considered the Armstrongs' neglect of their two younger children in the days just preceding the 21st of December. Thomas and Daisy had left their children in Collegeville, but in good hands, when they themselves went to Lake City to prepare for the crucial events just before the flood was due. But Dr. Armstrong's sister did not see it this way. On December 23 she filed a petition to have the two adult Armstrongs declared insane and to obtain custody of their children and their estate. Dr. Armstrong was examined by two court-appointed psychiatrists. Their report was unequivocal: they declared that, although the doctor might have some unusual ideas, he was "entirely normal." The petition was summarily dismissed and the Armstrong family, intact, was free to do whatever they wished. The doctor and his wife decided that it was necessary for them to leave Collegeville.

In the next two weeks the Armstrongs sold their home and wound up their affairs in Collegeville, and Thomas prepared for the role he was assuming — that of itinerant proselyter, spreading the teachings of the Guardians across the land. For the next several months the doctor visited interested groups in Virginia, Florida, and California, accompanied by his wife and youngest daughter, returning once or twice to Collegeville. When last we heard of him, early in the summer, he was still following his new vocation. He gave a talk before a large audience of flying saucer enthusiasts who were holding a convention at the College of Universal Wisdom in southern California.

The group of believers in Lake City was dispersed by forces outside their control — legal action or some accident of personal situation. And, while circumstances combined to pull the steadfast adherents apart, the group failed to win a single new convert. They were unskillful proselyters. It is interesting to speculate, however, on what they might have made of their opportunities had they been more effective apostles. For about a week they were headline news throughout the nation. Their ideas were not without popular appeal, and they received hundreds of visitors, telephone calls, and letters from seriously interested citizens, as well as offers of money (which they invariably refused). Events conspired to offer them a truly magnificent opportunity to grow in numbers. Had they been more effective, disconfirmation might have portended the beginning, not the end.

In most studies that rely heavily on participant observers for collecting data, these observers are known as such to the people being studied. In our investigation of the group which gathered about Dr. Armstrong and Marian Keech, our observers posed as ordinary members who believed as the others did. In short, our investigation was conducted without either the knowledge or the consent of the group members. This situation presented a number of problems that merit detailed discussion.

In our very first contact with the central figures of the group, their secrecy and general attitude toward nonbelievers made it clear that a study could not be conducted openly. Our basic problems were then obtaining entree for a sufficient number of observers to provide the needed coverage of members' activities, and keeping at an absolute minimum any influence which these observers might have on the beliefs and actions of members of the group. We tried to be nondirective, sympathetic listeners, passive participants who were inquisitive and eager to learn whatever others might want to tell us. As we shall point out later, our initial hope — to avoid *any* influence upon the movement — turned out to be somewhat unrealistic for reasons outside our control and inherent in the process of making such a study as this. The other problems of the study were of a more tactical nature: we had to be on the spot whenever something was happening in the group, and we also had to make opportunities for recording our observations before they were forgotten or distorted by subsequent events.

*Obtaining Entree.* We did not learn of the flood prediction until very late September and, owing to the pressure of other activities, could not arrange direct contact with the group until a week later. By the time we had acquired sufficient information to determine that the movement satisfied the conditions necessary to test our hypothesis, it was the beginning of November. Finding suitable observers and giving them even the briefest of training took another week or two, and it was almost that much longer before they could secure entree into the movement in Lake City and Collegeville. All this had to be done with the utmost dispatch, since it was vital to collect as much "pre-disconfirmation" data as possible and we could anticipate needing considerable time to establish ourselves well enough in the group so that we could safely proceed to ask relatively intimate questions of the various members. Finally, the training and supervising of observers was handicapped by the fact that the study was carried on in localities far from our home base.

Our first problem then was to obtain a quick but firm entree into the movement in two distant places. Because of the severe pressure of time we chose whichever technique for introducing observers promised to be most effective. Accordingly, the procedure varied from person to person and place to place. Our initial contact was with Mrs. Keech, whom one of the authors telephoned shortly after the newspaper story about her appeared in late September. He told her his name and said he had called to ask if he might talk with her about some of the things she had told the reporter, especially the matter of the predicted flood and flying saucers. He said he happened to be visiting Lake City "on business" and had telephoned on impulse because he and some friends in his home city had read the story and been interested. Mrs. Keech was reluctant to discuss any of her beliefs over the phone, or to give details on the extent of followership and similar matters. Since the caller could not conveniently visit her at that time he asked her if he might stop in on a subsequent trip and received an affirmative answer.

About ten days later, two of the authors made a trip to Lake City, primarily in order to learn as much as they could about the size of the movement if any, the activities of members, and so forth. One telephoned Mrs. Keech on arrival and made an appointment to call on her the following morning. He represented himself to be a businessman who had occasion to travel a good deal. Mrs. Keech seemed completely incurious about his occupation and readily accepted his statements that he and several of his friends had an "informal group" in Minneapolis that frequently "got together and discussed saucers and things like that."

She willingly began to talk about her experiences with "automatic writing," read aloud at great length from her notebooks full of messages, and, in general, was quite receptive, friendly, and talkative. She did seem reluctant to say much about the flood prediction and had to be questioned extensively before much information emerged. She was evasive on the question of how many "believers" there were in Lake City, and quite adamant in refusing to say what she and her followers (if any) were going to do about preparing for the cataclysm. Fortunately, Daisy Armstrong was present at the interview, visiting Mrs. Keech at the time, and supplied some answers that Mrs. Keech would not. She told the author about the Seekers in Collegeville, and made some reference to going to the Allegheny Mountains in late December.

In all, the author spent three hours interviewing the two women that morning, and returned that evening with his colleague, whom he introduced as a business associate from Minneapolis, for another three- or four-hour talk. Before the authors left, they made sure they could take the initiative to call again in Lake City or in Collegeville when they wanted further information. Thus it was easy to make the acquaintance of these two persons and to establish a basis for future contacts.

One of the authors called on the Armstrongs in Collegeville approximately three weeks later, this occasion having been chosen as the nearest convenient time for a visit, but still not so near the first contact as to arouse any wonder on the part of the Armstrongs about the speed and intensity of our interest in their activities. It was our hope, on this visit, to meet the members of the Seekers and to be invited to attend a meeting. We did meet a number of members and, in talking to the Armstrongs, picked up some important information about their plans for going to a mountain refuge just before the flood was to strike. On the basis of this information we decided to hire local observers in Collegeville, and, accordingly, secured the services of a male student in sociology to make the first approach.

We instructed this observer to attend the open meetings of the "elementary" Seekers (see Chapter III) at the Community Church and to attempt to get on good terms with Dr. Armstrong, with the aim of being invited to one of the Sunday afternoon meetings of the "advanced" Seekers. We have already reported the difficulty our observer experienced in arousing Dr. Armstrong's interest in him; all his efforts to stimulate an invitation to the "advanced" group meetings were having no success. Time was passing and we were losing opportunities for valuable observation. We therefore decided upon a strategem suggested to us by Dr. Armstrong's inquiry to our observer as to whether he had ever had any "psychic experiences." We decided to equip our representative with an "experience" with the supernatural.

The observer had told Dr. Armstrong of his having spent some time in Mexico, so we borrowed a folktale and set the scene there. The story our observer told was as follows: He and a companion had been driving between two Mexican cities. Toward dusk, they picked up an elderly peasant woman hitchhiking in their direction and let her occupy the rear seat. Soon she was talking to them, a long admonitory monologue full of warnings about disaster ahead. They paid little heed to her, and, after a time, she fell silent and, they assumed, slept. When they reached the outskirts of their home city, they turned to ask where she would get off, and found that she had disappeared! They had not stopped at all, and had been moving at a fast speed; they had heard no door open, no cry or noise of any kind from the rear once the old lady had stopped talking.

Dr. Armstrong's interest was immediately aroused, and he very quickly began to manifest much more friendliness toward our observer, and interest in him. The observer was invited to attend the next meeting of the Seekers at Dr. Armstrong's home and, from the point of view of gaining acceptance for our representative, the stratagem was a complete success.

At the same time that we were constructing this scheme for our male observer in Collegeville, we had decided to hire and train a young woman to act in the same capacity. Forewarned by his difficulties in approaching the Armstrongs through the medium of the elementary Seekers, we decided to arm our female observer with a "psychic experience" and to have her go directly to the Armstrong house to tell this story: A few nights previous to her call at the Armstrong home, our observer said, she had had a strange dream that disturbed her a good deal. She had consulted Dr. Armstrong professionally about a year ago, and he had urged her at that time to "get in tune with the universe" and this suggestion had stuck in her mind. Therefore, when she had the puzzling dream she had thought at once of going to him for advice and help. Her dream was as follows: "I was standing on the side of a hill. It wasn't a mountain, and yet it wasn't exactly a hill: and I looked up and there was a man standing on top of the hill with a light all around him. There were torrents of water, raging water all around, and the man reached down and lifted me up, up out of the water. I felt safe."

Mrs. Armstrong's reaction to this story was enthusiastic. She welcomed the observer warmly, and at once began to enlighten her visitor about the protectors from outer space. Within an hour,

our observer was informed about the belief system, had been told of the predicted flood, of the mission of the flying saucers, and like matters. When Dr. Armstrong came home from work, his wife proudly presented the observer as one who "had been sent," and the two Armstrongs began to interpret the "dream." During the next few days, our observer was pressed to retell her "dream" several more times to other members of the Seekers and finally was asked to tape-record it so it could be sent to Lake City or played to people in distant places. Again, our scheme had been successful for gaining entree into the group.

Unhappily, it had been too successful, for, in our effort to tailor a story to fit the beliefs of the members of the group, and thus gain their approval for our observers, we had done too well. We had unintentionally reinforced their beliefs that the Guardians were watching over humanity and were "sending" chosen people for special instruction about the cataclysm and the belief system. Dr. Armstrong's initial indifference to the male observer had led us to underestimate the powerful effect of the "dream." In all probability its effect was magnified by coming so close behind the male observer's story (they were separated by only two or three days).

In introducing themselves into the Lake City group, our observers there told stories that were quite unexciting, even commonplace. The male observer told Mrs. Keech that he had read the newspaper story about her in September and had intended to call on her earlier, but somehow had never got around to it. He had remained interested, however, though he was not quite sure what he wanted to know; he just wanted to know more than the newspaper account had given.

Mrs. Keech's response to this introduction was favorable, though not as enthusiastic as the Armstrongs' welcome of our Collegeville observers had been. She volunteered to tell the observer how she had begun to receive messages, how the messages related to flying saucers, what the significance of many of her writings were, and so on. She spent a couple of hours explaining these things, offered him refreshments, and, when he asked if he might return, told him: "My door is always open. Please feel free to come back."

Our female observer in Lake City was instructed to use a somewhat different approach, in order to avoid stretching a coincidence. She called a day or so before our male observer had and told Mrs. Keech the following story. She had been at a meeting of people interested in ethical and religious problems in the neighborhood where she lived and worked. The discussion had turned to flying saucers and a man seated next to her had remarked that if our observer really wanted to know about flying saucers, she should go visit Mrs. Keech, and had given her Mrs. Keech's address. The observer had thought about this piece of advice for a while and then, on impulse, had come to call. She seemed a little uneasy and said that she felt "sort of silly" and "didn't know exactly why she had come," but was "just curious about flying saucers."

Mrs. Keech again reacted favorably, inviting the young lady into the house to warm herself, and began to talk about flying saucers, about her communication with their occupants, her messages from Sananda, reincarnation, and the like. She told the story of the sice at Lyons field, mentioned the "war" between Atlantis and Mu, and offered to "get a lesson" from Sananda for our observer. In all, she spent about four hours talking about the belief system, without once mentioning the coming cataclysmic flood on December 21. This observer also asked if she might return and Mrs. Keech gave her permission, but warned her to telephone first, so that she would not come at a time when some other student was receiving a lesson.

In spite of the relatively ordinary, non-exotic stories that the Lake City observers told Mrs. Keech she subsequently made much the same use of their appearance on her doorstep as the Armstrongs had with the Collegeville observers. Her imagination embroidered the circumstances somewhat and, within a week of the first observer's call, Mrs. Keech was explaining to other members of the group that a girl had come to her door, upset, excited, wringing her hands, and so terrified that she could not speak; the girl had not known why she had come, and obviously she had been "sent" by the Guardians. Then, Mrs. Keech added, a man had also called, again not knowing why he was there, confused, upset, and unsure of his errand. She elaborated not only the bewilderment and emotionality of the observers but also her own warmth of response and comforting actions toward them. Her account was retold in Collegeville by the Armstrongs, just as their versions of our observers' visits to them were retold in Lake City. In both cases the visits were given as illustrations that "strange things are happening."

The members of the group who heard these accounts were impressed, it seemed to us, by this upsurge of membership within

239

a few days. There is little doubt that the addition of four new people to a fairly small group within ten days had an effect on the state of conviction among the existing members, especially since the four seem to have appeared when public apathy to the belief system was great and there were very few inquiries or new faces in either Collegeville or Lake City. Most important of all, perhaps, is that the four observers could not be traced through any mutual friends or acquaintances to existing group members and thus the most common and expected channel of recruitment was evidently not responsible for their appearance. It was an unfortunate and unavoidable set of events — we had no choice but to establish local observers in both cities where there were believers, to do it quickly, and to "push" as much as we dared to get our people well enough received so they could begin to move about in the groups, ask questions, and have a reasonable expectation of getting answers. We could not afford to have them remain peripheral members, or strangers, for very long.

One other observer, a man, did not make contact with the group until Christmas Day when he called at the Keech house, saying simply that he had read the newspaper accounts of recent happenings and had come out to learn more about what was going on. He had no problem of entree. As we have already pointed out, he was readily admitted and regarded as a spaceman, even though he told a most straightforward story of his earthly origin and occupation (unemployed IBM operator).

It seems clear that his appearance in the post-disconfirmation stage probably affected the state of conviction too, for he was the only new recruit the group attracted. The group imposed their own meaning on his visits. The new observer was introduced in order to maintain coverage. The regular observers and the authors had been "on duty" nearly full time for nearly ten days at that point, were exhausted, and had personal affairs to take care of.

*Maintaining Membership.* A major problem in acting as an observer was to become friendly enough, well enough accepted and integrated into group activity, to allow one to be present on significant occasions and to ask fairly personal questions of others, while still avoiding any act of commitment, proselyting, indication of conviction, or any act of directing the course of the movement. We have already shown how the mere joining of the group by the observers tended to heighten the conviction of at least the Armstrongs and Mrs. Keech, but a few examples of the kinds of situations the observers faced as members will illustrate the diffi-

240

culties they encountered and their attempts to cope with them. Actually, we were unable to achieve our goal of complete neutrality. At various points there arose situations in which the observers were forced to take some action and no matter what they might have done, their action would have had some effect on developments in the group.

One of the most obvious kinds of pressure on observers was to get them to take various kinds of responsibilities for recommending or taking action in the group. Most blatant was the situation that one of the authors encountered on November 23 when Marian Keech asked him, in fact commanded him, to lead the meeting that night. His solution was to suggest that the group meditate silently and wait for inspiration. The agonizing silence that followed was broken by Bertha's first plunge into mediumship (see Chapter III), an act that was undoubtedly made possible by the silence and by the author's failure to act himself. Twice again during that long meeting Marian Keech asked the author if he had "brought a message" for the group. By the time of his third refusal to act, he began to be concerned lest his apparent incapacity should injure the carefully nurtured rapport he had established in the group.

Both of our Lake City "local" observers were under pressure at various times in mid-December to quit their jobs and spend all their time with the group. One observer persistently avoided making any statement about his plans; the other waited until the 17th and then announced that her job had been terminated. Yet their evasion of these requests and their failure to quit their jobs at once were not only embarrassing to them and threatening to their rapport with the group, but also may have had the effect of making the members who had quit their jobs less sure they had done the right thing. In short, as members, the observers could not be neutral — any action had consequences.

Another form of demand for action was pressure on all the observers to take a stand when a division of opinion occurred in the group. Illustrative of this is the dilemma which the observers faced when during the meeting of December 4 Bertha brought meat into the Keech home after the Creator had revoked the vegetarian rule. While most members of the group proceeded to eat the meat, Mrs. Keech herself abstained. Any action of the observers had to be a choice between Sananda and the Creator. On this occasion the observers chose to abstain from eating the meat.

Another type of difficulty was faced by the observers when, on occasion, they were forced to deal directly with outsiders. During mid-December, especially from the 18th to the 20th, the Lake City observers were occasionally handed the task of answering the phone. When they could not avoid doing it, they were careful to ask for detailed instructions and meticulously followed them. Once or twice they were asked to discuss the belief system with callers. Ordinarily the observers tried to turn such occasions into interviews with the inquirers, but could not always avoid direct questions from the caller. Such questions were always personally embarrassing but became strategically difficult when a "real" member of the group was in a position to overhear the observer's answer. As far as we can tell, we fumbled our way through these latter crises without positively convincing any caller and without arousing any suspicions among members save those having to do with the observers' intelligence and knowledge of the belief system.

Occasionally the observers' well-hidden network of communication outside the group proved invaluable but led to unintended interpretations among the members of the group. Through these channels the authors learned of two meetings in Lake City that we had not been informed of "officially" by Mrs. Keech and we requested invitations to visit her on these days. It was clear from her subsequent remarks that she regarded our means of anticipating meetings as having supernatural origin. Once we had an observer change a personal plan that he had announced to Mrs. Keech in order to have him attend a meeting where we thought we might be shorthanded. Forced to give some account of his unexpected (and uninvited) appearance he had to say that he had changed his plans on impulse and, again, what might have been regarded by most people as a curious coincidence was interpreted by Mrs. Keech as a significant exercise of influence by the Guardians. It was omniscience of this sort that led Mrs. Keech to suspect that one of the authors had "his own channels of information" to the Guardians.

Finally, we shall describe an incident that strikingly highlights the utter impossibility of avoiding influence on the believers short of absolute refusal to participate in an activity. At the end of the December 3–4 meeting, Bertha sat for "private consultations" between the individual members and "the Creator" who spoke through her. All the observers dutifully asked a question or two of the Creator and accepted the answers passively, quitting the situation as soon as they politely could. The last observer to go through this ritual was not allowed to be merely passive and non-directive, however. The voice of the medium droned on for a few minutes and then said: "I am the Creator." Next the voice asked our observer: "What do you see when I say 'I am the Creator'?" To this the observer replied, "Nothing," whereupon the medium's voice explained: "That's not nothing; that's the void." The medium then pressed further: "Do you see a light in the void?" Our observer struggled with this impasse by answering, "A light in the void?" and got, as a reply, a fuller explanation of the "light that expands and covers the void" together with an increasing flood of elaboration that terminated when the medium called other members into the room and asserted that the observer had just been "allowed to witness Creation"! The medium further stated that this "event" was validation of her speaking with the Creator's voice since, every time her voice said "I am the Creator" our observer saw the vision of Creation! Against this sort of run-away invention even the most polished technique of nondirective response is powerless.

In spite of our best efforts, then, we did have some effects on the movement. We have perhaps overemphasized the effect of the observers by pulling out the major incidents that evidence our influence, but our presence alone, and some of our actions, did lend support to their convictions and their activities. On the other hand, at no time did we exercise any influence whatsoever on proselyting activity. We were meticulously concerned with this point and we were completely successful in avoiding any impact on our major dependent variable.

*The Observers and Their Task.* All observers were either students or staff members in departments of psychology or sociology, and all had had some previous experience in interviewing and observational technique.

We included one male and one female observer in each local team, so that we could exploit any advantages that a same-sex interviewer has in gathering data from a subject. It turned out to give us certain unanticipated advantages, too, for the female observers were able to pick up a great deal of information as part-time residents of the Keech and Armstrong households, a role that would have been much more difficult for a man to fill.

The assignment handed the observers was necessarily open-ended for the very good reason that the situation they were to observe was extremely fluid and unpredictable. The observers

243

were given very brief "training" in the objectives of the study and instructions about the kinds of information we were most interested in collecting. They were informed that we needed to know, about each individual in the movement, the degree to which he was sincerely convinced of the truth of the various components of the belief system; the kinds of actions he had taken (or failed to take) in committing himself to participation in the movement; and, finally, the extent to which he had engaged in proselyting or propagandizing for the belief system. In addition, the observers were instructed to note any activities or utterances of members that indicated changes or developments in the belief system, in plans for future action (particularly in regard to coping with the cataclysm), and any items of personal history that might throw light on how the members had become interested and active in the movement — especially if these items would throw further light on conviction, commitment, and proselyting. The first objectives of observation, then, were to determine whether or not a group of followers existed, who they were, and how convinced and committed they were.

The second important task, in the early phase of observation, was to discover what actions the members of the movement would take as the date of the cataclysm drew near. We knew that it would be essential to be present during the disconfirmation and recovery phases, and were greatly concerned about the initial plan of the group to go to the "safe places" in mountain ranges. Since we did not know how many people, or who, would be going to any particular place, or how many observers would be needed, we were greatly concerned about personnel, equipment, and travel facilities for accompanying the migrants and living with them for an indefinite period of disconfirmation on the side of a hill in midwinter.

Finally, since the ideology itself seemed changeable, and the inspirations of the leaders unpredictable, we had to be prepared for almost any contingency including the awful possibility that the date would be changed, postponed, or abandoned. It was a nerve-racking uncertainty that stayed with us right up till the midnight vigil on December 20.

Thus the job of observation differed from that encountered in a community study or the study of a stable, organized group holding regular meetings and having a fairly fixed plan of activity. We could not count on the regular recurrence of particular activities or interactions. With the exception of one or two of the

244

Seekers' meetings we rarely knew more than a few days ahead of time when any organized activity would take place, or where it would occur. The leaders themselves were unable to give planful coherence to their activities because of the other-worldly origin of their directives, and invariably shrugged off any question about the future by asserting that they were waiting for orders. Thus we had to grant as much responsibility and autonomy to our observers as possible and depend largely on their own initiative and acquaintance with the local situation to govern their actions. Problems of rigor and systematization in observation took a back seat in the hurly-burly of simply trying to keep up with a movement that often seemed to us to be ruled by whimsy.

For all practical purposes, the period of intensive observation began approximately one month before the predicted flood — i.e., on November 19. Between this date and the end of intensive observation on January 7, we conducted observations in Collegeville on 29 days and in Lake City on 31 days. Some of these visits or contacts were brief — only an hour or two, while others lasted up to twelve or fourteen hours of continuous observation. Coverage grew more intensive as the predicted date of the cataclysm drew nearer. In Collegeville there was daily observation from the 9th through the 24th of December, and in Lake City, from the 14th through the 27th of December. In both places there was at least one observer present at almost every waking hour between the 17th and the 22nd. Indeed, for this period, our female observers for all practical purposes resided in the Keech and Armstrong homes. When the Lake City observer told the group on the 17th that she no longer had a job, Mrs. Keech invited her to move in. In Collegeville, when the Armstrongs set out for Lake City on the 13th they simply assumed that our observer there would be willing to stay in their home and help look after their children. This observer was trapped and there was nothing to do about it.

It will be clear from this account of the extent of surveillance that we were fairly successful in arranging to have an observer present at the major events and developments in the movement and, when these were not correctly anticipated, to have someone on the scene shortly afterward to get an account of what had occurred from one or more of the participants. We are sure that we had a representative at every group meeting between the 20th of November and the 7th of January, and the only major "event" we did not cover at first hand was the Christmas carol sing on the lawn in front of Mrs. Keech's house on December 24.

Owing to observer fatigue we have a less complete account than we would like of the meeting (on December 12–13) between Marian Keech and Ella Lowell; but we believe we picked up the essential details and know the significance of the meeting. There were a few minor events during the observation period that we did not cover: one rump meeting at Bertha's home on December 5; the visit of the Armstrongs to Ella Lowell on December 6 (although we heard fairly complete tape recordings of the speeches of Dr. Browning on this occasion); a small private meeting on December 16 following the public lecture to the flying saucer club; and other events of this nature, whose significance was made clear to us by the participants' subsequent accounts.

Thorough coverage was both essential and difficult. Many of our observers' visits produced a relatively low yield of information (though scarcely any were completely barren) simply because nothing new had occurred since their previous call, or the members were engaged in biding their time — a rather unexciting activity. When no special event was taking place, the observers were usually able to draw out background information, cross-check rumors and reports among members, make inquiries about degree of conviction or proselyting activity, and, if nothing better offered itself, continue to build rapport.

The observational scheme was difficult to operate too because of the near impossibility of keeping a fresh, alert observer on duty at all times whenever something was likely to occur. Observing, in this study, was exhausting work. In addition to the strain created by having to play an accepting, passive role vis-à-vis an ideology that aroused constant incredulity, which had to be concealed, observers frequently had to stay in the group for long hours without having an opportunity to record what they learned. Sometimes, the long hours were imposed by Mrs. Keech or Bertha, who would make rules regarding constancy of attendance; sometimes circumstances stuck one observer with his task during a crucial phase when he was unable to summon a relief, or the relief could not appear.

Our observers had their own daily lives to care for as well as the job, and were subject to occasional bouts of illness or fatigue from lack of sleep. The job was frequently irritating because of the irrelevancies (from the point of view of our main interest) that occupied vast quantities of time during the all-night meetings, the repetitiousness of much that was said, and the incoherence of the congeries of beliefs that went into the melting pot of ideology. This last aspect was not only exhausting because of the strain imposed on attention and memory, but irritating because the observers felt responsible for keeping it all straight and setting it down as accurately as possible at a later time.

*Recording Observations.* The data collected by the observers was in the form of anecdotal accounts of events that took place in their presence; reports to them of actions that members had taken earlier or elsewhere; factual or attitudinal data elicited in interviews or conversations with members; and the content of talks or assertions made to the group as a whole. The circumstances of observation made it impossible to make notes openly except on a single occasion, the meeting of November 23, when the Creator ordered notes taken. It was also difficult to make notes privately or secretly, for the observers were rarely left alone inside the house and it was necessary to be ingenious enough to find excuses for leaving the group temporarily. One device used occasionally was to make notes in the bathroom. This was not entirely satisfactory, however, since too frequent trips there would probably arouse curiosity if not suspicion. Sometimes the bathroom was used in relays. On the morning of December 21, for example, when all our observers were very fatigued and unwilling to trust their memory too much, one would go make notes while the others stayed to listen.

Every so often it was possible for an observer to slip out on the back porch to make notes in the dark. During breaks in the meetings the observers would frequently take walks outdoors to get fresh air, thus providing another opportunity. For example, after Dr. Armstrong had finished urging one of the authors to shed his doubts at the critical time of 3:30 A.M. on December 21, Dr. Armstrong went back indoors but the author, pleading that he needed to think alone, stayed outdoors and wrote down the whole episode immediately.

At other times we had to depend upon memory to retain the substance of conversations, interviews and the like until we could dictate these observations into tape recorders. Every observer had access to such a machine, and was under instructions to dictate his observations as soon as possible after each contact. Ordinarily such dictation could be accomplished within a few hours after leaving the observation site, though from time to time an observer, exhausted by an all-night meeting, had to defer dictation until he had caught up on sleep. The greater part of our data was tape-recorded within three or four hours of the time the observer

ended his contact. During the period of round-the-clock coverage of the Lake City group (between the 17th and the 22nd of
December), we maintained a temporary headquarters in a hotel
about half a mile from Mrs. Keech's home, and the observers kept
three tape-recording machines busy absorbing their notes. Most
of the material obtained during this time was recorded within an
hour after leaving the house.

In all, the reports of the observers filled approximately sixty-
five reels of one-hour tapes, yielding almost one thousand pages
of typescript when they were transcribed; in addition, we accumulated about one hundred typewritten pages of material that
had been directly recorded. This latter material includes a variety
of things. When Marian Keech and Dr. Armstrong addressed the
Flying Saucer Club, we arranged to have a special assistant attend
this public meeting and he succeeded in recording almost the
entire session on a midget tape recorder.

Our verbatim material also includes many phone conversations.
From the evening of December 21 on, the group, expecting that
orders from the Guardians might come over the phone, tape-
recorded every incoming phone call. The group was quite happy
to let one of our observers borrow these tapes, which we then
transcribed. In addition, our observers in Collegeville were able
to transcribe many of the Ella Lowell tapes. We also have verbatim copies and sometimes the originals of many of Mrs. Keech's
most important messages.

The material we gathered, therefore, varies in accuracy from
verbatim transcriptions or written documents on the one hand to
a few reports that are simply summaries of the highlights of very
long meetings. For events before the beginning of direct observation we have had to rely largely on retrospective material.

We have quoted directly from documents and firsthand tape
recordings, but otherwise have used the direct quotation form
only when the observer either had an opportunity to make written notes on a conversation within a few minutes of its occurrence, or when he made an especial point of remembering an
important statement verbatim and putting it into his record with
assurances to that effect.

*Summary*. From the foregoing description as well as from the
report in the substantive chapters, it should be clear to the reader
that the procedures used in conducting this study departed from
the orthodoxy of social science in a number of respects. We

should like to summarize here some of these departures and the facts that made them necessary.

In the first place, it is clear that we were unable to rely on the standard array of technical tools of social psychology. Our material is largely qualitative rather than quantitative and even simple tabulations of what we observed would be difficult. Owing to the complete novelty and unpredictability of the movement, as well as to the pressure of time, we could not develop standard categories of events, actions, statements, feelings, and the like, and certainly could not subject the members of the group to any standardized measuring instrument, such as a questionnaire or structured interview, in order to compare indices before and after disconfirmation.

Actually we faced as much a job of detective work as of observation. We had to listen, probe, and query constantly to find out in the beginning who the members of the group were, how sincerely they believed the ideology, what actions they were taking that were consonant with their beliefs, and to what extent they were propagandizing or attempting to convince others. Later, we had to continue to accumulate this sort of data while further inquiring about what was going to happen next in the movement: when there would be another meeting, who was being invited, where the group (or individuals) were going to wait for the flood, and like questions. Furthermore, we had to conduct the entire inquiry covertly, without revealing our research purpose, pretending to be merely interested individuals who had been persuaded of the correctness of the belief system and yet taking a passive and uninfluential role in the group. Our data, in places, are less complete than we would like, our influence on the group somewhat greater than we would like. We were able, however, to collect enough information to tell a coherent story and, fortunately, the effects of disconfirmation were striking enough to provide for firm conclusions.

[1] P. Hughes, *A Popular History of the Catholic Church* (New York: Doubleday and Company, 1954), p. 10.

[2] Richard Heath, *Anabaptism: From Its Rise at Zwickau to Its Fall at Munster, 1521–1536* (London: Alexander and Shepheard, 1895), p. 119. This is one of the *Baptist Manuals: Historical and Biographical*, edited by George P. Gould.

[3] *Ibid.*, pp. 147–148.

[4] *Ibid.*, pp. 120–121.

[5] In describing the Sabbataian movement we shall follow the account given by H. Graetz, *History of the Jews* (Philadelphia: Jewish Publication Society of America, 1895), Vol. 5, pp. 118–167. This, in our judgment, is the best single source.

[6] Graetz, p. 122.

[7] *Ibid.*, pp. 134, 137.

[8] *Ibid.*, p. 146.

[9] *Ibid.*, pp. 147–148.

[10] *Ibid.*, p. 149.

[11] *The Memoirs of Gluckel of Hameln*, translated by Marvin Lowenthal (New York: Harper, 1932), pp. 45–46.

[12] C. E. Sears, *Days of Delusion — A Strange Bit of History* (Boston and New York: Houghton Mifflin, 1924).

[13] Francis D. Nichol, *The Midnight Cry* (Tacoma Park, Washington, D.C.: Review and Herald Publishing Company, 1944).

[14] *Ibid.*, p. 33.

[15] *Ibid.*, p. 101.

[16] *Ibid.*, pp. 124–125.

[17] *Brother Jonathan*, February 18, 1843, quoted in Nichol, p. 130.

[18] *Signs of the Times*, January 25, 1843, p. 147, quoted in Nichol, p. 126.

[19] Nichol, p. 126.

[20] Sears, p. 119.

[21] Nichol, p. 160n.

[22] Sears, pp. 140–141.

[23] *Ibid.*, p. 144.

[24] Nichol, p. 206.

[25] Sears, p. 147.

[26] *Advent Herald*, July 17, 1844, p. 188, quoted in Nichol, p. 208.

[27] *Advent Herald*, July 24, 1844, p. 200, quoted in Nichol, p. 208.

[28] Nichol, pp. 209–210.

[29] *Ibid.*, p. 213

[30] *Advent Herald*, October 30, 1844, p. 93, quoted in Nichol, p. 216.

[31] Sears, pp. 156–157.

[32] Nichol, p. 231.

[33] *The Midnight Cry*, October 19, 1844, p. 133, quoted in Nichol, p. 236.

[34] *The Midnight Cry*, October 3, 1844, p. 104, quoted in Nichol, p. 238

[35] Nichol, pp. 238–239.

[36] Hiram Edson, fragment of ms. on his life and experience, pp. 8, 9, quoted in Nichol, pp. 247–248.

[37] Luther Boutelle, *Life and Religious Experience*, pp. 67–68, quoted in Nichol, pp. 248–249.

[38] Unless otherwise identified, all quotations used in our discussion of Christianity are taken from essays in the collective work *Christianity in the Light of Modern Knowledge* (London and Glasgow: Blackie and Son, 1929). The specific essays from which quotations have been taken are the following: Francis Crawford Burkitt, F.B.A., D.D., "The Life of Jesus," pp. 198–256; Rev. Charles Anderson Scott, D.D., "The Theology of the New Testament," pp. 337–389; Rev. Canon David Capell Simpson, M.A., D.D., "Judaism, the Religion in Which Christ Was Educated," pp. 136–171.

[39] P. 335.

[40] P. 350.

[41] P. 165.

[42] P. 226.

[43] Graetz, Vol. 2, p. 166.

[44] The theory of dissonance and its implications are set forth in detail in a forthcoming book by Leon Festinger.

CPSIA information can be obtained at www.ICGtesting.com
Printed in the USA
BVOW010951230112

281053BV00002B/41/P